Dyslexia at College

This fully updated third edition contains practical and useful au...ce that will be invaluable for students with dyslexia, their parents and all of those involved in teaching and supporting them in their studies. The book:

- guides students through the process of applying for university, suggesting strategies for general organisation and for particular aspects of study

- outlines how to get the best personally and academically from higher education

- gives practical advice on setting up and using support facilities (both human and technological)

- is an accessible text for mainstream lecturers and tutors who need to be aware of the implications of the Disability Discrimination Act.

New chapters include 'Dyslexia plus', giving information on dyspraxia, attentional disorders, Asperger's syndrome, and the more controversial 'dyscalculia'. 'Out of college and into work' gives advice for students on the challenges they face after graduation. Appendices written by six former Bangor students tell how they coped with their dyslexia when they were at college and then later in life.

This book is an invaluable companion for any students with dyslexia and any professional working with them.

Liz Du Pré is Tutor/Coordinator for the Student Service at the Dyslexia Unit, University of Wales, Bangor and a member of The National Bureau for Students with Disabilities and The Association of Dyslexia Specialists in Higher Education.

Dorothy Gilroy was a pioneer in establishing and developing the service for dyslexic students at Bangor and advised many universities on good practice in the field.

Tim Miles is Professor Emeritus at the School of Psychology, University of Wales, Bangor.

Dyslexia at College

Third edition

Liz Du Pré, Dorothy Gilroy and Tim Miles

Routledge
Taylor & Francis Group

LONDON AND NEW YORK

First published 1986
Second edition published 1996
Third edition published 2008
by Routledge
2 Park Square, Milton Park, Abingdon, Oxon OX14 4RN

Simultaneously published in the USA and Canada
by Routledge
270 Madison Ave, New York, NY 10016

Routledge is an imprint of the Taylor & Francis Group, an informa business

© 2008 Elizabeth Du Pré, Dorothy Gilroy and Tim Miles

Typeset in Palatino by
HWA Text and Data Management, Tunbridge Wells

Printed and bound in Great Britain by
TJ International Ltd, Padstow, Cornwall

British Library Cataloguing in Publication Data
A catalogue record for this book is available from the British Library

Library of Congress Cataloging-in-Publication Data
A catalog record for this book has been requested

ISBN10: 0–415–40417–7 (hbk)
ISBN10: 0–415–40418–5 (pbk)

ISBN13: 978–0–415–40417–4 (hbk)
ISBN13: 978–0–415–40418–1 (pbk)

Contents

Preface to the third edition

It is with the greatest regret that the other two authors of this book report the death, on 5 September 2006, of our loved and respected colleague Dorothy Gilroy. Dorothy was co-author of the first two editions of this book and before her death had already played a major part in the writing of the third edition. She was not only tutor to the dyslexic students at Bangor. As part of her work she was known to visit them in their lodgings and even to help with the washing up; on one occasion she is reported to have hastened to Bangor railway station, where she succeeded in persuading an unhappy student not to abandon his college course.

As she makes clear in this book, the role of a tutor to dyslexic students can take many forms! We shall miss her greatly.

Since the second edition of this book appeared in 1996, the scene in Britain with regard to dyslexia has changed dramatically and continues to change. In this present edition we have tried to preserve the essential message of the first two editions while at the same time taking account of these new developments.

The main ways in which the dyslexia scene in Britain has changed are these. In the first place, there has been an increased understanding of what dyslexia is and how those who are dyslexic can best be helped. Side by side with this increased understanding, there have been technological advances – including in particular the techniques of magnetic resonance imaging (MRI) – which have confirmed the existence in dyslexia of distinctive brain organisations. These are varied and puzzling, and at present it is not possible for the findings to have any substantial influence on the provision of practical help. This is why the present book contains few references to developments in neurology and limits itself to what we have learned from our own observations and those of others.

With the increased understanding of dyslexia has come a major increase in the number of dyslexic students who have chosen to take courses in tertiary education at universities and colleges. In Chapter 5 we cite some statistics showing how striking this increase in numbers has been. At the same time there have been changes in the law. These are also described in Chapter 5 and referred to elsewhere in the book. Quite apart from anything to do with the needs of those who are dyslexic, there has been a greater public awareness of the needs of those who are in any way disabled. Although the message of this book is to encourage positive thinking about dyslexia, there is no doubt that in some sense dyslexic individuals are disabled by certain environments since there are some tasks which are more difficult for them than for their non-dyslexic peers. A discussion of the Disability Discrimination Acts will also be found in Chapter 5, along with information about the changes that universities and colleges are introducing as a response to the new requirements.

The Disabled Students' Allowance (DSA) had already figured in the second edition of this book, but there have subsequently been changes to the procedures for applying for it, and some clarification as to who is entitled to receive it (see in particular Chapter 3). Not surprisingly, since the 1996 edition of this book there have been technological advances of many different kinds. Many of these are of benefit to dyslexic students, and some of the more important ones have been set out in Chapter 16.

In this third edition, Chapter 1 has been substantially rewritten to take account of advances in our understanding of dyslexia. Chapter 2 is entirely new; it is entitled 'Dyslexia plus' and takes account of what may be called 'dyslexia-related' conditions: dyspraxia, attentional disorders, Asperger's syndrome and the more controversial 'dyscalculia'. There have been modifications and updating of references in the case of all of the other chapters. Chapter 21, 'Out of college and into work', is entirely new and it takes a forward look at the challenges which face dyslexic students after graduation.

Each chapter is provided with a short overview, indicating its content and its relevance to students, tutors or others involved in teaching and supporting dyslexic students. Where appropriate, documentation of the points made in the main text has been included in the form of notes to each chapter, along with extra comments which would have interrupted the flow of the argument in the main text. Recommended books on study skills and related topics are given in a separate section at the end, as is a list of the websites referred to throughout the book.

As in the previous editions, we have used 'he' and 'she' interchangeably on the grounds that students and tutors can be of either sex. Readers should make the necessary adjustments. They should also note that while we have called this book *Dyslexia at College*, the word 'college' should be understood to mean any institute of higher education, including universities and colleges of further education.

There are six appendices. These are written by former Bangor students, who have kindly described to us how they coped with their dyslexia when they were at college and/or their experiences later in life. We are very grateful to all six of them. We are also grateful for the many suggestions made to us by our colleagues at the university in Bangor. We should like to mention in particular Nikki Cameron, Ann Cooke and Elaine Miles (all from the Dyslexia Unit), Steph Tarn (from the university's Access Centre), Carolyn Donaldson-Hughes (Head of the Service for Disabled Students at Bangor), and finally Mike Du Pré who has learned to live with a laptop. Thank you to all of them.

Liz Du Pré
Tim Miles
September 2006

Authors' note

You are strongly advised to read this book only in *small* doses. We suggest you select from the table of contents those sections which are relevant to your needs on a particular occasion – do not try to read the book all at once!

The nature of dyslexia

By the time they have reached the age of about 16, most young people who have been assessed as dyslexic will be aware of their main strengths and weaknesses. For the benefit of their tutors and others involved in their teaching and support, however, we thought it would be helpful in this first chapter to indicate briefly what dyslexia is and, in particular, how it affects those who are taking – or are considering taking – degree courses at university or college. This chapter should also be of interest to those dyslexic students whose dyslexia has not yet been formally recognised or whose strengths and weaknesses have not been fully explained to them.

DYSLEXIC STRENGTHS AND WEAKNESSES

We have spoken of 'strengths and weaknesses'. It is important to give suitable prominence to both. Because of early struggles with reading and spelling, we know that many dyslexic students may have underestimated their own capabilities. The very word 'dyslexia' has negative connotations. It is for this reason that proposals have been made for a change in terminology – one which will enable those who are dyslexic to be viewed, and to view themselves, in a different light. Thus it has been suggested that they should be described not as 'disabled' but as 'differently abled' (**see note 1.1**). They have also been described as 'allomaths', which by derivation means 'learning in a different way' (**see note 1.2**). Some, such as Thomas West, have surmised that the distinctive brain organisation characteristic of dyslexia is associated with distinctive talents (**see note 1.3**).

West (1997) presents an impressive array of names of successful individuals who were either typically dyslexic or at least had dyslexic tendencies. West also points out that many of the clerical tasks which may have presented problems in the past can now be performed by computer. Certainly any terminology and any view of dyslexia which encourages positive thinking on the subject is to be greatly welcomed.

It is well established that on many types of task dyslexic students are no worse than their non-dyslexic peers. This applies, for instance, to many of the reasoning items in traditional intelligence tests, such as the ability to say how two or more things are alike. Suitably selected items from traditional intelligence tests are still useful in reassuring dyslexic students that they are certainly not stupid (**see note 1.4**). It is also a matter of familiar experience that many have outstanding gifts, for instance in art, architecture and the practical aspects of engineering. Perhaps surprisingly, weakness at reading and spelling does not prevent a sensitive appreciation of literature and poetry (**see note 1.5**).

For the rest of this chapter we shall be concentrating largely on the weaknesses of dyslexic students rather than on their strengths; if their needs are to be adequately met, it is essential that there is recognition of the aspects of study which may give rise to difficulties. It cannot be too much emphasised, however, that it is always important for dyslexic students and their tutors to think positively: the abilities of dyslexic people of all ages have too frequently been underestimated.

READING, WRITING AND SPELLING

Most dyslexic students have a history of lateness in learning to read and, even in adulthood, many continue to be poor spellers. The spellchecker on a computer, though useful, does not solve all problems, since the correct spelling offered by a computer is not always easy to recognise. The main disadvantage, however, which persists into adulthood, is a difficulty in dealing quickly with complex symbolic information – the memory easily becomes overloaded – and the effort needed in getting words and other symbols organised and ordered (**see note 1.6**).

For most dyslexic adults reading as such is not a major difficulty provided they are not under pressure of time and that there is not too much to hold in mind all at once. The main problem is that they are liable to remain *slow* readers and, unless they take plenty of time, there is a risk that they will *mis*read and therefore mistake the sense of what is written. With regard to slowness, it may take them longer than their non-dyslexic peers to read books or articles, to find the right place in a mathematical table or to check the times of buses or trains (**see note 1.7**). Those dyslexic students who can read reasonably adequately to themselves may nevertheless be very reluctant to read aloud (**see note 1.8**). There is more on reading and on strategies for coping with the academic reading load in **Chapter 11**.

With regard to misreading, there are some quite serious risks which we shall need to consider more fully when we come to discuss examination techniques (**see Chapters 18 and 19**). For instance, we know of a student in a physics examination who misread the direction of a vector line and wasted three-quarters of an hour before discovering his mistake. It is not that dyslexic students *cannot* read, but that they need to take extra care to avoid making mistakes which may seriously affect their understanding of what they read.

In addition, many dyslexic students make errors in writing – including the omission of words or parts of words and the transposition of letters. One student, instead of writing 'correlated', wrote 'corelatated' and when told that he had made a mistake said that he could see nothing wrong (**see note 1.9**). A graduate student, who had come to us for advice, afterwards sent a cheque and explained in his letter that it was a small 'denotation' to the Dyslexia Unit.

There was a problem in the past in that the handwriting of dyslexic students was sometimes hard to read and gave the impression of being immature; this in its turn could sometimes lead to their work receiving a lower mark than it might otherwise have done. Use of the word processor has now largely eliminated this source of unfairness, although some students report that their reliance on word processing means that the quality and fluency of their handwriting deteriorates rather than improves; this may be a concern in examinations for those dyslexic students who do not feel confident about using a word processor when there are time constraints.

Although correct spelling is not valued nowadays as much as it was in the past, a conscientious dyslexic student may spend precious time worrying over whether a particular word is spelled correctly or, even worse, choose a less effective word which is easier to spell in place of the word which he originally wanted. Those dyslexic students who wish to improve their spelling may like to refer to **Chapter 14**.

SPOKEN LANGUAGE

Dyslexic students are liable – more than others – to mispronounce words. For example, the following mispronunciations have been heard by us at a student discussion group: 'arriteration' for 'reiteration', 'simpler' for 'similar', 'relieve' for 'believe', 'pacific' for specific' and 'up the ball' instead of 'up the wall'. Unless one is specially on the look out for them, errors of this kind are not always noticed in ordinary conversation. However, they may have repercussions on spelling and in some cases may give rise to confusion – as in the case of the psychology student who was unsure whether a particular piece of research had been carried out by Bradley or by Baddeley.

NOTE-TAKING

If a dyslexic student attempts to write down in detail what is said in a lecture, it is very easy for his memory to become overloaded: if he tries to write at speed and at the same time devotes resources to understanding what is being said, the result may be that he succeeds in neither. For more on note-taking **see Chapter 11**.

ESSAYS

Planning and structuring essays is often a problem, not, indeed, because the dyslexic student has too little to say – usually quite the opposite is the case – but because of a limitation of the amount of material that he can hold in mind without writing it down. Essays written by dyslexic students, even though they may be full of good ideas, sometimes give the impression of a lack of planning and structure. There is more on essay writing in **Chapter 12**.

CALCULATION

Tutors should not be too surprised if some of their dyslexic students find difficulty over seemingly simple calculations. This can be true even in the case of those who can grasp highly complex mathematical ideas (**see note 1.10**). More will be said about mathematics in **Chapter 15**.

READING MUSICAL NOTATION

Many dyslexic people are gifted musicians, but, like the symbols of mathematics, the symbols used in musical notation may cause them problems; in particular, playing at first sight from a line of written music may not be easy, since it involves the absorption of a large amount of symbolic information in a short time. These problems are not insuperable, however, and it is sad if anyone is discouraged from playing music because of difficulties over musical notation (**note 1.11**).

SOCIAL PROBLEMS

These can take many forms. Many may seem minor to non-dyslexics, but may cause real unhappiness to those who live with them on a daily basis. For example, quite a number of students have told us of their embarrassment when they fail to remember someone's name. Several have found that learning to drive a car has highlighted their difficulties in following instructions over left and right. Some have told us that they avoid playing darts because, if they are asked to keep the score, they cannot carry out the calculations quickly enough. Most importantly, although dyslexic students may laugh about their present difficulties and speak of their earlier struggles without bitterness, it is important for tutors to remember that the scars may not have healed entirely (**see note 1.12**).

THE CAUSES OF DYSLEXIA

It is useful to think of dyslexia as a family of characteristics – what in medical terminology is called a 'syndrome'. A syndrome has been defined as 'a distinct group of symptoms or signs which, associated together, form a characteristic clinical picture or entity' (**note 1.13**). Those who have met and talked to even a few dyslexic people will recognise the underlying pattern.

The characteristics of dyslexia appear to be due to differences in the ways in which the brain is organised. There are many unanswered questions in this area, and there may be differences between one dyslexic individual and another. Dyslexia quite often runs in families, and this strongly suggests that a genetic factor is sometimes at work. In this book we need not be concerned with the neurology of dyslexia since not enough is yet known to provide firm (as opposed to speculative) justification for any changes to existing good practice. Thanks to modern technology in general, and to the techniques of magnetic resonance imaging (MRI), positron emission tomography (PET) and event-related potentials (ERP) studies in particular, knowledge is advancing at a fast rate, which means that theories are likely quickly to become out of date (**see note 1.14**). For the sake of completeness, however, we will mention two theories, not necessarily incompatible with each other, which currently command considerable support.

At the time of writing, a possible, though admittedly speculative, explanation is as follows (**note 1.15**). Researchers have divided the visual system of primates into two pathways, one containing relatively large cells (the magnocellular pathway), the other, smaller ones (the parvocellular pathway). The magnocellular system processes fast-moving, low-contrast information, while the parvocellular system processes slow-moving, high-contrast information. There may also be a similar division for the processing of sounds. Now, there is good evidence that a deficiency in the magnocellular system is associated with dyslexic difficulties. The suggestion is that on the auditory side this leads to difficulty in the ordering and recall of speech sounds. Thus, a widely held view of dyslexia is that it involves a weakness at the phonological level (where phonology is the study of speech sounds in so far as they convey meaning) (see note 1.16). If a person's ability to deal with fast-moving auditory or visual stimuli is inadequate, this could have subtle effects whenever that person is confronted with symbolic material – written words and letters of the alphabet, as well as algebraic symbols, symbols for chemical formulae, punctuation marks, musical notation and so on.

It is possible, therefore, that a deficient magnocellular system gives rise to phonological difficulties, which in their turn result in the familiar manifestations of dyslexia. However, as was noted above, once the function of a given symbol has been understood, dyslexic learners have no particular difficulty with comprehension. In general, dyslexic individuals show an imbalance of skills: they may have difficulty in taking in symbolic material when it is presented at speed, but they may be very successful at tasks that require good reasoning power – recognising patterns and similarities and being able to tell how things work.

An alternative view is that there are some differences in the structure of the cerebellum which give rise to dyslexic difficulties. This theory is associated in particular with the ideas of Fawcett and Nicolson (1994). One of their central points is that for those who are dyslexic a longer time is needed before skills become automatic, and this would include the development of phonological awareness. A particularly interesting contribution from these two researchers has been the formulation of the square-root rule. This is an attempt to explain in quantitative terms the amount of extra effort needed by someone who has dyslexic difficulties before a skill becomes automatic. Thus, if the average time needed in the case of a non-dyslexic for a skill to become automatic is 100 hours, then according to the square-root rule the same degree of proficiency will, on average, take a dyslexic person 1,000 hours to achieve (10 being the square root of 100, and 1,000 being 10 x 100). For further details **see note 1.17**).

Dyslexia, then, can be regarded as a syndrome or family of characteristics. It does not take exactly the same form in every individual, but the underlying pattern is not hard to recognise. It appears to be caused by differences in the way in which an individual's brain is organised. From the point of view of the college tutor, an important characteristic of dyslexic students is that they have an uneven balance of skills – some tasks, including the rapid processing of symbolic information, are hard for them – but it is particularly important that their talents should not be overlooked, and if dyslexic students are struggling it may often be helpful to say to them, 'These difficulties arise from the way in which you are made and *are not your fault.'*

CHECK POINTS FOR CHAPTER 1

Dyslexia can be seen as a syndrome or family of characteristics. While dyslexia does not take exactly the same form in every individual, the underlying pattern is not hard to recognise:

- Dyslexic people have an uneven balance of skills: the term 'differently abled' has been suggested in this respect.

- In particular, difficulties with the rapid processing of symbolic information affect the automaticity, accuracy and fluency of literacy skills; other tasks such as those involved in reading musical notation and certain areas of mathematics may also be affected.

- A dyslexic student's strengths may include good powers of reasoning – recognising patterns and similarities and being able to tell how things work.

- The characteristics of dyslexia appear to be due to differences in the ways in which the brain is organised.

- There are still many unanswered questions as to exactly what these differences in brain organisation are, and there may be differences between one dyslexic individual and another.

- Because of early struggles with reading and spelling, many dyslexic students underestimate their own capabilities and may still suffer from lack of self-esteem, despite having the strengths, talents and personal qualities which have helped them to achieve a place in university or college.

Chapter 2

Dyslexia plus

The title of this chapter highlights the fact that dyslexia is only one of a number of developmental differences – sometimes termed specific learning difficulties. Moreover, these may also overlap with dyslexia, to varying degrees. The chapter briefly describes aspects of AD(H)D, dyspraxia and Asperger's syndrome – with the aim of furthering understanding of the increasing neurodiversity amongst students in higher education and the challenge this presents to traditional concepts of teaching and assessment.

INTRODUCTION

As more has been understood about dyslexia, with the acknowledgment that the dyslexic pattern varies between individuals, so there has been recognition that there are a number of other developmental differences of which dyslexia is only one. (Some theorists have used the term 'developmental *anomolies*', but we prefer the word 'differences' since we regard 'anomolies' as question begging.) Moreover, there is often some degree of overlap between them (**see note 2.1**).

There is, now, growing awareness of what is termed the 'neurodiversity' of university and college students (**see note 2.2**). There is also more – though perhaps not yet enough – understanding of how these differences may affect students' learning and achievement. It is known, of course, that, like dyslexia, they are unrelated to intelligence and, as with dyslexia, the patterns of difference may include strengths as well as weaknesses.

As a result of increased awareness in schools and widening access to higher education, there are now more students with dyspraxia – also termed developmental co-ordination disorder (DCD), attentional disorders (attention deficit disorder, or ADD) and attention deficit hyperactivity disorder (AD(H)D) – and Asperger's syndrome. There are also students who have been described as 'dyscalculic' (**see note 2.3** and below). Many of these students have been previously recognised as dyslexic or dyspraxic, for example, and given appropriate support when they were at school. However, there are also students whose previous assessments may not have explicitly addressed the complexity of their difficulties, and still a large number who come to college with no previous formal assessment, despite having had varying degrees of difficulty during their time at school.

We have encountered many students who have entered college with previous assessments for dyslexia but who also have dyspraxic characteristics; others have been assessed as dyslexic but also have social and communication difficulties which perhaps lie on the autistic spectrum. One of the challenges for colleges and universities today is to increase understanding and awareness of this diversity, and to adapt their teaching, assessment and support so that these differences are catered for.

To ensure that these points are not neglected, we have added this chapter – Dyslexia plus – in the present book. We do not attempt to describe in detail how these differences affect a student undertaking higher education; that has been adequately done elsewhere (**see note 2.4** for further references and useful material). It may, however, be of help to both tutors and students if we give a brief description of some of the indications, particularly since in some contexts understanding may be a more constructive response than blaming.

AD(H)D

AD(H)D has been described as a persistent pattern of inattention and/or hyperactivity, and impulsivity:

- attention – inattention may occur in academic, occupational or social situations; AD(H)D students may fail to give close attention to details or may make seemingly careless mistakes in written work or other tasks; work may appear messy and disorganised, as if it were carried out with no considered thought;

- staying on task – people with AD(H)D often have difficulty in sustaining attention and find it hard to persist with tasks, moving from one task to another before any of them are completed;

- staying focused – being easily distracted, people with AD(H)D may often appear as if their mind is elsewhere or as if they did not hear what was just said; hyperactive students may constantly fidget, appear restless and easily distracted;

- taking turns – impulsivity may show itself in impatience or difficulty in delaying responses, for example by blurting out answers before questions have been completed.

For a student, these persistent characteristics can mean difficulties with study, with time management and planning, and with relationships with other students and staff. The word 'persistent' is important here. We can all be impulsive or inattentive without this implying the presence of AD(H)D. As with all the developmental differences, it is the overall pattern which is important, not any one individual episode.

DYSPRAXIA

Dyspraxia was sometimes known in the past as 'the clumsy child' syndrome and presents itself in a variety of different ways. The core difficulty is with skilled physical coordination. This may affect speech, general movement, spatial perception and fine-motor skills such as handwriting, tying knots, using paper clips etc. Some dyspraxic students describe themselves as 'still clumsy' – bumping into things, spilling drinks and so on. Those with severe dyspraxia would probably already have been given a medical assessment and support when they were younger from speech or occupational therapists.

Dyspraxia also affects students in more unexpected ways:

- organisation – e.g. paperwork and filing, keeping things tidy;

- time-management – estimating how long it will take to do things, meeting deadlines, getting to places on time, getting started on work;

- memory – forgetting things, losing things;

- attention and concentration – e.g. being sensitive to and easily distracted by sounds or lights;

- sequencing symbolic information – being able to remember the order of things, e.g. maths operations, or getting the right flow of ideas in essays;

- speech – pronunciation being affected or speech noticeably fast, loud or slow;

- reading – difficulties with tracking print or skimming and scanning text for information, in books or on a screen.

ASPERGER'S SYNDROME

Asperger's syndrome (AS) is usually regarded as being at the mild end of the autistic spectrum. AS students may be of high general intelligence but they have particular difficulties with social interaction and communication.

- social interaction – an AS student may have difficulty interacting with others, understanding what others are thinking and feeling and understanding what is appropriate behaviour in different social situations;

- language – AS students may be very literal in their use of language: this affects their understanding of what others mean, and their own communication; they may not be able to pick up 'between the lines' hints or meanings in conversation, or 'read' meaning implicit in others' facial expressions and body language;

- dealing with change – routine is very important to many of those with AS, who may be upset by unexpected changes or easily distracted by sounds, lights or by what others would think were unimportant details; related to this is the ability to become completely absorbed in topics of interest – almost to the point of seeming obsessed.

LUMPING AND SPLITTING

Researchers in these areas are regularly confronted with the problem of where to 'lump' and where to 'split', that is where to classify characteristics together, as exemplifying the same condition or syndrome, and where to separate them off. Thus, it is sometimes supposed that there is a separate syndrome, dyscalculia, for describing those with persistent and severe problems with calculation. The alternative view is that the manifestations which people call dyscalculia should all be regarded as part of the dyslexia syndrome. How to classify and where to draw boundaries is not made any easier by the fact that, as noted above, we often find overlap: a person may, for instance, have signs both of dyslexia and of AD(H)D. If a student appears to have difficulty in attending to what is going on in a lecture, this could be part of the AD(H)D picture, or it could be part of his dyslexia in that his memory becomes easily overloaded.

DO WE NEED LABELS?

The importance of a label is that it can – to an extent – explain why someone has a particular pattern of strengths and weaknesses, and indicate both what ought to be done and what to expect in the future. For many people, an assessment which explains to them why they have had particular struggles and difficulties can come as a relief after years of frustration and feelings of inadequacy. Not least, under the current funding system for higher education in Britain, obtaining the label may open the door to support.

In contrast, if the wrong label is given, the resultant misunderstanding can be disastrous. However, just because two people have been given the same label (such as 'dyslexia'), it by no means follows that they have the same needs. It would be a serious mistake to promote a one-size-fits-all treatment for dyslexia – or for any other of the diverse conditions described here.

There is the further complication that sometimes the indicators may occur in a very mild form: unless they are causing significant inconvenience, no action is necessary. There is a risk, however, that what seemed like a minor inconvenience at one stage in a student's career may, at another stage when demands have changed, give rise to major problems.

It is important, therefore, that the label should not be allowed to steal the show; the key question for universities and colleges is: 'What are this person's needs or, rather, what barriers to success does she experience in her studies?' because the way she best learns – and can demonstrate her learning – is one that does not have an easy fit with traditional methods of teaching and assessment (**see note 2.5**). These ideas are discussed further in **Chapter 5**.

CHECK POINTS FOR CHAPTER 2

Dyslexia is not uncommonly accompanied by characteristics of other developmental differences:

- **AD(H)D** – characterised by differences in aspects of attention and impulsivity;

- **dyspraxia** – characterised by differences in aspects of motor control and coordination;

- **Asperger's syndrome** – characterised by differences in aspects of social relationships and communication;

- like dyslexia, these specific differences are unrelated to general intelligence;

- the patterns of difference may include strengths as well as weaknesses;

- at their mildest, there is what can be termed a subtle interchange with 'normality';

- labels may be useful in so far as they help us to understand our behaviour and individual patterns of strength and difficulties.

The term 'neurodiversity' is increasingly used to emphasise the positive aspects of the differences between us; in particular, it points to the need for our social and cultural institutions (including colleges and universities) to ensure that, as far as is possible, their practices accommodate – and aim to include rather than exclude – such diversity.

Chapter 3

Understanding your assessment

In this chapter we make suggestions for students as to how the information obtained as a result of an assessment for dyslexia can be put to best use. If you have already been assessed for dyslexia, and have no particular queries about the assessment or the written report, you could skip the first sections here. You may, however, be interested in the final sections about the Disabled Students' Allowance, and about adjustments which may be made for you on your course.

INTRODUCTION

Many dyslexic students will, before they reach college, already have had assessments indicating that they are dyslexic and making suitable recommendations. Not all dyslexic students, however, will have received such assessments (**see note 3.1**). We have come across plenty of students, particularly older ones, whose dyslexia has been recognised only after the start of their college courses. In some cases tutors or lecturers have suggested to students that they might be dyslexic on the basis of their essays or other written work; in some cases the students themselves have wondered if they are dyslexic and have come forward for assessment.

HAVING AN ASSESSMENT FOR DYSLEXIA

There may, of course, be students who for various reasons are poor spellers but who do not have the other typical signs associated with dyslexia. Their difficulties may be the result of other factors, such as a prolonged absence from school at an important stage. In view of this, many colleges operate what has been called a screening or preliminary informal assessment: this is a preliminary assessment to determine the nature and extent of a student's difficulties before sending him on for formal assessment.

During the formal assessment itself, you are asked to carry out a number of tasks or tests. Their aim is to find out both your strong and your weak points. Even the word 'test' may be off-putting for some people, particularly if they have had unpleasant experiences with testing in the past. However, in this case there is no need to feel threatened. You are in no way being got at, and you will normally find that the person who carries out the test is glad to talk to you about the results and willing to answer your questions. If she does not wish to do so, you should ask your dyslexia tutor to talk through your report with you when you receive it.

READING AND SPELLING TESTS

The assessment will almost certainly include tests of reading and spelling. Your results on these tests will give you an indication of the level of reading and spelling that you have reached. The key question which you need to ask is whether this level is adequate for your needs. If it is not, then you would be wise to look for further help either before your course starts or, if you have already started it, as something additional to your existing studies.

If you decide that it is possible to do something about your weaknesses, as it certainly is in the case of reading and spelling, and that the effort is worth it, then the assessment has helped you.

Your performance may be scored in terms of percentiles. If you are in, say, the 50th percentile, this means that half of your fellow students will have scored higher than you on the test and half lower. If you are in the 95th percentile, only 5 per cent of them will have scored higher; if you are in the 5th percentile, only 5 per cent of them will have scored lower.

In all scores of this kind you are being compared with other people. Such comparisons can be useful *for some purposes*. However, there may also be times when it is more appropriate to compare your *present score* with the score which you yourself obtained *on an earlier occasion*, for example if you want to know whether your reading has improved (**see note 3.2**).

It is possible, though this is less common nowadays, that your performance will be described in terms of a reading age and of a spelling age. If, for example, you have a reading age of 11 years, this means that your reading is on a level with that of a typical (non-dyslexic) 11-year-old. It does not, of course, mean that your mentality is in other ways like that of an 11-year-old! You should remember that most 11-year-olds are fairly adequate readers; and if you have a reading age of 12 years and a spelling age of 11 and a half years you will not have too much difficulty with college courses.

If you are interested, you may like to talk to the person who did the testing about how the scores were obtained. Some reading tests involve the identification of single words, whereas others involve making sense of a passage of prose – in which case there is a certain amount of scope for guessing from the context. In the case of single-word reading the usual procedure is to award one point for each word correctly read; it is worth remembering that this method of scoring does not differentiate between near misses and total failures. There is the same limitation in the case of spelling. In general, a reading age and a spelling age can normally be regarded as a reasonably accurate indicator of your performance on a given occasion, but you should of course always remember that *numerical scores do not tell us everything*.

INTELLIGENCE TESTS

This is also true if you are given an intelligence test, now often called 'tests of cognitive ability'. There is evidence that suggests that those who are successful in some of these tests are also likely to be successful in the skills which are needed in studying for a degree. However, for various reasons, scores on intelligence tests are somewhat controversial things (**see note 3.3**), particularly in the case of those who are dyslexic. We therefore offer some words of caution. Whatever else, if your tester uses the traditional concept of IQ, do not regard the resultant figure as something cast in tablets of stone. Several decades ago it was widely believed that every individual possessed something called an IQ (intelligence quotient), which was assumed to be something that could not change and which imposed a ceiling on what the person could achieve. As a result, people came to regard the IQ figure as being of crucial importance, and this attitude has still not entirely disappeared.

Such thinking has always seemed to us defeatist, since there is reason to think that many different kinds of learning are possible given the right environment (**see note 3.4**). In particular, many dyslexic students have surprised us – and sometimes, we suspect, themselves – by what they were able to achieve despite having a relatively poor academic record before they came to college and/or an allegedly low IQ figure. Traditional intelligence tests – which were devised before dyslexia was widely understood – contain some items that are weighted against those who are dyslexic (for example tests in which you have to recall strings of digits). Far from being measures of intelligence, these items are actually tapping typical dyslexic difficulties (**note 3.5**); an overall IQ figure may therefore be an underestimation of a dyslexic student's ability.

Remember then that as intelligence tests test a variety of skills it is possible that your performance may be uneven. This is yet another reason why giving your 'total' performance in terms of an IQ figure can be misleading. The exact spread of your scores is something that you can usefully discuss with the assessor or your dyslexia tutor. One can say in general that, if you are dyslexic, it is likely that there will be a marked contrast between your intelligence test scores and your ability to spell and write essays – but this is not always the case.

You would certainly be right to feel encouraged if you find that you have come out with high scores on an intelligence test – it is all too easy for dyslexic students to underestimate their abilities; but in our experience we have often found that low scores give a misleading picture. There are also questions about the narrowness of the aspects of intelligence that these tests address; some theorists prefer to broaden the concept of intelligence and speak of 'multiple intelligences' (**see note 3.6**).

Our advice, therefore, is that if you are keen to take an academic course and are willing to put in the required effort a relatively low score on your reading, spelling and intelligence tests should not discourage you from doing so. If a course genuinely turns out to be too difficult for you, this will almost certainly become apparent in a matter of weeks: for many people it is better to try something and fail than not to attempt it and then wonder for evermore whether they should have done so.

OTHER TESTS

Accurate information about your strengths and weaknesses can also be valuable if you are given tests other than those of reading, spelling and intelligence, for example the Bangor Dyslexia Test (**note 3.7**). This particular test can often help you to understand more about the kinds of things which you have found difficult and about why it has been necessary for you to think out particular compensatory strategies. Some students have found, after being given this test, that various earlier events in their lives fitted together as part of their dyslexia. For example, if, on the basis of what they do on the Bangor Dyslexia Test, the tester discusses with them their difficulty in remembering verbal instructions or telephone numbers, this may remind them that when they were much younger they were reprimanded for failing to convey a message accurately from the school to their parents. It is only now that they realise that their failure was a direct consequence of their dyslexia. Thus, the items which show up a memory weakness may give a valuable insight into the reason for some of the problems you may have experienced, and you should be able to talk to your tutor about ways of coping with these (**see note 3.8**).

WHY HAVE AN ASSESSMENT?

One of us (TRM) has met a famous dyslexic actor who reported both that he tended to be late for appointments and that he could not remember names. People had regarded this simply as arrogance; but he said that when he realised he was dyslexic he felt forgiven. In general, you may well find as a result of your assessment that you have gained a much better understanding of the part which your dyslexia has played in your life. You may be better aware of your strengths and feel encouraged to work out further strategies for coping with your weaknesses.

A formal dyslexia assessment is of course essential for students who want to apply for the Disabled Students' Allowance (see below) because those in charge of the money need to be satisfied that you are a genuine applicant. It will also be important if you wish to request adjustments, for example to exam arrangements on your course. As a general rule, if you plan to take college courses, your dyslexia assessment report should have been written, or updated, after your sixteenth birthday, and within two years of your starting the course; your assessment report must also contain the results of a specified range of tests if you wish to be considered for the Disabled Students' Allowance (**see note 3.9**).

A WORD OF ADVICE

If, as still occasionally happens, you are assessed by someone who in your view does not fully understand about dyslexia, do not worry too much: such people, though they are a dwindling number, are still to be found. In some cases, perhaps through lack of experience, through misunderstanding or simply through excessive caution, they may express reservations about the term 'dyslexia'. If you meet such a person, the sensible response, in our view, is to make use of such information as she gives you – reading scores, spelling scores, intelligence scores and the like – without necessarily accepting the inferences which she draws. This general principle applies, of course, to any counselling situation. Counsellors are only human – and even with the best of intentions they do not always get things right (**see note 3.10**).

THE DISABLED STUDENTS' ALLOWANCE

Now for some good news! Many students who are assessed as dyslexic can claim a Disabled Students' Allowance (DSA); this funds support to help you through your course. Do not, incidentally, be put off by the word 'disabled'. As was pointed out in Chapter 1, it is perhaps more helpful to think of dyslexics not as 'disabled' but as 'differently abled' and to remember that, despite your other capabilities, if your reading and writing are not fluent, you are to an extent *dis*-abled by an academic environment which places a premium on these skills. When people speak of the Disabled Students' Allowance, the term 'disabled' is used in this context for administrative purposes, as an indication that you might benefit from support in meeting academic demands.

The DSA (**see note 3.11**) is a three-part allowance which consists of:

- a general allowance intended to cover extra costs (e.g. for extra photocopying) incurred by specific aspects of dyslexia which make it difficult for you to study;

- an allowance for payment to non-medical helpers (e.g. those who provide note-taking or special tutorial help);

- a further allowance for equipment such as specialist software, a word processor and so on.

Your dyslexia assessment report may make specific recommendations, for example it may indicate the study support that you need, the type of computer equipment that you need, whether you should benefit from adjustments to examination provision, whether you would be helped by coloured filters or lenses (**see Chapter 11**) and so on. It is possible that the cost of this support will be met through the DSA. To apply for this, you should contact the Student Support officers in your Local Authority (LA) in the first instance; they will be able to tell you what to do next (**see note 3.12**).

You then need to have an Assessment of Study Needs, at an Access Centre. If there is one attached to your chosen university, it might be best to go there. This will be paid for. The Assessment of Study Needs is *not* more tests. Rather, it is an informal discussion with experienced assessors to establish the equipment and support you will need on your course as a direct result of your dyslexia. Recommendations are drawn up by the assessors, and when you have seen and agreed to them they will be sent to your LA, or the Student Loan Company, for approval. Recommendations are also made for the university or college, regarding adjustments that you need arising from the way the course is taught and assessed.

ADJUSTMENTS TO TEACHING AND ASSESSMENT

You will be able to hand both your dyslexia assessment report and your Study Needs Assessment report to your college staff, and the relevant sections will indicate to them what adjustments are needed, particularly with regard to teaching methods and arrangements for examinations. The intention is that you should not be in any way disadvantaged in your studies as a result of your dyslexia. Procedures vary at different institutions, but it is likely that staff will discuss with you adjustments to the way that you are taught and assessed which might be put into place to support you. Examples of such adjustments might be ensuring that you have copies of outline notes of lectures beforehand or consideration of your specific difficulties when your work is marked. With your permission, your department and the examinations office will be involved in arranging such adjustments (**see Chapter 5**).

CHECK POINTS FOR CHAPTER 3

There are several important points to note about having an assessment for dyslexia:

- It may help you to understand why you have had particular difficulties.

- Your scores on the various tests will show you where your strengths and weaknesses lie.

- Remember that overall IQ scores may be misleading.

- Don't be discouraged if the report says that you have low reading and/or spelling ages.

- Make sure that you are able to discuss the report, either with the person who assessed you or with your dyslexia support tutor.

- If you want to apply for the Disabled Students' Allowance, your assessment report must be no more than two years old, and it must show the results of a certain range of tests.

- You will also need an up-to-date report if you want any adjustments to be made to the way your course is taught and assessed.

Chapter 4

The move to higher education

This chapter is for students and those advising them (possibly parents and teachers): we outline issues to consider when choosing a degree course. You will also find guidance on making applications and advice on disclosing dyslexia and on going for interviews.

THE STUDENT'S WISHES

When choices relating to degree courses and career come up, the central consideration must of course be the student's own wishes. Much sensitivity is needed, however, on the part of parents and teachers if they are to strike the right balance between positively encouraging her on the one hand, which is often very welcome, and putting her under undue pressure, which is not.

The first suggestion we would like to make to anyone who is thinking of going to college is: do not be afraid of taking risks. In our experience the ability of a dyslexic student is often underestimated – and this not merely by her teachers but often also by herself. We have frequently met parents who secretly felt that their son or daughter was very bright and well capable of taking academic courses but were reluctant to say this in public, particularly if unsympathetic teachers and educational psychologists – claiming to be realistic – had told them that they were overambitious. There may be a completely sincere wish to save the student from disappointment (**see note 4.1**). Yet is it not sometimes kinder to encourage a person to attempt something, even if there is risk of failure, than to allow her to go through the rest of her life wondering if she should have made the attempt? We have met many dyslexic students who derived tremendous encouragement from knowing that there were those who were prepared to back them against the odds and in spite of their weak examination results.

This has been particularly relevant in the case of mature students on Access courses, which are designed to prepare students for degree study; these students have often come back into education with few traditional qualifications and therefore might be expected to find academic work difficult.

Of course, there are risks for some dyslexic students if they attempt college courses. However, such risks seem fully justified, provided the student is aware of them, is willing to work hard and is prepared for possible disappointments. It can often be a greater error for a dyslexic student to set her sights too low than to set them too high (**see note 4.2**). If your interests are academic, there is every reason for you to try for a place at college where you will find that you are one among many dyslexic students and that there is now a great deal of understanding and support (**see Chapter 5**).

ROUTES TO HIGHER EDUCATION

Parents and prospective students should make themselves aware of the various routes into higher education. Since the second edition of this book was published in 1996, access to study at degree level in Britain has widened, and there have been other changes (**see Chapter 5**) which have led to better opportunities for dyslexic students to display their abilities; those living in other parts of the world may well be able to explore similar possibilities.

A dyslexic student with only a small number of passes at GCSE (General Certificate of Secondary Education) may like to consider courses in a local college (these colleges were originally called Colleges of Further Education – FE Colleges or Technical Colleges) (**see note 4.3**). Sixth-form colleges are also broadening their range of courses. There are vocational step-by-step courses, such as Foundation courses (including technicians and pre-apprenticeship courses), which can lead on to Edexcel or baccalaureate diplomas,

General National Vocational Qualifications (GNVQs) or BTEC courses at varying levels. Students may progress to HND (Higher National Diploma) courses, to higher-level NVQ courses or to other courses that lead to a degree (**see note 4.4**).

Older students who may not have been successful at school may find that an ACCESS course leading to higher education is their best option. These courses are designed for mature students who wish to return to learning. They contain core skills, such as information technology, study skills and mathematics, all of which develop the basic abilities needed for higher education.

Many local colleges are now offering students the chance to study for a degree. The learning environment in such colleges can be very supportive, and dyslexic students should look at a local college's higher-education prospectus if they feel wary about moving away from home. Other prospective students may wish to consider studying for a degree with the Open University (**see note 4.5**).

It is also worth noting that the degree courses at some of the new universities often follow the same principles as Edexcel, baccalaureate and GNVQ courses: they tend to be more practical and less theoretical and academic than traditional university courses. Many of them are tested by continuous assessment, and the students who take them are encouraged to use many different methods of collecting, collating and presenting information. Some of them are structured on a sandwich basis, with their students spending a proportion of their time working in industry. This can give them work experience and provide them with the necessary practical training. Moreover, as with some of the lower-level courses, assessment techniques are likely to contain a relatively large oral element, along with evaluation of students' work experience and their ability to respond to real-life situations. There is less emphasis on the formal written word, and the final grading does not place undue reliance on examinations of the traditional type.

CHOOSING YOUR DEGREE COURSE

It is very important that you spend time thinking carefully about what degree course you want to do. There is a CD-ROM published by the University and College Admissions System (UCAS) which contains a full guide to all courses on offer (**see note 4.6**). You can also find out about courses, universities and possible (eventual) career opportunities from some excellent comprehensive guides (**see note 4.7**).

Many dyslexic people have skills and sensitivity in the field of human relationships, and for them some forms of nursing or teaching, social work, probation work and the like may often be a good choice. Many, too, may wish to make use of their gifts in the area of art or design, while others have talents for working with computers and for software design: at Bangor there are always a good number of dyslexic students on computer science courses.

When you start to make enquiries, you should look in particular at the content of courses, at the way in which different ones are organised and at the methods of assessment used. You will usually find course tutors and admissions tutors very willing to offer help and advice, and, if it is at all possible, you should look round the departments and talk to students who are already on the course. Most colleges now have support services for dyslexic students which produce their own publicity leaflets, and there may be information available in the university's prospectus and website. However, there is variation between one institution and another, and you should also remember that there are likely to be many different attitudes to dyslexia, not merely within the same institution but even within the same department.

At degree level, it is essential that you should feel genuinely committed to your chosen subject. At the same time, you need to be realistic about your difficulties. Thus, if you find writing essays very difficult, you will need to check carefully on the amount of written work that the course involves. Most courses now are organised on a modular basis, which gives students some flexibility in their choices;

but you should check what you are committing yourself to before undertaking a particular module.

A few subjects, such as physics or computer science, require mathematics at a high level (for instance a knowledge of calculus), while there are some which need a knowledge of basic mathematics because of the use which they make of statistics. These include, among others, psychology, economics, education, agriculture, biological sciences, sociology and business studies. Do not rule out the idea of taking such courses because you feel that you have problems with mathematics. There may be parts of mathematics that you have missed out on at school, but these can be learned. Indeed, there is no reason why those who are keen should not do a degree in mathematics (**see note 4.8**). There are admittedly difficulties in the early stages, for example in holding figures in mind so that one can carry out calculations. These difficulties, however, can be overcome, in which case the way is open for challenging and enjoyable academic work. Those who have found mathematics a struggle may like to bear in mind some of the things that are discussed in **Chapter 14**.

There have been dyslexic students who have qualified as doctors or dentists; it seems likely that a good understanding of anatomical and physiological processes can to some extent compensate for relative inefficiency at learning by rote the necessary medical terms; there is, however, a considerable amount of rote learning involved in this training. Many technical and drug terms will be spelt out by the computer, but the ability to read such words correctly is essential. We know of a dyslexic surgeon who claims that his high visuo-spatial abilities actually put him at an advantage in certain forms of surgery in comparison with his colleagues (**see note 4.9**).

Engineering calls for less by way of language skills than some subjects, and, although written examinations have to be passed and clear thinking is essential, it is possible for a dyslexic student to show in his examination answers that he understands a particular issue, even if he cannot spell correctly or express himself very easily. Chemistry, physics, mathematics and computer science may present certain difficulties because of the amount of symbolism involved, but once the symbols are learned – which will probably take extra time – a dyslexic student may well be extremely successful. We know also of many dyslexic students who have honours degrees in biological subjects and we have first-hand evidence of many who have achieved honours degrees in psychology.

With arts subjects, there is inevitably more to do by way of reading the relevant literature and writing essays, and it is unavoidable that students will have to spend very much more time over written assignments than do non-dyslexics. Degrees in English, history, sociology, economics and the like are by no means ruled out, however, and we have met a number of dyslexic students who have been successful in business studies (indeed some dyslexic people have proved to be very successful in running their own businesses: think of Richard Branson).

Philosophy has sometimes been a struggle, and although we know of a small number of dyslexic barristers or trainees, some dyslexic people might find law difficult because of the amount of reading and rote learning involved. Foreign languages are also likely to be hard going because of the effort needed in mastering the spelling systems of languages additional to English. If, however, there is a one–one correspondence between letters and sounds, as there is in Spanish, Italian, Welsh and (to some extent) German, learning to spell in these languages may not be too difficult. French, however, and the Scandinavian languages are likely to be hard. Nevertheless, in no case should a particular course be ruled out without careful consideration of a student's individual wishes and aptitudes.

We know many dyslexic students who have trained as teachers. It is sometimes supposed that there is risk of embarrassment for them if they write up a word which the class can see is misspelled. However, it could also be argued that a conscientious teacher will usually be able to forestall possible difficulties by suitable preparation. For example, if he is writing a report on a child, he can check his spellings with a dictionary, and if he writes a misspelled word on the board in front of the class – well, it does not seem to us a major disaster if he has to admit that his spelling is not as good as he would wish. After all, it is widely agreed that to retain the pupils' respect one need not present oneself as being infallible (**see note 4.10**). Some dyslexic students have said they would like to specialise in the teaching of dyslexic children. However, most specialised training courses, not unreasonably, require that applicants should have had some ordinary classroom experience first.

HOW IS THE COURSE TAUGHT?

There are various other factors to think about in choosing a course, apart from its content. There may be advantages in being at a small college or in a small department where students are personally known to the tutors. Lectures to a very large audience, particularly if they involve a large amount of overhead projector or PowerPoint slides, can be quite daunting for dyslexic students. Find out whether lecturers provide handouts of lecture notes or outlines of the main points to be covered in lectures; ask too whether lecture notes are published on the university's intranet. It is also wise to find out what are the methods of teaching: some, though not all, dyslexic students enjoy taking part in oral discussions, and those who do so may like to choose departments where there are regular group meetings and tutorials.

HOW IS THE COURSE ASSESSED?

Also, since most dyslexic students are likely to do themselves better justice if they are assessed in untimed conditions, it is sensible to apply to a department which does not rely solely on timed written examinations. The majority of departments nowadays award marks on the basis of continuous assessment and take into account performance on projects, dissertations and the like. It is worthwhile to check how often examinations are held; in modular courses this is usually twice a year, which allows for a staggered revision load. There may be recommendations for adjustments to examination provision (for example extra time, use of a word processor) written into your dyslexia assessment report, or your Assessment of Study Needs for the DSA. It would be sensible to confirm that these adjustments will be available on your new course and to find out whether your specific difficulties will be considered when your work is marked: contact the dyslexia support staff, or the department you are joining, to discuss this.

WHERE DO YOU WANT TO BE?

Another consideration is environment. You need to ask yourself whether you prefer a country setting or a town one. Often a smaller place or a campus university is easier to get around and involves less travelling stress. In view of the extra amount of work dyslexic students need to do, it is sensible not to live too far away from the institution as travelling to and from lectures can take up valuable time. Those who feel the need for continuing support from their parents should choose a university or college that is reasonably near home.

FILLING IN THE UCAS FORM

A problem which may cause heart searching is that of how to fill in the application form. (This is commonly the *UCAS form*.) There is much useful information on this in *Applying to Higher Education for Dyslexic Students* (**see note 4.6**). The form is complicated and you should certainly ask for help in filling it in; your school or college may assist you in making an online application, but, if you need to apply on paper, it will help you to photocopy the application form so you have a rough copy on which you can make alterations.

Some of the entries are relatively straightforward, for example address of parent or guardian (though who can say that anything is straightforward if you are dyslexic, and if a form contains a complicated mass of symbols?). On the form you have to indicate your qualifications and your choice of different universities or colleges. You are also asked to write a personal statement, in which you set out your reasons for applying for your chosen subject and outline your personal experiences and interests. If you refer to your dyslexia in this section (see below), we advise you to do so as positively as you can, and to mention your strengths, what strategies you have to cope with your dyslexia and how you plan to cope with it when you get to college. The same point is important if you are being interviewed. David McLoughlin and his colleagues (**see note 4.11**) have said that what makes dyslexic adults do well are:

- a desire to succeed

- being sure of their goal

- being willing to take action to overcome their difficulties.

This last point could be particularly important if you are to convince the admissions officer that you are a well-rounded person and that you have the ability and determination to complete the course.

At the end of the UCAS form a referee, usually your head teacher or someone of similar status, has to write a confidential report on your suitability to take a college course. In this report, it is normal practice nowadays for the referee to refer to an applicant's dyslexia.

DISCLOSING DYSLEXIA

This brings us to the question: 'Should you yourself mention on the UCAS form that you are dyslexic?'

If you are likely to need *any* kind of adjustment to the way the course is taught and assessed, or if you will need some form of support, the answer is 'yes'. There is now plenty of evidence that dyslexic students are perfectly capable of obtaining high-class degrees, and it is hard to believe that any selectors are so ill-informed that they would regard dyslexia as such to be a barrier to admission. Indeed, the opposite may well be the case, since a dyslexic student with relatively low grades in his examinations – where inevitably the odds are stacked against him for reasons given in Chapter 1 – is likely to be a better prospect, particularly in terms of creative ability and seriousness of purpose, than a non-dyslexic student whose grades are somewhat higher. This is a factor that we know selectors have increasingly come to appreciate.

A further point is this. There is now a section at the beginning of the form where you can indicate that you have a disability. In a later section you are asked to follow this up by indicating what special arrangements you are likely to require (exam provisions, study support etc.). You also have to sign a statement saying that what you have put on the form is true. Clearly, therefore, if you do not disclose your dyslexia you cannot in that case expect your university or college to make any adjustments. On the other hand, if you do disclose it, the support services will be able to contact you, discuss with you the adjustments you need and advise you on applying for the DSA so that you can have these arrangements in place as soon as you start your course.

TAKING MORE TIME?

Some students take a gap year before going on to university. This gives them the chance to recharge their batteries after an intensive A-level course and perhaps to gain some valuable experience in voluntary work – or, indeed, paid work (**see note 4.12**). Admissions tutors welcome the idea of a gap year but like to see it used positively. Students may also like to bear in mind that if they are over 21 they are classed as *mature* students, and this may affect their financial status as a student.

The report of the Kershaw Committee (**see note 4.13**) contains recommendations that have relevance today:

> where ... a university student is dyslexic he should be permitted to stay at the university for an extra year beyond the ordinary duration of his course. The alternative might well be a final examination level which would not reflect his true capacity.

Dyslexic students should not hesitate to discuss with their tutors the question of taking extra time over their courses. The issue is one which needs to be worked out separately for each individual. It is not necessary in the case of every dyslexic student, but our experience suggests that for some students it is extremely beneficial, particularly for those students who feel themselves overwhelmed by the amount of material to be covered or who tire easily. In a three-year course, the break is likely to be most useful between the second and third years. During this time, the student can consolidate what he has learned in the first two years and perhaps also take an advance look at some of the topics to be covered in the final year. Above all, however, he can have a change of scene and a rest so that he does not feel under too much pressure.

We know other students who have arranged with their university to take one or two years of their degree on a part-time basis. A drawback to an extra year is that it will, of course, involve extending the student loan.

INTERVIEWS

If your application form indicates that you are likely to have severe difficulties in meeting course requirements, we recommend to selectors that they invite you for an informal interview. This gives an opportunity for a joint exploration of what the course involves, whether it covers the areas in which you are genuinely interested and what adjustments to course delivery and assessment would be advisable to give you the best possible opportunity for success.

Remember that the purpose of the interview is not to catch you out but to determine whether a particular course is suitable for you; be careful, then, not to read more into a question than the questioner intended, particularly if this 'more' is perceived as threatening (**see note 4.14**).

For dyslexic applicants mock interviews are likely to be of special help. What is involved here is that a careers adviser or teacher takes on the role of interviewer and asks searching questions similar to those which you are likely to be asked at the interview proper. Indeed, it is useful if the 'interviewer' asks extra-difficult questions; then, if such questions occur in the real interview, you will not be taken unawares. One function of the mock interview is to give you practice at formulating your ideas, and if you are used to the procedure you will find the real interview less of a strain. Many of us fail to find the right words if we are under pressure; with dyslexia, there is the added risk of mispronunciation, stumbling or going blank.

If you are asked about dyslexia, it is probably wise if you talk about it as objectively as possible, neither playing it down nor making too much of it. There is no reason why you should not indicate that there are certain tasks that you still find difficult, but you should also talk about the compensatory strategies you have found useful.

THE GOOD NEWS

What is good news is that, as we have already indicated, the whole scene for dyslexic students has altered beyond recognition over the last 20 years. The next chapter looks at how things have changed – and are still changing.

CHECK POINTS FOR CHAPTER 4

Dyslexic students – you should aim high. Think carefully about what degree course you will take, and where you will choose to do it.

Think about:

- how the course is taught;
- how it is assessed;
- where you want to be – where would it suit you best to live?;
- the support that is available;
- disclosing dyslexia when you apply;
- discussing dyslexia and any needs you have;
- taking more time to complete a course.

Chapter 5

Changes to the landscape

This chapter has good news for dyslexic students. It outlines the changes which are happening in higher education, as a result of legislation, that are particularly relevant to you. It is important to understand how adjustments can be made to support you in your studies, and how you can contribute to the debate about change for the future.

INTRODUCTION

In the years from about 1980 onwards there were a number of important changes in universities and colleges in Britain. From the point of view of those interested in dyslexia the most dramatic change was the increase in the number of dyslexic students in higher education: in 1981 there were probably around 100 students at university in Britain who were recognised as dyslexic; in 1994 there were around 5,000; in 2003 there were more than 42,000, including nearly 4,500 postgraduate students (**see note 5.1**). In response to this rise in numbers there has been a rise both in the public's understanding of dyslexia and in the availability of support for dyslexic students in schools, colleges and universities.

The existence of the Disabled Students' Allowance (DSA) has meant that students can get help to enable them to progress through a university course more easily. Skill, the National Bureau for Students with Disabilities, has been of particular support to dyslexic students, and its staff offer advice both to them and to their tutors. There is also ADO, the Adult Dyslexia Organisation, which works for dyslexic students as well as adults in the workplace (**see note 5.2**). To some extent the growth of all this support has been the result of the successes of small numbers of dyslexic students who, from the 1970s onwards, beat the system and worked their way to college despite all kinds of initial disadvantages (in the appendices at the back of this book you can read contributions from a few of these students).

Perhaps most important of all are the changed – and still changing – expectations of what dyslexic students can achieve and especially expectations about how universities and colleges can adapt and adjust so as to give the students the best possible opportunity for success. This was reflected in the extension in 2001 of the original Disability Discrimination Act (DDA) 1995 to apply to education (**see note 5.3**).

WHAT HAS CHANGED?

It is now unlawful for universities and colleges to discriminate against disabled applicants, potential applicants or students in either of two ways:

- by treating them 'less favourably' than other people or
- by failing to make a 'reasonable adjustment' when they are placed at a 'substantial disadvantage' compared to other people.

Institutions are expected to make what are called 'anticipatory adjustments'. This means that if they can reasonably expect certain students to need particular adjustments they should plan ahead to ensure that the changes are made. In this respect, institutions are expected to do what is 'reasonable': what is reasonable will depend on all the individual circumstances of the case, including the need to maintain academic standards, resources available, the cost of the adjustments and so on (**see note 5.4**).

WHAT DOES THIS MEAN FOR DYSLEXIC STUDENTS?

The introduction of the DDA has meant that universities and colleges have needed to consider what adjustments are needed for a range of students, and this includes dyslexic students (**see note 5.5**). Put simply, the idea is that students should not be faced with unnecessary barriers to their learning – or to their being able to demonstrate what they have learned. Adjustments are the changes that are made to various aspects of the way in which a university or college operates to level the playing field and, as far as is possible, to eliminate the effect of any difficulties (related in this case to dyslexia) that stand in the way of a student's success. As we noted in **Chapter 3**, if you have an assessment of study needs for the DSA, recommendations will be made as to the adjustments that could reasonably be made for you; but even if you are not applying for the DSA your college will still need to discuss with you what adjustments are needed.

SOME BASIC ADJUSTMENTS CAN MAKE A GREAT DEAL OF DIFFERENCE

Adjustments to teaching and assessment methods are considered on the basis of an individual student's needs, and of course they will also depend on the requirements of the course that they are taking. However, there are a number of basic adjustments which can be made which will benefit most dyslexic students as well as many other disabled students and, it is generally agreed, they would be seen as good practice with regard to students in general. Listed here are just some of the adjustments which are often recommended for dyslexic students. A fuller list has been published by the Association of Dyslexia Specialists in Higher Education (ADSHE) (**see note 5.6**).

For lectures, tutorials and practical sessions

Information should be available, wherever possible, *online* in advance of the session, so that students can prepare themselves.

- for lectures, this might be a basic outline of what the lecture will contain, along with a glossary of new terms and pointers to the main background reading (specifying chapters of books, articles and so on);

- most dyslexic students find it easier too if they have copies of any PowerPoint presentations so that during the lecture they have less copying to do and can annotate the points;

- for tutorials, advance reading lists are useful if they prioritise essential texts;

- for practical sessions, instructions available in advance mean that students can read through them in their own time rather than try to read them at speed in a busy laboratory.

Students should be permitted to make recordings of sessions, *for personal use*, and in tutorials dyslexic students should not be asked to read aloud on the spot.

Reading for study

- dyslexic students benefit from having prioritised reading lists; as they take more time to read than non-dyslexic students, it is very helpful if they are able to target the most important sources;

- dyslexic students generally benefit from having extended loans on library books;

- it is important that library staff are aware of the difficulties that many dyslexic students have in locating books and that they are available to give advice where needed.

Written coursework

- it is sensible if deadlines for assignments are staggered and advertised well in advance;

- extensions to deadlines for individual pieces of work might be considered, so long as this does not compound the problem, recognising that if a dyslexic student has misjudged how long he needs to complete the necessary research and writing he is unlikely to be able to complete the work satisfactorily under last-minute pressure;

- work should be marked with consideration for the individual student's difficulties, in so far as learning outcomes allow; this means departments need to be very clear and specific about what they are looking for in assessed work;

- where this is possible, feedback that is word processed is generally easier to read.

Examinations and timed assessments

- most dyslexic students need more time than non-dyslexic students in timed examinations: this may be for reading questions, planning and writing answers or checking over their writing;

- again, work should be marked with consideration for a student's dyslexic difficulties, where learning outcomes allow.

In **Chapters 17** and **20** there is further and full discussion about what may be reasonable adjustments in examinations for students with dyslexic difficulties.

ALTERNATIVE ASSESSMENTS

We are not giving a great deal of space in this chapter to adjustments to the examination system, partly because these are discussed later in the book but also because there is increasing understanding that making such adjustments may not be the best way forward in the long term.

The number of adjustments recommended has greatly increased, and the examination offices of many colleges and universities are finding them increasingly difficult to implement, as they involve extra people, extra rooms, extra equipment, time and cost. Quite apart from these considerations, it is becoming clear that alternative forms of assessment, requiring students to demonstrate the same learning but in a different format, might both eliminate many of these administrative problems *and* give all students a chance to do justice to their knowledge and understanding (**see note 5.7**). A range of alternative assessments has been suggested, from which course designers can choose those most appropriate for assessing learning outcomes on different courses (**see note 5.8**). These include, for example:

- critical diaries, learning logs and journals (written or taped)

- portfolios

- posters

- short-answer tests (rather than essays)

- online multiple-attempt tests

- oral/taped record of seminar presentation (rather than essays)

- dissertations presented on video or DVD

- coursework with discussion elements.

It would be good to think that, when the next edition of this book is published, more fundamentally inclusive and fair alternative assessment arrangements will have been built into course planning so that *all* students in higher education have an equal opportunity to do justice to their abilities, skills and knowledge. In schools, to some extent, and in local colleges, many of these assessment arrangements are already in place (**see Chapter 4**). Higher education lags behind in some respects, although changes are beginning (**see note 5.9**) to be made.

THE ROLE OF DYSLEXIC STUDENTS IN CONTINUING CHANGE

Something that is now very clear is that you, as a dyslexic student, have an important role to play in the ongoing process of the changes we have described. This has been recognised by the government in the process of implementing the Disability Equality Duty (DED), which is a central part of the most recent Disability Discrimination Act 2005 (**see note 5.10**). This new duty requires public institutions and authorities, including universities, to address issues of discrimination by improving policies and services as a whole for all disabled people.

Most important, as part of this duty, universities and colleges have to create their own disability equality scheme, and this process must involve disabled people – staff, students and visitors – through meetings and forums and so on. Thus, you have the opportunity to contribute to the process of change by bringing to the discussions your own perspectives on the university experience. Find out about this at your university or college – your voice will be valued and your contributions might help to shape the future.

CHECK POINTS FOR CHAPTER 5

There have been important changes to the landscape of higher education in Britain, as far as disabled students are concerned; this includes students with specific learning difficulties – in particular dyslexia:

- Over ten years the number of students with dyslexia who are studying for degrees has increased almost ten-fold.

- The legislation that has been introduced (in particular the extension of the Disability Discrimination Act into education in 2001) has meant that universities and colleges are now bound to make adjustments so that such students should not be faced with unnecessary barriers to their learning – or to their being able to demonstrate what they have learned.

- Our experience is that some very basic and straightforward adjustments to the way in which courses are taught and assessed can make a great deal of difference to students' experiences of higher education, and to their achievement.

- As these adjustments – which should be anticipatory – gradually become more commonplace, the learning environment will become more inclusive.

- The requirements of the Disability Equality Duty highlight the need for universities and colleges to involve disabled students – including those with dyslexia and other specific learning difficulties – in influencing the process of change for the future.

Chapter 6

Preparations for college

This chapter gives very practical advice to students getting ready to start college. You will possibly be leaving home for the first time, and leaving behind sources of support you were hardly aware were there. Find out here what you can do to prepare for independent life.

A LOOK AHEAD TO POSSIBLE DIFFICULTIES

Many students aged 18 and 19, when they go to college, will be leaving home for the first time. This can be exciting and challenging, but the start of a new life inevitably has its complexities. Similarly, mature students, maybe newly assessed as dyslexic, will now be undertaking a much more complicated life style, for instance they may be commuting into college on top of running a home and family. There may even be some doubts and misunderstandings to cope with from family and friends. In our experience, if it is possible for students to develop some habits of planning and organisation (don't groan!), the early months at college can be much easier. It is, of course, a bonus if you can start on this before you go to college; but it is never too late to learn, even if you are part way through your course. We begin with a comment about attitude: **think positive**. We have given some of our students a poster with the following words:

**NO NEGATIVE THOUGHTS:
I CAN DO IT.**

It is very easy if you are dyslexic to feel bad about yourself and to develop a low self-image. If things start going wrong, you tend to blame yourself – and perhaps your dyslexia as well. If you forget something and blame yourself for always being forgetful, you are more than likely to forget something again – and so it goes on.

Watch out, therefore, for the negative thoughts; look at what you have already achieved in getting to college; realise that most new students – and those well on in their courses – forget things, muddle dates and go through patches of disorganisation. It is not all down to your dyslexia!

Next, a word of caution. If you tell a dyslexic student that he needs to be 'tidy' and 'structured', this can sometimes be perceived as threatening. Many people get through their work quite successfully with a considerable amount of chaos in their lives; they may find that too much order imposes too rigid a discipline and this is too stressful to deal with (**see note 6.1**). On the other hand, we have seen dyslexic students unable to cope with their work and almost come to a standstill because they cannot sort out their muddle. What we have to say on organisation, therefore, will not necessarily apply to everyone; but you can ask yourself if it is relevant to your particular circumstances.

Large numbers of students, whether dyslexic or not, find their first few weeks in college rather bewildering. Even those who have been away from home before may not be used to the responsibility of organising their lives independently. 'Life', said one student, 'was so easy when you were 14 – everything was planned or done for you; all you had to do was toe the line!' This was said as he clutched a bag of dirty washing, a file of notes for an overdue essay and a demand from his mother for some communication. To make matters worse, he had just broken his spectacles.

For the dyslexic student there are extra difficulties. You are likely to be confronted with forms to fill in, with seemingly complicated messages on noticeboards telling you where to be at a given time, with unfamiliar acronyms, such as NUS (National Union of Students) and BURPS (Bangor University Role Play Society), and with a bewildering array of invitations to join political and religious groups, sports clubs, aerobics classes and the like. You may also have to deal for the first time with an unfamiliar bus service – perhaps one that has a very complicated timetable.

Even for such apparently simple tasks as reading a message or filling in a form, it is known that a dyslexic person needs more time than a non-dyslexic (**see Chapter 1, note 1.7**). The problem is likely to be aggravated if you are under pressure of time or if there is jostling round a noticeboard. You may even feel nagging doubts as to whether you should have come to college at all, particularly if you had to make your choice in the face of discouragement from teachers, friends or relatives. Occasionally we have met students who went for several weeks without getting in touch with their homes – partly, it seems, because they felt that they could not cope with letter writing or even, surprising as it may seem to the rest of us, because they could not get around to phoning. Many of our students put off doing the paperwork for the Disabled Students' Allowance (**see Chapter 3**) – it seems to be just too much hassle. If you can make plans in advance to forestall some of these difficulties, then life when you reach college is likely to be much easier for you.

LEARNING TO BE INDEPENDENT

From talking to dyslexic students we have noticed that many of them have had at least one person as a prop during their school career. This 'prop' is often a parent or other relative, or sometimes a teacher, a tutor or a member of a local Dyslexia Association. Such a person will have guided them in a variety of ways, for instance by showing them how to fill in forms, by reminding them of appointments, by supplying them with addresses and telephone numbers or by making suggestions as to how they might plan their studies and revision.

We suggest, therefore, that while you are still at school – or as soon as possible thereafter – you **make yourself aware of the help that you get from these various sources**, with a view to making yourself gradually more independent. This need not be too hurried a process, and so long as you are at home you will always know that there is someone to turn to for help if necessary. It is likely, in fact, that when you reach college you will find fellow students who are willing to assist you; but this may take time, particularly if you are hesitant at first to tell people that you are dyslexic.

If you have become used to filling in forms, to writing letters, to organising your own bank account etc. before going to college there will be less need for you to be dependent on others. In the next few sections we offer some suggestions as to how prospective students can prepare themselves for greater independence.

FILING

One of the things you can usefully do is to spend five to ten minutes each day training yourself to tidy and sort out papers. Few people ever file things perfectly, but it should be possible to have drawers, files or boxes, preferably labelled in colour, for different kinds of paperwork. It is all too easy to let muddle accumulate, and if this muddle continues during your college days there is a risk that your desk will contain a disordered mess of undated lecture notes, uncompleted essays, unanswered letters, out-of-date invitations to meetings or social events, bills, paper clips, rubber bands, unwashed handkerchiefs and … you name it! If the chaos has gone beyond a certain point, it is a very daunting task, particularly if you are dyslexic, to set to work and sort it out – the more so as you may well not know where to begin! In this connection some readers may remember a delightful poem by A.A. Milne (**see note 6.2**) about an old sailor who was shipwrecked. His plight was that he 'had so many things that he wanted to do' yet '*never* could think which he ought to do first'. He in fact ended up by doing none of them and got away with it. Regrettably, we cannot advise college students to follow his example.

Before you go to college, **try to get into the habit of keeping your desk tidy** so that you know where to find things. You will then be better prepared to deal with all the paperwork which is likely to confront you when you start your college course. As we know to our cost, this is the kind of advice which it is easier to preach than to practise. One of us (TRM) had a grandmother who used to admonish him by saying, 'A place for everything and everything in its place' – but few of the family had much success in bringing this state of affairs about!

MEMORY JOGGERS

Many dyslexic students grumble about their poor short-term memories. Unfortunately, they have to use them constantly at college. If you cannot remember things, we suggest that you work out ways of jogging your memory.

- A notebook or organiser (see next section) is likely to be very useful.

- Try leaving yourself notes where you will see them: small yellow sticky labels are excellent for this purpose.

- One student writes on the mirror every night (with a whiteboard pen); another props a list up by the kettle.

- If you have a poor short-term memory, it may help you to try to develop the habit of writing down anything important that crops up during the day –you may be able to store notes to yourself on your mobile, or on your computer.

Even if you do not consult your memory joggers, the very fact that they are there relieves you from the worry of wondering what you have to remember.

OTHER AIDS

We recommend that, well ahead of going to college, you train yourself to use:

- a noticeboard

- a planner calendar

- an in-tray or a set of stacking trays

- a personal filing system

- a diary, notebook or filofax

- an address book

- an electronic organiser

- a kitchen pinger.

These and other aids can mostly be found in stationers, computer shops or office suppliers, and if you are at a college or at a large school with a business studies department, you may find that the staff can offer useful suggestions. If these aids are used intelligently, certain routines – for example the filing of personal correspondence as soon as it is received – will become a habit, and therefore take less effort. The following are suggestions as to ways in which the different aids might be used:

The noticeboard

What we have in mind is a small portable board made of cork or wood which can be placed on a desk or hung on the wall. You can pin onto it slips of paper noting urgent messages, reminders, and the like – for example timetables, telephone numbers, important spellings, lists of equipment needed for laboratory classes, details of the opening hours of the library, and things which you might otherwise forget, such as 'Mum's birthday – *Friday* – post card on Wednesday'. You can use highlighters, coloured stars or stickers to make things stand out. Posters can also be attractive on the eye, and they offer a change from the none-too-legible entries in diaries or notebooks. Some students we know have used medium sized whiteboards as noticeboards – and they can come in handy for study too.

The planner calendar (Figure 1)

This enables you to enter events for a year ahead (or for six months if you buy a 'half year' calendar) and to remind yourself of them

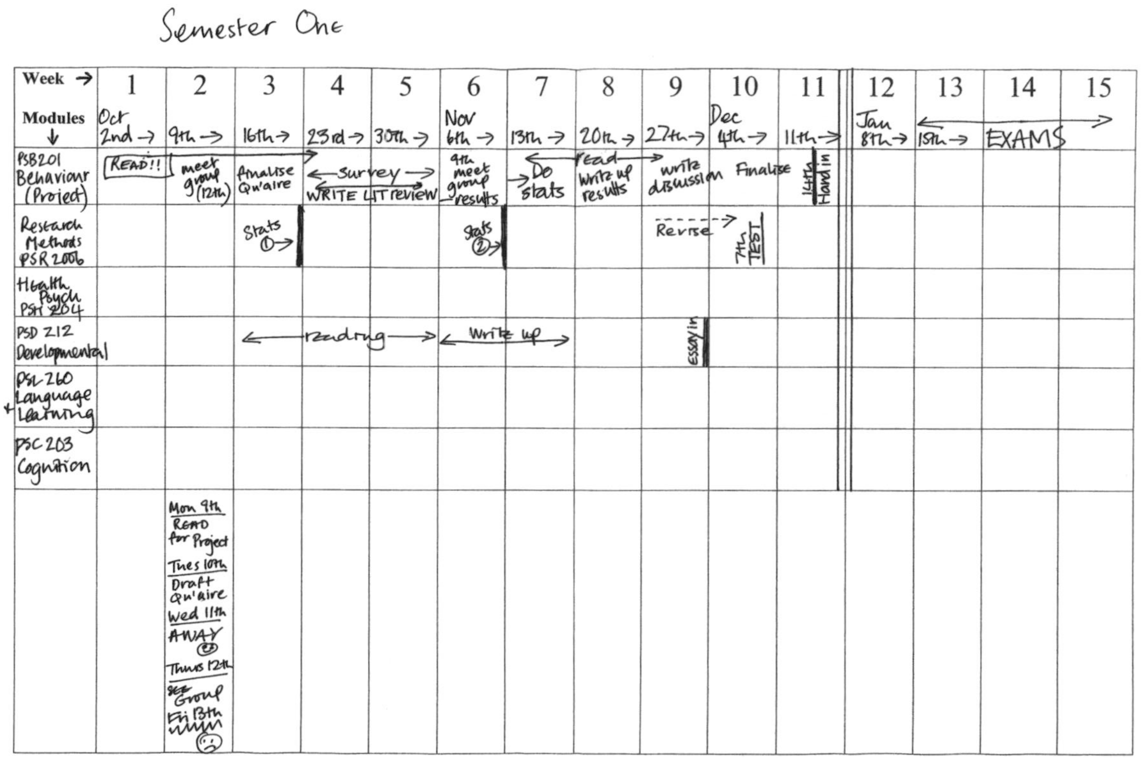

Semester One

Week →	1	2	3	4	5	6	7	8	9	10	11	12	13	14	15
Modules ↓	Oct 2nd →	9th →	16th →	23rd →	30th →	Nov 6th →	13th →	20th →	27th →	Dec 4th →	11th →	Jan 8th →	15th →		→
PS8201 Behaviour (Project)	READ!!	meet group (12th)	Analyse Q'naire	←Survey→ WRITE LIT REVIEW		4th meet group results		Read write up results	write discussion	Finalise	Hand in 11th			EXAMS	
Research Methods PSR 2006			Stats ① →			Stats ② →	Do stats								
Health Psych PSR 2014									Revise →	Test #					
PSD 212 Developmental			← Reading →			← Write up →			Essay in						
PSC 260 Language + Learning															
PSC 203 Cognition															
	Mon 9th Read for Project / Tues 10th Draft Qu'aire / Wed 11th AWAY @ / Thurs 12th / Group Fri 13th mmm ☺														

Figure 1 Example of a (partly filled in) planning chart. If you use colour coding, it is even easier to see what needs doing and when

in plenty of time. Some planners are designed specifically for the academic year. Buy one with large clear spaces so that there is room to write. It is also possible to buy plastic-covered charts and use magnetic shapes and wipe-off pens. Different colours can be used for different kinds of activity; and some events – for example, family birthdays and dates of holidays – can be entered before you leave home. A major advantage of a planner calendar is that you can see your term's work as a pattern; and where there is a cluster of hand-in dates you can try to stagger your work (**see also Chapter 10**).

The in-tray or set of stacking trays

These can be bought from a stationer's and may be made of wire mesh or plastic. Some students, however, may prefer to construct their own trays – one of our students uses empty cereal packets. The advantage of such trays is that all unanswered correspondence can be put into one of them. Thus if, as may sometimes happen, a complicated letter arrives and you have no time to read it then and there, you will know that it is in a place where you can easily find it, and you can reply to it when more time is available. Labelled stacked trays can hold notepaper, envelopes, college correspondence – all within view and yet sorted.

The personal file

A suitable file, which might perhaps unfold like a concertina, can be bought from any office supplier or stationer – they make useful birthday presents! It is likely to be of most help if it is divided into sections. For example, there might be separate sections for your birth certificate, passport, bills, receipts, bank and credit card, correspondence over your student loan, membership cards for clubs and societies, and so on. Plastic clip-on or slide-on headings can be used to name each section of the file.

The diary, notebook or Filofax

This is essential at sixth form level and, indeed, earlier. It is helpful if
you develop the habit of writing down every date, book, suggestion,
reference etc. which you meet during your working day, and it can
contain a list of tasks which need to be completed. A spiral bound
notebook is often useful because used pages can easily be torn out
and discarded. You may also find it useful to insert at the front of
the notebook the letters of the alphabet set out in order; this will
help you when dealing with telephone directories, index references,
library catalogues etc. One of our dyslexic students calls her
notebook 'my external brain'.

It is, however, better not to acquire too many notebooks since this
may be confusing. When you reach college, your master plan will
probably be the planner calendar in your room. When you are away
from your room you will need to make entries in a diary. If this can
serve the dual purpose of notebook and reference book there is less
risk of having 'things to remember' scattered in too many different
places (**see note 6.3**).

A filofax can be very useful as it is already quite well organised
and replacement sections can be bought each year. Many sections
will be ongoing from year to year, and this saves tedious copying
out.

The address book

This is an essential aid to memory. Before leaving home, you should
check that you have written down all the addresses etc. that you
are likely to need for the next few months. If you have a problem
remembering the initial letter of any awkward names, write them
down at the front of the address book. Sticky labels with the
addresses of relatives and friends printed on them are also useful –
particularly if your handwriting is not very legible! Addresses can be
added onto a 'label' template on your computer. Under stress, some
dyslexic students may find even the seemingly simple task of writing
an envelope very demanding, and any device that saves time and

energy is to be welcomed. If your parents are in a benevolent mood they may even be induced to provide stamped addressed envelopes!

The electronic organiser – or your mobile phone

Many dyslexic students use electronic organisers or PDAs (Personal Digital Assistants – **see Chapter 16**). Many of you now have mobile phones which include calendars and so on. You can enter important dates and times into these and they can be made to ring at pre-programmed times to remind you of things you need to remember.

The kitchen pinger

Some students seem to lose track of time; they get absorbed in their work or on even possibly drop off to sleep for a while. They find a kitchen pinger can act as an alarm clock: it can remind them when they have only ten minutes to go before going out and it can be used for timing study sessions.

FINANCE

Again, before you leave home, you can do a lot of useful preparation here. You should make sure that you know how a bank account operates and how to use a cash point. Develop a consistent signature and practise it regularly. (For some students this may not be as easy as it seems, particularly if they find themselves being watched by someone as they sign their name.) A number of our students have reported embarrassing moments when, because of untidy writing, the signatures on their cheques have seemed not to tally with those on their cheque cards. There may also be certain numbers that remain difficult to spell – for example, 'eleven', 'eight' and 'forty' – and some students may find it useful to write these words down in a diary or in their chequebook. Thankfully – for many – writing cheques is rarely necessary these days.

You may also need to know your cash point or pin number. Here a mnemonic seems desirable, as it might be risky to have the number in writing anywhere near the cash card. And make sure, if you choose your own number, that it is not one that others might guess.

If you qualify for the Disabled Students' Allowance (DSA), it is a good idea to set in motion the application as soon as you have a conditional acceptance from a college; this will save you having yet another job to do when you actually arrive. For more information about the DSA **see Chapter 3**.

Give a little time to thinking ahead and working out how much money you will have to spend. Whatever funds you have to start with, there will be certain things you have to pay for: rent, food etc. Try to picture roughly what you will then have to spend, on a weekly basis, on other things you will need: social life, clothes, books and so on. If you have this rough idea of your finances at the start, there will be less chance of a huge shock later on (**see note 6.4**)!

TRAVEL

Many students go abroad during their years in college. You can avoid considerable worry if you are equipped with a passport before you leave home. The paperwork involved in filling in an application form for a passport may be extremely laborious and time consuming for a dyslexic student, particularly if you have to make your application during the pre-vacation examination period. Train and bus timetables can also be somewhat daunting: make sure in particular that you fully understand the 24-hour notation, e.g. that '1600' is the same as '4 p.m.'.

Take with you to college a supply of passport-size photographs; and if forms have been sent to you in advance, it is a good idea to fill them in before you go, to save an extra job when you are under pressure later.

SPOKEN LANGUAGE

You will almost certainly find that the ability to speak fluently is an extremely useful skill during your time at college. After all, it is through our spoken communication that most people get to know us.

Here is an example. One of our students was outstanding in her spoken answers to questions about her laboratory work. She then wrote an essay for which she got a poor mark. When she went to see her tutor, he instantly realized the difference between her oral and written ability, looked more deeply into her essay and then upgraded it. She had proved herself orally.

In general, oral communication is becoming more important in assessment. It is common practice to give *vivas*, and, as will be seen in **Chapter 16**, some students in examinations speak their answers to an amanuensis (a person who writes down their response) or record their answers onto tape. Almost all courses include presentations, when students present a topic to (sometimes) quite a large group, and seminars may be an important part of many courses: students are expected to lead or contribute to the group discussion. This can gives you the chance to do well without relying on the written word.

Practice at oral communication will also give you confidence if you wish to speak in a debate or chair a committee. Most of our communication is through the spoken word, and in the case of dyslexic students the use of spoken language provides the opportunity of demonstrating your knowledge and understanding.

Slight mispronunciations and other errors sometimes occur in the dyslexic people's speech, and we suggest that you listen to words carefully, as this will enable you to say them accurately. This may also help your spelling; and, conversely, if you know the spelling of a word you will be better able to say it accurately (**see note 6.5**).

Reading aloud can be a real ordeal for dyslexic students; at college, you may sometimes have to read work in a tutorial group. As a preparation it is a good idea before you go to college to give yourself plenty of regular practice at reading aloud. A member of your family or a friend may sometimes be available to listen and to comment, or, if no one is around, it is always possible for you to read into a tape recorder and afterwards monitor your performance by comparing it with the printed text. This will require self discipline and is not easy to do, but it is worth it.

WRITTEN LANGUAGE

In many first year college courses the student has to take several different subjects, usually now organised into modules. If you have taken a practical or science-based course before going to college, you may find the written work difficult to cope with. Prospective students should be aware of this and make every effort to keep up their written English (or other language) during the pre-university period. It might be worth going to an evening class in writing skills at a local college, or doing a short correspondence course.

Students who have taken a year off should also try to get back into the writing habit before they return to academic work. Mature students should consider a pre-university course – ideally an Access course. These courses often provide the chance for practice in note-taking and essay writing. The Open University also has various courses in essay writing and study skills.

In our experience, it is quite possible for dyslexic students to learn to write grammatically and to punctuate. If they are weak in these areas, it may not be because the required skills are beyond them; it may rather be that because they had so much else to cope with in their early teens they did not pick up things which their non-dyslexic classmates learned as they went along.

Prospective students need to concentrate in particular on:

- précis writing

- paraphrasing

- note-taking.

Précis writing forces you to think out carefully what are the key ideas in a particular passage and to express them clearly and concisely. *Paraphrasing* involves similar demands but makes you consider the style of the original and be critical of your own attempts to represent what has been said. A good newspaper or journal can be used as practice material. *Note-taking* will be very important at college; it makes similar demands with regard to the grasping of key ideas and the selection of concise phrases; in addition, it is something which has to be done at speed. A possible exercise is to listen to talks on radio or television and to write down the important points.

All in all, the message is: do not let your writing skills deteriorate through lack of practice – use and improve them if you can, before you come to college. If possible too, learn to touch type – this will be an invaluable skill for life, but especially for academic study.

USING EMAIL

When you start your course, you will be given a college email address, and you will be expected to check your college emails regularly, as lecturers, tutors and administrators will email you with important notices – almost from the beginning. It is really important that you learn how to use the college email, and become confident with it. You will need to train yourself to get into the habit of checking your email regularly, and opening, reading, replying to, and deleting messages, or storing them in folders. We have seen students let their email inbox build up until it is so unmanageable that they never want to open it and, when they do, it is hard to find the important messages.

WRITING LETTERS – AND EMAILS

Students sometimes need to compose more formal business-type letters during their time in college. Rightly or wrongly, many people set considerable store by the layout and appearance of such letters, and these are things which some students cannot achieve without a lot of practice. Reference books are available on this topic (**see note 6.6**), and in addition it is worthwhile for the prospective student to obtain guidance from teachers or parents.

A helpful suggestion, in our view, is that you should try to put yourself in the position of the person who will receive the letter. Assume that he or she is a busy person who does not have time for non-essential details, and it is therefore important to say what you have to say in as clear and concise a form as possible. As a check, see if you have stated the purpose of the letter clearly at the start and then given all necessary details. You should also check that the letter reads courteously. Sensitivity to shades of meaning is important here. We were recently told of an executive who instructed his secretary to check why a colleague had not replied to a letter. Her draft began:

Dear Mr Smith

Why haven't you replied to my letter?

It is true, in a sense, that this was what she had been told to ask, but the wording is sharp and aggressive. A dyslexic person may not readily pick up nuances of this kind, but he can certainly be trained to do so. In this case the letter could perhaps have started:

Dear Mr Smith,

I am rather concerned about my last letter and I think it is possible that you may not have received it.

It may also be useful if you include in your spelling notebook a list of words likely to be needed in letters. Some of the important ones are: 'grateful', 'reference', 'acknowledgement', 'enquiry', 'advertisement', 'faithfully' and 'sincerely'. These words should be available to you in advance, otherwise the flow of the letter may become interrupted while you stop to think about their spellings. You can create your own letter heading and store a sample letter with useful phrases in it on your computer.

In the case of important letters, you should use clean, unlined notepaper of consistent size. We have met students, both dyslexic and non-dyslexic, who clearly had no idea of the extent to which recipients can be put off by a scruffy-looking letter.

In the case of emails, much of the advice about style applies here too: there will be times when you need to write more formal emails, which will be very similar to the formal letters we have talked about.

Be careful when you are writing a more formal email, to spell-check it; if your email does not have this facility, write the email as a word document first, then copy it over.

AND FINALLY...

Before you leave home, do make time to read carefully the information which the college has sent you. This may tell you when and where to register for courses, how to join the Students' Union and much else. You may find it helpful to mark the important points with a highlighter pen, and all relevant times and dates should be entered as soon as possible into your diary.

It is also useful if you have a map of the college and its precincts and mark on it your lodgings or hall of residence, the relevant lecture rooms or laboratories, the Students' Union building, the library, and so on.

If it is at all possible, you should make a short visit to the college before your course starts so that you can become familiar with the layout of the campus. During your first days in college, continually having to ask directions to places may be an extra worry. If you then receive complicated verbal instructions ('first left; then second right, and then it's the third door on your left when you've been through the arch'), this will certainly add to your confusion at the very time when you have all sorts of other things to think about. In this matter, as in so many others, careful preparation at an early stage can save worry and embarrassment later on.

CHECK POINTS FOR CHAPTER 6

The message of this chapter is think positively and think ahead. Prepare for independent life and study at college by thinking about:

- filing;

- memory joggers (e.g. notebook, mobile phone);

- other aids (such as a noticeboard, planner calendar, diary, address book, organiser);

- finance and budgeting;

- travel;

- spoken language;

- written language;

- using email;

- writing letters – and emails;

- familiarising yourself with any information that has been sent to you – the map of the college and important dates and times in the first week.

Chapter 7

Social and academic relationships

Here are some tips for new students starting at college. This is practical advice on familiarising yourself with people and places, establishing a routine and asking for support if necessary. This chapter also addresses the issues involved with telling other people about dyslexia and discusses how best to work with your tutors. There is advice, too, on dealing with stress.

ESTABLISHING A ROUTINE

During your first few days in college, you are likely to meet many new people. Think carefully about how you will cope with this. Do you have difficulty, for example, in remembering the things that you are told? You may well find yourself being given far more information than you can possibly remember – people's names, addresses, room numbers, email addresses, passwords, phone numbers and much else.

In the case of names you can try to fix them in your mind by repeating a particular name when it is said to you and by using it when you speak to the person concerned. It may also be possible for you to call to mind an obvious feature of that person or to think of other people with that name.

As for addresses, you will probably find it helpful to write all relevant material in your diary or notebook. If you have a mobile, you can use that to store names and numbers. Some of you may have electronic organisers (or PDAs: personal digital assistants, **see**

Chapter 16), which are very useful for storing names and addresses, important dates, timetables etc. It is also useful to carry a map of the college around with you; if you need to remember where someone lives (or where you yourself live), you can make a suitable highlight or mark on it.

You should make sure that you locate the important university buildings: several dyslexic students have missed their first lecture by going to the wrong place. Perhaps mark the plan of the university campus with your own colour coding, arrows and highlights.

If you find a diary hard to use, we suggest that you carry with you a simple day-to-day calendar and write all appointments down, highlighting the times. It will probably help if you adopt a set routine: this could include checking your notebook, mobile, diary or calendar each day before going out and emptying your in-tray at least twice a week. You may well find that such a routine helps you socially as well as academically, since it will be a safeguard against missed appointments and the like, which can be very irritating to the person on the receiving end. Look carefully at dates and times, and in the early days at college leave extra time to find your way to appointments or classes. If at all possible, dyslexia should not be seen as an excuse for being unpunctual. Over the years we have had many telephone calls from tutors, administration officers, Access Centre assessors and so on asking where a student is.

With mobile phones many students are able to keep very closely in touch with their family; if you do not phone often, try to contact your family at a regular time each week. Most of us know to our cost that if things are not done at fixed times there is a risk that they will not be done at all.

DO I TELL OTHER STUDENTS THAT I AM DYSLEXIC?

We have met students who have worried considerably over this point. Some of them have wondered whether telling others they are dyslexic would make them different from other students in some uncomfortable sense or give the impression that they were looking for preferential treatment. Some may have been the victims of such accusations when they were at school, and so it is understandable if they do not wish to run the risk of something similar happening at college. From time to time we have met students who, quite understandably, wish to make a fresh start and leave their dyslexia behind. To quote one student, 'So much was made of my dyslexia when I was at school that I was determined, when I came to college, to forget it.'

A few students – perhaps as a result of some misunderstanding about what dyslexia is – feel ashamed of being dyslexic and for this or some other reason do not wish any mention of dyslexia to go into their records. These are all points which you may wish to talk about with a counsellor or with other dyslexic students.

We strongly believe that telling is the wisest policy. Not only may keeping your dyslexia secret involve you in all kinds of stress; more importantly, it is our experience that almost all students, when they learn that someone is dyslexic, have been extremely supportive. Most students have dyslexic friends, are interested in learning more about dyslexia and are glad if they can help at all. Since this book was first written, many more dyslexic young people have shown how successful they can be at school and college (**see Chapters 5 and 18**), and there is a much greater general understanding about the issues than there used to be.

Nevertheless, you may sometimes be asked what dyslexia is, and it is worth giving thought as to how best to explain. You could say, for instance, that dyslexics may be talented in all kinds of ways but that they have difficulty in the processing of symbols and language. If necessary, you could add that dyslexia has a physical basis and quite often runs in families. One of our students likes to be called a 'right-brained person'. This is an interesting, though maybe not a scientific, way of looking at dyslexia. There is a good discussion on this in Goodwin and Thomson's book, *Making Dyslexia Work for You* (**see note 7.1**).

Very occasionally we have heard seemingly unsympathetic comments, for example one student said in a loud voice, 'There are an awful lot of dyslexics around here.' (Remember, of course, that even this remark may simply have been made on the spur of the moment with no hostile intention.) If by any chance you meet with hostility – which can occur, though we do not believe it to be very frequent – perhaps your answer could be that there is no reason why there shouldn't be dyslexics at college, and you could explain that there were not so many in the past simply because they did not get the chance to use their ability.

If someone makes a snide comment about the 'free computer' you were recommended to have through the Disabled Students' Allowance (DSA), you could well find this upsetting. However, you may like to point out that a student has to be very carefully assessed in order to get the DSA, and you may even like to quote the words of the dyslexic student who said, 'I'd rather be not dyslexic, and do without the computer.'

If comments are made in a semi-joking way, take them lightly; some dyslexic students can be very sensitive and perhaps overreact to what seem cruel jokes. It is better not to turn nasty but to make up your mind that at some convenient stage in the future you will have a chat to the person who has made the comment. You might also offer to share your computer with other students – we have known several students who have done this with very positive results.

It is also very important that you should not give the impression of being self-centred about your dyslexia or of being unwilling to take an interest in the needs of others. Some students with a problem (not just dyslexia) relate everything back to their difficulty and blame it for every mishap they encounter. Although this is to some extent understandable, it can be most off-putting for others. Almost everyone has difficulties of some kind – and it is therefore up to you to take an interest and try to be helpful.

COPING WITH STRESS

Your social relationships can also be affected if you allow yourself to harbour bitter attitudes. Some of our dyslexic students have, not unreasonably, felt very bitter towards their schools, where they were perhaps discouraged or put into the wrong stream. There may be all kinds of scars from the past (**see note 7.2**), and sometimes a student's very success at college opens these up, for instance resentment towards those of their teachers who had not recognised their ability. In the case of mature students who have been recently assessed, there may be feelings of deep regret over their 'wasted years'. Bitterness is a negative feeling, however. If you can – and we know it is not easy – it is better to forget, forgive and determine to do your best in *this* stage of your career rather than dwell on the past. We have in fact found that many of our students after graduation have taken a genuine pride in telling their schools about their degrees – and this can be good for future generations of dyslexic students from the school. You might read or watch on video what other dyslexic people have said about being dyslexic – Richard Branson, for example.

Stress may occur when a combination of academic and personal demands accumulate and you feel both tired and under pressure – there is just too much to cope with. Dyslexic students are particularly prone to this kind of stress, and what distinguishes them from the non-dyslexic student is that they seem extra vulnerable – and the stress in its turn seems to make the dyslexia worse (**see note 7.3**).

It is important that you should realise this and watch out for signs of feeling under too much pressure. Some students become very tired – things become fuzzy or blurry; others can be very tense, while for others things can get out of proportion and the smallest event can seem a catastrophe. Some students can almost come to a standstill when acutely stressed and their work will then deteriorate. Others show their tension by being overactive – in which case the mind may become confused and make irrational jumps: it is hard for the student to unscramble his thoughts, and his work in general becomes disjointed.

Many students have found that learning about stress management has been very useful. Dyslexic students under stress may find it difficult to organise things or give them a structure. It is important in that case to decide which are the most important things to do, or prioritise. This involves creating a list of the essential tasks to be done so that you can work through them steadily and systematically, taking one thing at a time (**see note 7.4**).

Some colleges run yoga or relaxation/meditation sessions. Music can be very soothing, and there are also relaxation tapes (**see note 7.5**). Some of our students practise reflexology or aromatherapy. If the stress symptoms become too strong, it is wise to seek help from a counsellor. There will almost certainly be a counselling service in your college.

Communicating with other dyslexic students in a student group can also be very helpful – see the section on group meetings in **Chapter 8**.

Finally, as part of 'dealing with stress', may we throw in some grandmotherly advice? Make sure that you eat properly and that you take regular exercise, or at the very least allow yourself relaxation of some kind. We have in fact found that dyslexic students can be prone to ongoing illnesses – sore throats, asthma, colds and, more extremely, glandular fever or even ME (myalgic encephalomyelitis). Dyslexia can be fatiguing to live with, and perhaps the extra strain it places upon the whole coping mechanisms of the body can lead to a student becoming physically run down. Then, as a result, it is harder to keep up with the work. If possible, try to prevent this by building up your strength with healthy eating. This does not necessarily involve cooking: there are all kinds of foods where cooking is not needed, for instance cheese, salads, wholemeal bread, bananas, raw vegetables and yoghurt. Several of our students go swimming or to a gym once or twice a week – and we much recommend it. If you think it would help, you could read some of the material written for students on the subject of health (**see note 7.6**). Our overall advice is that you will function much better if you take care of yourself.

COLLABORATION BETWEEN STUDENT AND TUTOR

Dyslexic students should make a special effort to get to know their tutors and to get on good terms with them early in their course. If things go well, there is every chance of effective collaboration.

There are, of course, different types of tutor. The terminology at different colleges may vary, but the three main types are as follows. (As in the rest of the book 'he' and 'she' are used indiscriminately. Please make the necessary adjustments.)

- First, there is your **academic tutor**. It is his job, primarily, to help you with your academic studies. This is not to say that he will not try to help you in other ways should the occasion arise, but primarily he is there to help you over your choice of reading, over your written work and the like. You may, of course, have different academic tutors for different parts of your course.

- Second, there is your **personal tutor**. (Some colleges used in the past to speak of 'moral' tutors, but this term is now largely obsolete.) He is the person to approach on personal matters, for instance changes of course, difficulty over finding accommodation or inability to get down to work. He will usually be a member of your department and may therefore also be advising you on your academic work, but his prime role is to help you in the event of difficulties other than those which arise from your academic studies.

- Third, both here and in other chapters, we shall be referring to the **support tutor**. This is the role that two of us (DEG and LDP) have played in relation to the dyslexic students at Bangor. There are many forms of support available for students, and there are likely to be other support tutors, e.g. for visually impaired or deaf students.

Many colleges now have support tutors for dyslexic students, and their job is principally to provide a service which these students can use. This is a point to which we shall return in the next chapter. Help is also available from doctors, from chaplains, from student counsellors, from hall wardens, from student services and the Students' Union. In all cases, if useful relationships are to be established, there needs to be effort on both sides – both by the student and by the tutors and advisers.

You will probably find that there are some lecturers and academic tutors who do not have a clear idea about what dyslexia is: if there is a chance to discuss your dyslexia with them, it is wise to think out clearly in advance what needs to be said. In particular, you will need to explain your difficulties and be prepared to make suggestions as to how the tutor can be of most help. It could well be useful if you take along a copy of your dyslexia assessment report or DSA Assessment of Study Needs report so that the tutor can read it; you should, of course, make sure that you understand what it says so that you can explain it to your tutor.

If there are any feelings of strain, it should be remembered by both parties that it is the other who may be feeling uncertain or shy. For example, a student may be in the position where he has to come forward and ask for help yet may find it difficult to admit, even to himself, that any help is needed. In these circumstances, what seems like an abrupt or aggressive manner may be a cover for feelings of insecurity. Similarly, the tutor may naturally be a shy person or may act aggressively because he is inwardly unsure as to what help he should be trying to give.

There are further complications. The student may well have had some hassle from his teachers at an earlier age: they may have accused him of being lazy or careless, or even have implied that he was using his dyslexia as an excuse for doing no work. If this has happened, it is hardly surprising if the student assumes – perhaps without any serious reflection – that his college tutors are going to treat him in the same way. It follows that remarks which they make in all innocence may be misinterpreted. To tell a dyslexic student that his spelling is poor, for example, may be no more than the truth; but, if it is adequate for his needs, the comment is unnecessary and, if it is not, something more constructive is called for.

Similarly, if the tutor is unfamiliar with dyslexia, it is very easy to assume, wrongly, that if the student hands in a seemingly scrappy, untidy and poorly spelled piece of work it is because he has not taken enough trouble. It is far more likely, if his work gives this impression, that he has in fact put in considerable effort and that he has reverted to his earlier weakness of failing to express his ideas adequately in writing. It is good if tutors bear in mind what it is like to have language difficulties in a language-based environment. It may also be helpful if tutors ask the student how long he took over a particular piece of work. Regular checks on the student's progress are particularly important, since if things are not going well the cost of delay may be very heavy.

If tutors have heard the word 'dyslexia' but have not had it explained to them, they may be under the mistaken impression that a dyslexic student is a weak student, or they may be misled, as a result of the student's obvious competence in some areas, into assuming that his alleged difficulties are a fiction. In this connection we should like to emphasise the harm that can be done if tutors give the impression that they are questioning the genuineness of the difficulty; a sensitive person can find this very demoralising. It is possible, too, that things which a tutor says light-heartedly may nevertheless be misunderstood. This happened once when a tutor told a student that he ought to have been in the secret service since so much of what he wrote was in code. Although no malice was intended, this particular student found the remark very wounding; and it is important that tutors remember that dyslexic students may be extra sensitive to criticism because of their earlier failures. It is also possible for a tutor unfamiliar with dyslexia to write off a dyslexic student as 'stupid' through being unaware of the kinds of thing which can happen on a bad day (**see note 7.7**).

SOME PRACTICAL MATTERS

There are many ways in which academic tutors and lecturers can give practical support, and it may be that when the students start at college some form of learning support plan will be drawn up to outline any necessary adjustments (**see Chapter 5**), which should be put in place to remove any unnecessary barriers to their successfully accessing the course. For example, if a student has had difficulty with note-taking, copies of lecture notes or OHP (overhead projector)/PowerPoint presentations will be valuable. In many institutions these are made available on the internal intranet, before a lecture, and they can be of benefit to all students, not only those with dyslexic difficulties.

Some students have indicated to us that they would have been helped if the lecturer could have repeated or clarified something that she had said in the lecture but that they were hesitant to approach her. It is not always appropriate for a student to interrupt a formal lecture: you could approach her at the end of the lecture; though, if she is looking busy or harassed, it may be best to email and ask for an appointment later. If you feel unsure of yourself, you can always ask, 'Do you mind if …?' or 'Would it be a trouble to you if …?' etc. We believe that there are few lecturers who are so busy or so unsociable that they would be unwilling to respond to requests of this kind, and many of us who are ourselves lecturers positively welcome it if members of the audience approach us afterwards.

If a later appointment is fixed, it is important to be punctual – some dyslexic students do not have a very secure sense of time. It is also important not to overstay your welcome – some dyslexic people do not pick up what may be called the 'being-busy vibes'. Occasionally we have met students who, perhaps because they were over-anxious, have gone into a tutor's room and been quite aggressive or pushy. This can easily put the tutor's back up, and will not do the cause of dyslexic students any good. We have also had students who have telephoned their academic tutors late at night or at weekends. Although your anxiety is understandable, this is not the right thing to do.

From time to time, we have met academic staff who did not appreciate that their relationship to a dyslexic student needs to be a professional one. In such a relationship, the student is no less entitled to confidentiality than when he confers with his doctor, solicitor or student counsellor. It is therefore quite improper, for example, for a tutor to proclaim in a lecture or exam room, 'I knew you might not follow this because you are dyslexic' or 'Which of you are dyslexic? Come and sit at the front.' Few students object to it being publicly known that they are dyslexic, but the choice is theirs, not the tutor's.

As we indicated at the start of this chapter, there are some students who decide not to let it be generally known that they are dyslexic. If you are a student who feels like this, it may still be wise to take your personal tutor into your confidence. If it is your wish, he will probably say little to you about your dyslexia, but it will help neither him nor you to deny its existence. At the opposite extreme, as we have said, are those who attribute every minor incident of forgetfulness to their dyslexia – not realising that we all forget things. Perhaps the most important task for tutors and counsellors is to help students to view their dyslexia realistically, making neither too much of it nor too little. It is very important that tutor and student should work as a team and jointly try to ensure that common sense is not thrown out of the window.

CHECK POINTS FOR CHAPTER 7

When you start at college you will need to:

- find the time to establish a routine and familiarise yourself with people, places and the new timetable;

- think about how to explain dyslexia to others who may not know much or understand;

- recognise signs of stress and learn to deal with stress;

- look after yourself;

- give thought to establishing good relationships with your tutors.

Chapter 8

Organising a support service

This chapter will be of interest to staff involved in setting up and providing support for dyslexic students (and students with other specific learning difficulties). Although support services vary in their structure from college to college, there are certain common issues: the need for publicity about available support, the resources that should be available, the types of support that may be offered and the role of the support tutor. In what follows, 'you' should be understood to mean the support tutor.

INTRODUCTION

Support services for dyslexic students in higher education have developed steadily in recent years, evolving with the increasing numbers and range of students studying at this level (**see note 8.1**), and also as institutions respond to the requirements of the Disability Discrimination Act (DDA) 2005 (**see note 8.2**). Many of these students will have had support and provision at school or at a previous college and will therefore expect a similar service in their degree studies.

Any support service for dyslexic students should, of course, operate within the framework of other student services: the Disability Service, the Counselling Service, the Careers Service and the like, but dyslexic students (and, of course, those with other specific learning difficulties) are likely to have certain distinctive needs. Depending on the framework of student services in your institution, an all-round dyslexia support service *may* be involved in:

- advising students on claiming the Disabled Students' Allowance (DSA) (and possibly participating in assessments of study needs for this);

- drawing up learning agreements for students, to set out necessary adjustments, in conjunction with their departments;

- arranging or directing students, note-taking support, reading services etc. and liaising over library and examination adjustments;

- giving preliminary (screening) assessments (before referring on for full assessment) to students who have never before been assessed as having specific learning difficulties;

- providing information for and receiving visits from prospective students and their parents.

From time to time, support tutors may also need to undertake awareness-raising among their colleagues, and advise on how inclusive teaching and assessment methods may be implemented. All this will, of course, be additional to the core work of what we consider to be traditional study support.

Support services vary according to the type of student, the size of the institution, the staff available and, of course, the budget. Within a support service, too, the help offered to a student *needs to be flexible*: there are, for example, students who require to be taught academic skills by means of a structured programme; there are those who have worked out their own strategies and who wish to consolidate them; and there are also those who, for all kinds of good reasons, simply need to drop in for an informal chat. We have found that many younger students have already been taught a considerable amount about study skills and need little assistance, whereas mature students, especially those recently assessed, are often very anxious to receive as much help and guidance as they can get. In some cases what starts by ostensibly being a tutorial in essay writing or on study techniques may well turn into a counselling session. It is important, therefore, that the tutor or counsellor be sensitive to the student's needs at a given time.

The needs of dyslexic students are likely to be fairly complex, since they may well need counselling as well as academic support. You may have to help them, for example, over their study habits or over the management of their time. It is important for some students that, when it is provided, support be on a regular, organised basis. It should not only cater for their academic needs; it should also deal, for instance, with the feelings of doubt and anxiety which many of them experience when they reach college, and with the last-minute panics which sometimes arise as they approach examinations.

PUBLICITY

In any large institution communicating with students can be a problem. If you are the organiser of a service for dyslexic students, you should therefore explore every possible means of publicising what is available. In particular, the need is for clear and simple information which reaches as many students as possible, raises their awareness of dyslexia (and other learning differences) and tells them about the support available. Many students – and prospective students – will search university websites; so the support service information should be easily accessible.

Publicity for prospective students

It should be possible to contact prospective students directly if they indicate on the UCAS form that they are dyslexic, or to send information via the academic office which administers the UCAS applications.

Prospective students should be clear about what support is available, and they should be invited to contact the support service to discuss any queries they have. They should be strongly encouraged to contact the service to discuss, in particular, any support that will need arranging ready for the start of their course – having notes taken for them in lectures, for example. At times it will be necessary to involve the academic department in consideration of any adjustments needed, as they may (rarely) not be considered 'reasonable' with regard to the requirements of the particular course. For example, it may not be considered reasonable to disregard spelling errors in the work of a student on a language course if accurate spelling is seen to be a necessary demonstration of achievement. Prospective students and their parents may be invited to visit the support tutor/service on a general or departmental Open Day, and they should be advised to find out if they are eligible for the DSA (**see Chapter 3**) and encouraged to apply for this several months before they start at college. In all of these ways it is possible for students to be well prepared when they start the course and familiar with the support service. In their turn, staff will have been able to follow up initial contacts with more information and advice, to the point when students begin their new course.

There will be other students who arrive at college knowing that they are dyslexic but not having disclosed this when they applied; others may have wondered if they are dyslexic or had it suggested to them on a previous course. It is important that these students should be aware of the existence of a dyslexia support service: this should be included in the college's prospectus and on the university's website, with further information on hand when students register for their courses.

Publicity within the college

In addition, a comprehensive system of publicity should be established within the college. Handouts and posters should be designed, and the wording should be friendly and informal – for example, 'Drop in for a talk.' An indication of the form of the service which is being provided should be shown on the poster. Dyslexic students are often extremely sensitive and will hesitate to enter a group situation until they have first established a firm contact with the tutor. They will also need to be assured that the service is entirely confidential and that they can approach the tutor without necessarily being identified as dyslexic. A notice such as 'Dyslexic Students' Meeting' should never be displayed (**see note 8.3**).

Publicity about dyslexia and the support service should be distributed to all areas of the college, including individual departments, the library, the Students' Union, the rooms where students register for courses, the administration offices, Student Health, Student Services, Counselling, Nightline, the chaplain, the students' shop, halls of residence, eating places etc. Reference to the service should be made in the relevant student diary, calendar, newspaper or handbook. There should be easily accessible information on the university/college intranet. Explanatory letters should be sent to all heads of departments, personal and academic tutors, chaplains and others concerned with student support. Even if a dyslexic student makes only infrequent use of this service, it is important that he know of its existence.

RESOURCES

As a minimum, some kind of room should be set aside for the use of the support tutor(s). You should also retain an emergency meeting place if your room is not always available. A kettle and a box of tissues are often useful! A discreet waiting room is also important.

Ideally, part of the student service should comprise a resource base, and even a study area. The resource base would contain study materials, information on dyslexia, books of all kinds and spelling dictionaries. There should be equipment for the student to use, including computers and software, spellcheckers and Dictaphones. There could also be materials with which the student could experiment – coloured paper, plastic overlays and cards and posters for revision. This is the ideal; however, practicalities – such as cost, staffing, administering a loan service (some students are not very good at returning books), security and insurance – could make this prohibitive in terms of money.

Because concentration is not always easy for dyslexic students, many of them welcome somewhere quiet to work. Some, in fact, prefer total silence; others like to have music on in the background. It may also be useful if a room is provided in which they can revise together and learn study techniques from each other.

THE WORK OF A SUPPORT TUTOR – TYPES OF SUPPORT

The increasing numbers of dyslexic students place heavy demands upon support tutors, and in many institutions the services of freelance tutors are bought in. It may also be possible to draw on expertise within the college. Generally, but not always, tutorial support can paid for out of the DSA. Students have sometimes set up their own self-help groups – these will be discussed later on in this section. We suggest, however, that the followings patterns act as a basis for support.

One-to-one meetings

The simplest way for support tutors to operate is to be available to see students on a one-to-one basis at a fixed time during the week. If this method is used, every effort should be made to ensure constancy and regularity, since it is an extra difficulty for dyslexic students if the time and venue of the meeting are continually being changed. Their first visit may be difficult for them and you should be aware that for many students it takes a great deal of courage to come forward asking for help. See **Chapter 9** for more discussion on what may need to be included when working with individual students.

While we have found that many students have benefited from one-to-one guidance on ways of studying their subject, there have been others for whom simply the possibility of such guidance has been a reassurance. In the words of one of them, 'I may not come very often but I always know you are there.' It is important that the support service as a whole is able to respond with flexibility in this respect: while some students will want a regular weekly session, others may not feel they need this and may prefer to come in less frequently – or they may be able to find the level of support they normally need within their academic department. Still others will have wanted to work as independently as possible and may come in only when they feel they need advice. Also, as students proceed through their courses, their needs change, and students who have not been in for a year or two may appear for advice or support in their final year. A regular newsletter or group email (using the BCC blind-copy option on the email) sent to all students will ensure that they do not forget that support is there if they should need it.

Some colleges provide mentors who may be people with training in general study skills – and who can also give one-to-one support (**see note 8.4**). In some cases it is possible for a postgraduate student, provided he has had suitable training, to give help with such things as spelling, statistics or essay writing. It is also possible that a 'buddy' service may be in operation: in that case another student 'chums' a dyslexic student, perhaps taking notes for him or helping him with reading. This can either be for free or, where appropriate, for a payment which might be arranged through the DSA.

Group meetings

Another way of working is to have group meetings, perhaps weekly, or twice or three times a term, according to demand. These can operate as small, formal classes or as study groups with a set topic to be addressed and discussed. For first-year students a discussion of dyslexia can be a useful starting point and may be followed, for instance, by an introduction to the concept of learning styles, before study skills are tackled. There may then be discussions of note-taking, essay writing, reading up material for assignments, giving presentations, dealing with stress or of improving one's spelling etc. As examinations approach, we have found that time spent on revision, memorisation and examination techniques is particularly valued. Speakers other than the support tutor, including other dyslexic students or ex-students, can be brought in both to address the group and to participate in discussion. You will be guaranteed to learn about successful strategies as students pool their own ideas, which you can, in turn, suggest to other students. We have found it useful to note down hints and tips suggested and discussed in group sessions and circulate these by email to all the dyslexic students.

However, besides formal teaching, of which most students have plenty every academic day, something more informal may also be of help. For example, as a support tutor you could give a brief lecture on an everyday topic – pollution, the monarchy, the local area, sport etc. – while the students would be encouraged to take notes, to compare what they have written with what has been written by others, to discuss what is good or bad in each and, individually or jointly, to produce a set of notes which, with the tutor's guidance, is better than any of them could have produced individually. In these circumstances a really interesting learning situation can develop: each student will have his own approach and the various different techniques can be pooled and discussed.

Perhaps the most positive aspect of a meeting of dyslexic students, however, is the remarkable group atmosphere that emerges. In our experience every group, without exception, has developed its own distinctive feelings of togetherness. For some dyslexic students this may be their first meeting with others who are dyslexic. They can offer each other quite striking personal support. We have also found that the second- and third-year students have fostered and guided the first-year students, offering them help with their studies, their examinations and their approach to the academic staff. The group can be particularly supportive to any one of its members who may have a problem. A student may storm in, smarting from the latest insult and find complete understanding, immediate sympathy and many practical suggestions as to how to cope with it. Students are always pleased to find that some of their difficulties are not just theirs but are shared by the others.

We have also found that as a group the students worry about any of their members who may not have attended for a while. They are all willing to offer each other their devices for coping with dyslexia in day-to-day life. Generally, they all understand each other; and this is clearly a vital factor in the successful working of the group.

It is of particular benefit to the less experienced students to know that others have gone before and not only coped and survived but actually succeeded. Some of our previous students have written back to the group with encouraging stories of their successes (**see note 8.5**). We have also found that a discussion of someone else's problems can help a student to get his own problems into perspective. In general, a study group can act as an important lifeline

for students who wish to open up and discuss their problems with
each other.

From your point of view, too, as support tutor, the experience
may be a rewarding one. Although if you are not yourself dyslexic
you are in a sense an outsider, your understanding of the problems
can be very much enhanced simply by careful and sympathetic
observation of the ways in which the students interact with each
other. There is the possible difficulty that you may sometimes have
to listen to harsh criticism of your academic colleagues, if a student
believes them to have been unsympathetic, or even embarrassing
praise. In these circumstances it is probably wise, if the necessity
arises, for you to make clear that for professional reasons you may
not discuss the merits or otherwise of individuals; but this need not
prevent you from discussing how the student feels about people
who have come into his life. It is, of course, widely agreed among
counsellors that they should not take sides with a client in finding
fault with a particular person, even though they may make clear that
they understand the client's feelings about that person.

It may sometimes be possible for you to use your outsider role
in guiding the group. We have found that now and then there is a
tendency among certain students to have a good moan. This may
at times be necessary, but it can become very negative and be off-
putting to other students. At some point you may like to announce
humorously that there is a ban on negative comments and that only
positive thinking is permitted (**see note 8.6**).

Our students at Bangor have set up their own self-help groups
outside the main group, working with computers, sorting out notes,
revising and so on. There is a strong informal network among them.
We have discussed whether they would like to run their student
study group as a total self-help group. This raises the question of
the type of support which they need; the consensus is that they feel
that it is valuable to have a tutor who will present ideas and patterns
from the outside and who will prepare materials, obtain books,
help with work and liaise with their academic tutors and others.
We feel that it would place heavy demands on dyslexic students if

the support group were run solely by students, although there is certainly a place for student-led groups alongside tutor-led groups.

There are always students who for various reasons do not wish to participate in group work. It may have been the flavour of such meetings which they disliked; indeed, one student said that the meetings 'smacked of Alcoholics Anonymous'. In our experience it is wise that all students known to be dyslexic should be informed if a group meeting is to take place; but it should be clearly understood that there is no pressure on anyone to attend it.

Instant help

Another way in which you can help your students is to let them have your mobile/telephone number. This will enable them to get in touch with you at any time if they feel depressed, frustrated, muddled or unable to cope. Obviously, this is more feasible in a smaller college. Dyslexic students find it difficult at times to deal with pressure, and stresses may accumulate until their thinking becomes befuddled and the various problems begin to seem insurmountable. At this stage they may call for help, and if you are readily available you will be in a position to go immediately and listen. In this situation it is perhaps better to meet in a less formal setting, for instance in a pub or coffee-bar.

It has been our experience that stress is more common at certain times of the year than at others. The third or fourth week of the first term is often a bad point for first-year students, and pressures often seem to mount in February or March: it is the mid-year low point – one set of modular exams has just been completed and the next modules have started with an new workload; at this time also students are often run down after the winter. Any examination times are, of course, almost always stressful. Some dyslexic students withdraw into a shell at bad times and cannot cry for help. It is important that you should know where to find your students, and, if you have not seen a student for some time, you could perhaps contact them casually to check that all is well. It is always possible that problems may have accumulated. On various such occasions tutors have found themselves doing the washing up, re-filing notes, helping with application forms, writing a letter and taking home a load of washing.

There is no reason why all these forms of support should not be available concurrently; and, again, it is important to recognise that dyslexic students may need different kinds of help at different stages of their course.

THE TUTOR AS COUNSELLOR

Although a support service may be seen principally in terms of academic support, it will have become obvious that there is also a strong need for a service which can provide for integrated personal help and advice. Problems with study trigger off anxiety; a student becomes tense and many underlying insecurities may well up from the past (see Chapter 9).

Hence, a session with a student may involve study skills to cope with the immediate problem but also some discussion of past difficulties: into that might come problems with personal life, which could easily have got out of proportion because of the general stress under which the student is labouring. In such a state, it seems that a dyslexic student may jump from one thing to another – all her problems crowd in together and she cannot structure either her thoughts or her work. This can easily happen if she is under pressure or has too much work to do.

Although in general we use the words 'adviser' or 'tutor' with regard to study, we do also refer to 'counsellor'. A distinction can usefully be drawn in this connection between 'generalist' and 'specialist' counselling. A counsellor with generalist skills is a trained listener who helps the client to talk through possible courses of action but does not have the specialist skills of, say, a doctor, solicitor or college lecturer. These have expert skills in their own particular areas and can advise accordingly. In contrast, a generalist counsellor is not that kind of expert.

Now it seems to us that if you are to act as tutor to dyslexic students you need to be *both* a generalist *and* a specialist counsellor – generalist in that you need to be a good listener but specialist in that you need to have a knowledge of dyslexia (**see note 8.7**). Your job is both to deal with the anxieties that the students bring up and to know what aspects of their academic work they are likely to find easy and difficult; it is also to know when a student would be best served if he were able to get advice from the college's counselling service (**see note 8.8**).

Finally, bear in mind that dyslexic students are often highly sensitive and can easily become upset by negative criticism, for example it may take a student months to come to terms with some severe comments on his use of grammar. Occasionally, too, you may come across a student who has not wanted to admit to his dyslexia but who finds that he cannot cope on his own and therefore, *almost against his wishes,* has to come forward to seek help. This can often cause a loss of face. Such a student can sometimes be quite aggressive until he has settled down, and it is important for you, as his tutor, to understand the reasons for this.

CHECK POINTS FOR CHAPTER 8

The remit of a support service for dyslexic students and those with other specific learning difficulties may include:

- work related to the Disabled Students' Allowance, liaison with the wider institution over necessary adjustments and support, first-time assessment of students who request advice on their difficulties and advice for prospective students and their parents.

The support service will need to consider:

- publicity – providing information for prospective students, dyslexic students and the wider student body;

- resources – including space, materials and staff time;

- the types of support which students will benefit from – individual support and advice on a regular or 'as needed' basis and support groups (tutor-lead or self-help);

- the role of support tutors – recognising that study support for dyslexic students may often be more than delivery of study skills.

Chapter 9

Study skills and the support tutor

This chapter offers broad guidance to support tutors on helping students with their studies. The abilities and needs of each student are different; the work of supporting students towards independence will in some cases be less than straightforward and may take unpredictable turns. In what follows, 'you' again means the support tutor.

ON BEING BOTH COUNSELLOR AND ACADEMIC TUTOR

We believe that the roles of counsellor and adviser on study skills are inextricably intertwined. In the words of Dr Gerald Hales:

> We cannot – we must not – separate an individual's dyslexia from other aspects of existence [in this case – study] and some assessment of the effects on personal structures is, and should be, a part of our service to the individual dyslexic person.

(see note 9.1)

Thus, your aim as the support tutor should be to support the student as a person: this means encouraging her motivation by developing her self-confidence and feelings of self-worth while at the same time supporting her ongoing academic work – coursework, dissertations and essay writing. Alongside this, it is important to help the student to develop her own strategies so that she will gradually acquire sufficient self-awareness to monitor and control her own learning (**see note 9.2**).

You should also encourage the student to think positively about herself, about the way she studies and about what she is expecting as a result. It is important that she should go into a period of work actively, thinking about her aims, rather than just reading and writing passively or mindlessly. Visualising herself 'where she wants to be' – and the steps to achieving this end – can be a useful strategy to learn (**see note 9.3**).

WORKING WITH STUDENTS

In the first two or three meetings, the support tutor and the student might decide to look at the student's assessment reports. These might include a report from a psychologist or specialist teacher and, if this is available, the report from the DSA Assessment of Study Needs. You could then discuss how she approaches her work, what study strategies have worked well for her, what support – if any – she has had in the past and what support will best suit her needs now. This could be particular aspects of study skills, for example reading techniques or revision strategies, support with ongoing work which could involve advice on strategies for written assignments or strategies for proofreading, spelling difficulties, problems in organising her life, requests for help with form filling and so on. At times the support tutor may need to liaise with the teaching staff in the student's department; then, provided the student agrees, it is good practice to inform the department of the work that is being done.

While it may be possible to make some kind of initial very broad-brush plan for the sessions, the tutor's approach needs to be flexible and responsive, and at times it will be necessary to review progress and negotiate with the student what type and level of support will be appropriate as her skills develop and course demands change. There is a limit to the extent that goals and targets for tutorial support can be planned for in any detail. The overall goal will always be to build students' confidence and give them the ability to take their learning into their own hands, seeing the support tutor as just another resource which they may independently choose to use.

It is not always easy working on essays and assignments with dyslexic students, and the tutor needs to look carefully at the skills required by the student. There is the initial research; a required skill in essay writing is that students learn to use research resources correctly. The tutor should discuss with the student what information and ideas are needed for the particular assignment – not give her a list of resources to seek out. At the same time, we have taken dyslexic students into the library and worked with them at the computer to show them how to access books and periodicals. Again, it is important for students to be taught the general principles of how to plan essays so that they can eventually produce their own plans; there is a danger, however, that a tutor faced with a hopelessly organised essay can take it over and restructure it instead of helping the student to do the restructuring herself.

Finally, it often happens that the tutor finds herself in danger of becoming simply a proofreader. For many students these last checks are at the end of an exhausting process and they just want to get the essay in; some universities do offer a simple proofreading service, perhaps through email, and the use of this should probably have to be endorsed on the student's essay. We would suggest that the support tutor discusses this with the student and whenever possible includes a teaching element when the student is reaching the final stages of completing the essay. This can be done by getting a copy of the essay before the student comes in for her session and selecting the major points of spelling, punctuation and grammar etc. to discuss. Support tutors should not be seen as copy-editors; however, the nature of dyslexia is such that there is commonly a ceiling to the extent to which many students are able to identify certain errors through independent proofreading, and a tutor needs to make a judgement, based on their knowledge of that student, as to the nature and degree of support she should be given.

In the dyslexic student's eyes you may well be the most stable and caring person she will encounter in what could be stressful weeks in a college term. In your whole approach to the student, therefore, you need to be calm and unrushed –and punctual! If you can, you should develop a relationship with the student that will help you to understand her abilities and needs. It is therefore important to know your student – in order to find out what strengths to build on, what difficulties to work on and what causes of stress are likely to affect her academic performance. Some students come to us only if they have a personal problem which may be interfering with their work and, once one knows the student, the first question could be, 'How are you?' or 'Is everything all right?'

Although it is a mistake to probe uninvited into personal relationships or family background, in practice what often happens is that we are given accounts of difficulty with living arrangements, of flatmates not understanding or of problems with money. It is plain in such cases that the student needs a listener who appreciates that these things are worse because she is dyslexic and who can see that they interfere with her study. What the student reveals at such times should normally be regarded as confidential. What might be discussed are the student's feelings and, if appropriate, the possible ways in which the student might deal with these feelings as well as with the situation itself.

Situations may arise where it is necessary for you to discuss the student's relationship with other students. As we have seen, some people are very open about being dyslexic, while some go to great lengths to conceal it. It is useful if you and the student jointly discuss ways of telling the outside world what it is like to be dyslexic. This is the type of topic which can be discussed in a student support group and such a pooling of ideas can be very valuable.

BUILDING A STUDENT'S CONFIDENCE AND INDEPENDENCE

As a support tutor you should never forget the extent to which many dyslexic students have low self-esteem (**see note 9.4**). It is therefore important that you do your best to encourage your students and give them confidence. There is little doubt that people who think badly of themselves make poor learners (**see note 9.5**). It follows that you should **look at your students' strengths and make them aware of these**. Dyslexic students desperately need self-respect.

In this regard, a further look at the student's assessment report may be useful. In some cases the student may not have had it explained to her: many students may still be unclear as to what dyslexia is. It is possible to work through the report to help her to reflect on and develop strategies for learning and to increase her self-understanding.

Ginny Stacey has spoken of dyslexic brains 'being wired differently' (**see note 9.6**); this can mean a different pattern of skills and hence a different approach to work. It can sometimes be useful to talk, with provisos, about left-brain and right-brain activity, or auditory/visual learning styles (**see note 9.7**). This may help the student to get to know herself, to develop metacognitive awareness, by reviewing her own thinking and learning processes, and to understand the way in which her memory works best. You should discuss how to study, how to relax and how to plan a work session. Many dyslexic people have good days and bad days; the bad days need to be talked through and some kind of coping strategy worked out. Above all, it is important to convince your student that she is not 'thick' but rather has a different and distinctive individual approach to learning.

Many students will tell the support tutor of difficulties which they have had with their mainstream staff. They sometimes get these difficulties out of proportion, and it may therefore be important to give them the confidence to go and seek help. A possible strategy is to talk to them about how to approach other tutors. It is particularly useful if you can help to make them aware of the pressures that there are nowadays on most mainstream staff – though not in such a way that they are deterred from approaching them.

For whatever reason, there are some people whose interpersonal perceptions are not very acute. To these students, their own problems are paramount; they may be tense or anxious, and if they also have poor language skills the result may be an abrupt or seemingly aggressive manner of confronting their tutors. As we have noted, you will often find that you need to act as a link between the student and your fellow staff. A procedure which we often use is to obtain the student's permission to approach other staff and then do so on the understanding that all correspondence between ourselves and her other tutors is open for her to see. Finally, she will probably experience certain struggles within a structured college environment, and within that environment you can act as the buffer and stabilising influence.

HOW FAR SHOULD THE SUPPORT TUTOR TAKE OVER?

We should like to consider this question by citing a particular example. One of us (DEG) worked with a final-year student who came in looking pale and thin and very stressed. It was late January. He had six essays to hand in, a dissertation of 9,000 words to complete and application forms for jobs to fill in. There were finals coming up and he had not been eating. He said that he was 'working all the time but not getting anywhere' and that his mind had 'gone all blurry'. In fact, the essays and the dissertation did not have to be in until the second week in May and the application forms were to be completed by the end of March. Because there was so much looming, however, it seemed that he was unable to impose a structure to help him deal with the various tasks.

We therefore discussed each part of what lay ahead and broke his work and his timetable down into manageable chunks. Since as a final-year student he had only four lectures a week, we decided to split the week into two sections – either all the mornings as one section and all the afternoons as the other or two blocks of two and a half days each. One of the blocks would be spent on the dissertation, the other on the essays.

We also decided that he would do an essay to a deadline every two weeks and that he would hand them in to DEG. We worked out that he would be able to complete the dissertation by mid-March and that he could then start revision. We photocopied the application forms and he decided that he would take them one at a time.

There were still two days each week free, and we discussed the importance of time out without feeling guilty. We also had a chat about the least stressful way of keeping oneself fed. After all this

DEG asked him if he wanted her to write it down for him (it might have seemed patronising to do so peremptorily). He in fact said that he did, and he actually asked for it to be put on a postcard so that he could keep it in his pocket and look at it when he needed to. This procedure worked.

From this example it can be seen that coping with college life, both academic and personal, makes it virtually essential for the student to have some structure in his weekly routine. Study at college can be much more open-ended than study at school, and students have more responsibility for their own private work. There seems to be more free time to fill in; there is no set homework timetable, and submission dates for essays are often set weeks ahead. This can involve planning and time-management tasks which can be very stressful for dyslexic students. In addition, the organising of their studies may place many demands upon their memory – and there is usually much diverse information to process during an academic week.

Our dyslexic students have often described themselves as having 'blurred brains' or, to use an expression coined by Ginny Stacey (**see note 9.8**), 'muddle in our minds'. One could perhaps speak of an 'overcrowding' or 'overloading' of the brain so that, as in our example above, the student cannot sort out his thoughts into clear structures, particularly when he is under stress. When such a student comes forward for help, you will need to assess how far to impose a structure for him and how capable he is both of organising his work and of sticking to the plan.

Work with an individual dyslexic student or group of students should be a dialogue: the tutor can present structure, ideas and strategies from the outside, but each student may have his own strengths and difficulties. The study skills handouts which we provide for our students (of which examples are given below) are very simple: they present general ideas which can be discussed and adapted according to individual needs.

THREE SAMPLE WORKSHEETS

Here are three examples of the work sheets which we use. They are kept simple for two main reasons:

- In the first place they can function as discussion points, either with individuals or with groups; this means that the students can then add their own ideas and strategies while you, as tutor, go over each point with your comments.

- Second, dyslexic students have so much complicated material to process during their working week that it is a relief to have something which is both challenging and simple.

1 A WORKSHEET ON BASICS STUDY SKILLS

BASIC STUDY SKILLS

1. Plan out your work
    Work for short periods of time
    Be clear and realistic about what you aim for in any one
    period of work
    Look forward to finishing
    Take a timed break

2. Never work when you are tired (the mistakes will get worse)
    What are your best times for working?

3. Can you keep tidy ... how?
    Colour coding
    Folders for each subject
    Desk – in-trays for work to do now and later

4. How can I learn?
    Noticeboard, posters (subconscious learning)
    Record and listen
    Mind-maps
    Colour
    Shape

---

2 A WORKSHEET ON TAKING NOTES

TAKING NOTES IN LECTURES

1.   Why is the lecturer lecturing?
    - ideas
    - facts
    - for exams
    - ask the lecturer
    - ask other students
2.   Look at the lecturer's programme:
    - pick out key words
    - read around it
    - prepare key spellings/names
3.   Prepare shorthand:
    - What ideas have you? (*Shks* for 'Shakespeare'; *envr* for 'environment')
4.   Techniques
    - headings
    - sub-headings
    - key words
    - signposts
    - bullets, mapping or both?
5.   How to get extra help?
    - approaching lecturers? how?
    - what about recording?
    - friends? notetaker?
    - photocopying notes?
6.   Labelling, dating and organising notes:
    - just do it!

3 A WORKSHEET ON APPROACHING A SESSION OF WORK

GETTING GOING

1. What is my goal tonight?
2. Avoid those chasing thoughts
3. Can I monitor myself?
4. Am I controlling my work patterns?
5. No negative thoughts
6. Am I getting tired?
7. Relax … do something else

CHECK POINTS FOR CHAPTER 9

Depending on the abilities and needs of individual students, the support tutor's work may involve:

- helping students to understand their strengths and weaknesses;

- guidance – to varying extents – with organisation and time management;

- advice on strategies for study;

- support with various stages of the student's ongoing work.

Less predictably, there may be a need for the support tutor to:

- recognise that the effects of dyslexia on a student may impinge on wider aspects of a student's life: encourage the student to use strategies to deal with this;

- liaise with mainstream academic staff;

- act as a stabilising influence for students who are experiencing particular 'ups and downs'.

Chapter 10

Organising yourself and your time

Helping yourself to concentrate

The main message for students here is that if you can manage your study by organising yourself you will find that concentration comes more easily. There are some simple strategies to help you manage your time and your work so that you can feel positive, stay in control – and have a social life too.

TIME MANAGEMENT AND SELF-ORGANISATION

When you first look at your lecture timetable, you will be amazed at how much spare time you will seem to have compared to what you had at school. However, one of the aims of university is for students to take responsibility for their work, and thus learn to manage their time, both academically and socially. When the essays and practical write-ups start coming in, you will soon realise what a lot there is to do.

From the time you first come to college you are likely to achieve more if you plan in detail how to spend your time rather than leave matters to chance. If you, either alone or with a tutor, can create a structure or framework for your studies, it is likely that you will work better, feel more in control and so feel more confident. Your teachers may have done this for you in school, and such a framework exists in many courses offered by local colleges. For degree courses, however, long-term planning is needed and there may be no one standing over you to make you get on with your work.

You will probably find it helpful to work out a timetable.

MAKING A TIMETABLE

- To start with, there will be a number of hours during the week that are committed in advance – those in which there are lectures, practical classes, tutorials and the like. You could colour code these so that you can tell what they are at a glance.

- Time also needs to be set aside for meals and for regular social activities, such as club meetings, going to the gym, sport, social events, meeting friends etc.

- This still leaves a large number of hours available for private study. Do not make the mistake of thinking that private study can be fitted in at odd moments. It is best if it can be built into your timetable. Once a particular slot has been set aside, it should be regarded as firm a commitment as attendance at lectures.

- Study hours should be integrated with the lecturing timetable; for example, if there is an hour between classes, this may be the right time for carrying out certain tasks in the library or printing out some work that you have done on computer.

Taking a longer view, a planner calendar is valuable to ensure that study plans are made well in advance, as it is difficult for a dyslexic student to dash off an essay or revise for an exam at the last moment.

MAKING A PLANNER CALENDAR

- You can find models on the Internet or create your own.

- Some students use large sheets of card or A3 paper, divided into columns, with a column for each week of the term or semester. Then subjects or modules are listed on the left, each in a separate row (see page 52).

- Deadlines for handing in work should be marked in as soon as they are known, along with dates of tests, examinations and the like; then work backwards from the hand-in dates, or tests etc., plotting out what you need to do in the weeks beforehand.

- You can then visualise how the tasks, and the work you need to do for them, are spread out.

Although this seems very unfair, most dyslexic students need to spend longer hours than a non-dyslexic student on their work; both the reading-up of research and the completion of written assignments may take twice as long and more. It may also be more difficult for you to catch up in the same way as the non-dyslexic student does, for example by copying reams of missed lecture notes or by staying up all night to complete an essay. You may think that you have loads of time, but remember that it is easy to underestimate how long something will take you, and if you overestimate how long you will need, and get a task underway *early*, any unexpected contingencies – being laid up with flu, a visit from a friend etc. – will not be a catastrophe.

WHEN TO STUDY

It is important to aim at regular controlled working hours and to avoid putting off work or missing classes.

- As a rough guide **we recommend a total working week of about 40 to 50 hours.** If you spend fewer hours than this on your studies, there is a risk – because of the time needed for reading things up, for checking what you have written etc. – that you will find that you are not keeping up with the workload. We have seen students who have started to drop behind, who then cannot face the accumulated backlog and who end up not knowing where to turn to sort it all out. On the other hand, if you spend more hours than this, you may become overstrained, and in any case it is a pity to miss out on social life and college activities. We have come across many dyslexic students who work too hard and become very run down – you need to be like the tortoise in the fable and plod solidly along.

- **Many students can work better at certain times of day.** You should consider which times best suit you, and allocate your time accordingly. If you find reading very tiring, you should aim to do the bulk of it when you are at your freshest, and the same, of course, applies to other things which you may find difficult or laborious, such as completing essays or transcribing formulae.

- If it is possible (and we understand that sometimes it is impossible), avoid working when you are tired, rushed or under pressure. If you feel like this, you will not produce your best work and again there is a risk that the dyslexic errors will multiply. You should try to plan to avoid such pressure. Late-night study is liable to be extremely tiring, and if – unavoidably – some catching-up time is needed, you should consider whether it might not be better to get some sleep and start early the next day rather than make yourself very tired working into the small hours.

- **It is unwise to work for too long at a single stretch.** We have found, on the whole, that dyslexic students can achieve good results if they continue for about an hour, but after that their work deteriorates. In that case, it is not worth continuing, since the errors associated with dyslexia tend to multiply. This is particularly so if you are working on the computer, which can place strain on the eyes, hands and back, apart from the brain.

- **You should learn to watch out for signs of tiredness:** the ideas do not come as quickly, the handwriting gets worse, the keyboard errors multiply. Take a short break and move away from the workplace. If you can work to a rhythm of, say, 50 minutes study and ten minutes break, you will find that you can cover a large amount of ground and yet still remain fresh at the end of it.

- Similarly, **regular but limited amounts of study each day are likely to do you more good than occasional days of intense effort.** The time taken off work is important because it gives you the chance to relax and unwind.

- **In addition to shorter breaks, your time off should include one whole day per week as well as one complete evening and one afternoon.** It is important that these should genuinely be periods of relaxation and that you should look forward to them. Some dyslexic students have found yoga classes very beneficial. If periods of work and periods of relaxation are not clearly distinguished, you may find yourself half-working instead of working at full stretch – and then worrying during your spare time because you feel you ought to be working. As a result you may end up achieving very little.

- **Time is precious and you should try to get straight down to work.** You should be aware of the risk of erosion of study time. Five minutes here, ten minutes there, an extra break for coffee – these never seem very much, but together they can result in a serious loss of time.

- Some students may find themselves unwittingly making use of **avoidance tactics** – finding excuses for not getting down to work. It is important that you should recognise when you are doing this. It helps, for example, to keep your desk tidy and organised, with spare pens and pencils so that there will be no time wasted at the start of a period of study in looking for the things that you need.

A fixed time should be set aside each week to check over lecture notes. You should make sure that you understand them, and remember that you will want them to make sense when you come back to them for revision before exams. You might consider transferring them onto a digital recorder. Whether or not you do this, it will certainly save a large amount of time later if you date them and, when they are complete, catalogue them; and you will probably find that colour coding with felt pens will help you when you try to find things later. File your notes carefully, as it is difficult to sort out a mass of notes long after the lecture.

Nowadays, you can expect that most lecturers will provide an outline of their lecturing syllabus (often called the module outline). Make sure that you look at this: it will help you if you can use some of your private study time to look ahead, in order to gain maximum benefit from future lectures. You can obtain some knowledge of what is to come by a brief scan of the outline, and if possible you should try to familiarise yourself with any names, specialist words or diagrams which are going to be used; this will save you from having to puzzle over these during the lecture.

All these points are matters of common sense; but it is easy in the stress of the moment to forget them, and it is very important that tutor and student work as a team and to ensure by their joint efforts that common sense is not thrown out of the window.

WHAT IF THERE SEEMS TO BE TOO MUCH TO DO?

Finally, you may at some stage in your college career feel overwhelmed if large amounts of written work have not been completed. You may feel that you cannot cope and may even consider giving up your course. If this happens, you should talk to your dyslexia tutor or your academic tutor or perhaps a student counsellor; you might even have a chat to a fellow student. The simplest procedure is to make a list of priorities, with help if necessary, and to work steadily through them. You may well find it daunting if you try to look at all the tasks together.

If the pressures seem too great, it is a good idea to take a complete break, such as a weekend away. You can then slowly 'retrain' in your studying: one student restarted with just ten minutes, three times a day, and built up from there. It is also useful at these times to practise relaxation as this helps you to unwind, particularly last thing at night. If you find that you cannot sleep, it is important not to worry: in our experience, worries over not sleeping can sometimes be more damaging than the actual lack of sleep (**see note 10.1**). Try to work out ways of combating the problem: practise relaxation during the day so that you can use the same strategies at night, treat yourself to a warm drink or listen to music. Some people find it useful to have a notebook by their bed to capture thoughts they might otherwise forget. Above all, have a calm and methodical approach: if you and your tutor deal with your problems one by one, they are likely to seem much less overwhelming.

WHERE TO STUDY

You need to think carefully about the place where you can best study. It should, if possible, be somewhere where there are no distractions. If you use your own room, it should be organised so that it contains both a place to work and a place for relaxing. All students, not least dyslexic students, require breaks in their studies, and a cup of coffee over a desk covered in papers or by a keyboard is not really enough. You will have a much better break if you move away to a different environment, if only to sit in an armchair by the window.

If you decide that your own room is not a good place for study – you may, for example, want to escape from the computer for a while – you could consider the college library or perhaps somewhere in your department. Your tutor or some of the other students may have helpful suggestions. Some universities have study rooms set aside for students who need access to specialist equipment or software. Some of our students meet together about once a week in groups, checking notes and discussing work, and this is something they have found very useful.

CONCENTRATION

Concentration is perhaps at the heart of coping with all aspects of study skills. Many of our students report difficulties with concentration, both in lectures and in private study. It is a problem for all students, but perhaps dyslexic students have extra difficulty because of their limitations in short-term memory and their relatively slow speed of working. In the words of some students, there are 'too many chasing thoughts'.

Poor concentration can be caused by worry and stress, by fatigue, by inactive or passive methods of studying and by negative, self-critical thoughts, such as questioning the value of what you are doing or expecting not to do well.

THINK POSITIVE

When you are studying, at home or in the library, become aware of your signs of tiredness or stress and make sure that you have a good break so that you can relax. Do not forget the positive value of doing things that you enjoy when you are not working. You will then be better able to return to your work; and the happier you feel, the more you will enjoy it. All this means, of course, that you need to plan ahead sensibly.

CHECK POINTS FOR CHAPTER 10

You will be better able to concentrate if you take control and organise yourself and your time.

- Choose times for working when you work best.

- Plan your work into manageable chunks.

- Plan your allocation of time – taking breaks and deciding time limits.

- Avoid distraction; work in a place where you will not be distracted.

You should therefore try to:

- deal with one task at a time – keep a list for 'floating thoughts';

- avoid looking too far ahead, but be clear about what you need to do and by when;

- prioritise – forget irrelevant details;

- have a clear desk – no clutter, since muddle can cause stress;

- watch out for delaying tactics – get started!

Chapter 11

Taking notes in lectures and from books

Strategies for reading

Here are some practical suggestions for students about making
the most of your lectures and your reading – together these
will be your main sources of information. Get the best from
both by using active learning strategies and taking time to
reflect on what you already know and what you expect to
learn – and then by reviewing what you have learned.

LECTURES

A university lecture is different from a lesson in a school. The
lecturer delivers his information, usually without interruption. Most
lectures last for at least 50 minutes and are often quite specialised.
The lecturer may move quickly to get through all his information
(which will be the result of hours if not years of research!). He may
use overhead projector (OHP) or PowerPoint presentations, but
lecturers in some subjects such as maths, physics and economics may
use a black/white board. Most students find that taking notes is both
tiring and difficult. For dyslexic students it can be quite hard going
as you have to listen, look at visuals and copy down what is often
new terminology.

For various reasons you may have difficulty with note-taking:
you may, for instance, have a slow writing speed, be slow at taking
in what is said or be delayed in writing things down because of
uncertainties over spelling. It is sometimes possible to have someone
to take notes for you – paid for out of the Disabled Students'
Allowance (DSA). Alternatively, your lecturers may agree to provide
you with copies of lecture notes: this may be seen as a reasonable

adjustment under the terms of the Disability Discrimination Act 2005, and many lecturers make some form of notes available to all students on the college intranet. Your college support advisers will discuss these possibilities with you.

Other means are also possible, though not all dyslexic students will want to make use of them. One is to **photocopy another student's notes**, though this can be expensive – and your fellow student's notes may not be wholly reliable! If a first-year course has not changed very much since the previous year, there may be useful material in the notes of second- and third-year students, who, as has been pointed out already, are often very glad to help.

Like reading, however, note-taking is a skill that can be improved with practice (**see note 11.1**). In this connection, Burton distinguishes two extremes – 'the eager first-year student who tries to take everything down and the exasperated second-year student who has given up the unequal struggle and doesn't take notes at all' (**see note 11.2**). Both these extremes are unsatisfactory. No student – least of all a dyslexic student – will be able to write down all the points made in a lecture, but we suggest that you try to sift out the important ones, making sure that they are not forgotten. First of all, it is worth considering how you can prepare yourself in advance.

PREPARING FOR LECTURES

Read your module/course handbook carefully. Here you will find an outline of the lecture programme, which will help you to work out beforehand which topics are coming up. You might also find that some lecturers have ready prepared handouts and that others put a summary of the lecture on the university intranet.

Here are some general hints as to how to get the most out of lectures.

- Be prepared for lecturers to be different in their styles and expectations.

- As in the case of reading, it is a good idea to work out why the lecturer is lecturing. Is it to present you with ideas to make you think and do further reading – something which is more likely to be the case in arts subjects? Is it to present you with facts and the latest research which you might not easily find for yourself – something which is more common in science subjects? Is it to reinforce what you can find in the course textbook?

- How necessary are the lecture notes for the examinations? We know one lecturer who tells her students that they will not pass their exams unless they are fully familiar with her lecture notes; we know of another who has put all his notes in outline on disk but tells the students that they must attend his classes to pick up the necessary details – and that the combination of both will provide all that is needed for the exams. In contrast, other lecturers have emphasised the need for originality and have said that there is no point in attending a lecture unless it sets you thinking.

- As we have already suggested, you will probably find it useful to read up in advance on the subject matter of the next few lectures; this will make you familiar with the main topics and key words and prevent the spelling of new or difficult words from becoming a major problem. You could try writing a list of these words on a small piece of paper and have them near you in the lecture. If the lecture notes are available to download before the lecture, this gives you the chance to look through them and prepare yourself. If you print them out, you can add your own notes during the lecture.

NOTE-TAKING IN LECTURES

A good lecturer will normally write up new technical terms and the like, either on the board or using an OHP. If, however, for any reason, a lecturer is not in the habit of doing so, you can help yourself by developing **your own shorthand**. Commonly occurring words, such as 'compare' and 'result in' and specialised words belonging to your particular discipline, such as 'hypothesis', 'monarchy', 'streptococcus' etc., can be represented by abbreviations or even by arrows, stars and so on. It is important, obviously, that such shorthand expressions should not be so cryptic that you are baffled by them when you come to do your revision. See the end of **Chapter 9** for the example of an advice sheet on taking notes.

There is no point in wasting your energy in writing down the lecturer's jokes and asides; and if a student makes a conscious effort to distinguish the essentials from the incidentals then taking notes, like reading, will become very much easier. We suggest that you aim to **jot down the key words** which represent the key themes of the lecture.

Linear notes

These key words might be represented in **linear note form**, with headings, sub-headings and bullet points listed in order. Use arrows ($\rightarrow$) and stars (*) to help emphasise particular points, while the use of ampersands (&) saves writing out the word 'and' in full. You can then work vertically down the page, leaving yourself plenty of space. If you can make your notes look like the note pages at the end of **Chapter 9**, then there is every chance that they will be easy to follow. Some students use a double-paged pad to take down lecture notes: they put the key words on the left-hand page, then move across to the right-hand page to add in the details. Others write on one side of each sheet only so that when the notes are filed each left-hand page is empty, ready to add in more notes and comments at revision time.

During the lecture itself, we suggest that you **leave plenty of space** by writing on alternate lines and by leaving wide margins (compare also the section in **Chapter 12** on getting across what you want to say). This means that the relatively cryptic jottings which you might have made during the lecture can be expanded when you return to the subject during your own study periods.

Mapped notes

As an alternative to linear notes, some dyslexic students have found Tony Buzan's **concept map/mind-map** method of taking notes very effective (**see note 11.3**). Here, rather like a spider-gram, the main point is written in the centre of the page and the pattern of ideas works outwards from this; cross-links and cross-references can easily be added and the further expansion of ideas will continue outwards. An example of a mind-map summary of a biology lecture is given in Figure 2.

For a full map, it is easier to use an A3 size drawing pad, and to turn the paper sideways and work horizontally. The total pattern of notes can form a diagram which you may remember from its visual or graphic rather than its verbal representation, and this may be easier to use for revision. In general, not so many words are used, which is easier both in time and effort, but some training and practice in mind-mapping is necessary so that you learn how to present the key concepts before filling in with details.

The mind-map also makes you think in terms of concepts or key words rather than sentences which have unnecessary padding. After

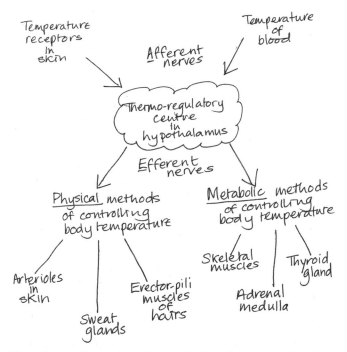

Figure 2 Notes in mind-map form from a biology lecture on the reflex control of body temperature

a lecture, you can go over them and add colour, signs and symbols, even drawings.

Mixing the styles

Some of our students use mind-maps all the time – for note-taking, for planning essays and for revision – and find them really creative. Other students find that mapping really does not suit them – they prefer a linear style, especially for taking notes in lectures. Quite a number of students use a mixture of both styles, adapting their notes to the content of the lecture and the style of the lecturer as they go along. In this way mind-maps can be used for just part of a lecture and afterwards be built into linear notes. This again adds interest to the vertical linear pattern.

Whatever method of note-taking you use, if you find difficulty in spelling some of the words used by the lecturer, it may be helpful to use a pencil or different coloured pen to indicate such words – or at least some approximate representation of them. If you are using a laptop, you might put a * by them. If you spend five minutes wondering if it should be 'Enistine', 'Insteine' or 'Einstein', you may easily lose the thread of the lecture, whereas you can sort out spellings at your leisure afterwards.

LISTENING FOR SIGNPOSTS

You should try to make use of the **signposts** provided by the lecturer. First of all, listen carefully to the first few sentences of the lecture: it is likely that in them the lecturer will state the purpose of the lecture and indicate his treatment of the topic. Similarly, listen particularly carefully to the end of the lecture where he may sum up the points he has raised. (This means that you should not be late for the lecture or start to pack up before he has finished.) Listen also for signposts within the lecture when the lecturer may say, for instance: 'There are three main aspects of ...' or 'This can be developed in two contrasting ways ...' You can then number your points and subdivide your notes accordingly or at any rate ask the lecturer for further help on where the subdivisions come if he has not made this fully clear.

LISTENING AGAIN

It is also possible to combine written notes with the use of a sound recording. Quite a few students now record their lectures, and some university departments are beginning to produce podcasts of lectures which you can download from the intranet.

Recording has to be thought out carefully. It is sensible to check with the lecturer that he knows that you will be recording his lectures: permission to record lectures *for personal use only* is generally seen to be a reasonable adjustment for dyslexic students (**see note 11.4**). Some lecturers, however, may not be happy to be recorded – perhaps because it would make them feel uncomfortable or insecure – in which case you should perhaps discuss the issue with your dyslexia tutor or the Disability Adviser.

Tapes, mini-discs and digital recorders can often be paid for out of the Disabled Students' Allowance (DSA). Whichever you use, it is best also to use a good external microphone which will pick up voice only and not register all the background shuffling and coughing. You will need to sit near the front of the class. It is, of course, still useful to supplement the recording with your own notes, as this will ensure that you continue to concentrate on the lecture.

During the lecture, you can **note down key words**, which will act as a reminder of the important points made. You can then reconstruct further details of the lecture by yourself, talking round the key words and, perhaps, recording yourself. This procedure places emphasis, once again, on understanding rather than on the transcription as such. Indeed, if you find yourself unable to talk round the key words this may be an indication that you have not fully understood the main points of the lecture, and you will need to follow this up as soon as you can by talking to the lecturer or your friends, or by looking in the course books.

If you are satisfied that you have recorded the lecture suitably, you can then label the tape or disc and store it so that you can easily find it again when you need to revise. You will need to be organised about this. You can download the recordings onto your computer if you have a digital recorder, and then listen to them on an MP3 player. In Bangor, some lectures are being distributed centrally as podcasts – and this is likely to be a growing trend. If you have been doing a large amount of reading for revision, then listening may be a welcome change.

A word of warning: do not do what one of our students did. She recorded all her lectures and then sat down each evening to write them out in full. A few weeks into her first term she panicked because she was getting behind – the recordings were piling up; she was becoming very tired and she felt she 'didn't have a life'. After talking this through with her tutor, she decided to save the recordings and simply listen to them if she needed them for revision, or to jump to any important parts of the lecture that she had missed and particularly needed to hear again. With a digital recorder you can mark the important points so that you can find them again quickly.

NOTE-TAKING FROM TEXT

For the general approach to extracting material from text we suggest that you look at the section on reading below.

This is very much easier than taking notes from a lecture, since you can work at your own speed and return to a particular passage if you wish to study it further. However, the same general principles apply. First of all, again, **think about why you are taking notes**, whether they are background reading, whether they are to supplement lecture notes or whether they are for an essay. It is particularly important that you should consider what information you are looking for; it is no use copying straight from a book without giving any thought to the subject matter – and for revision purposes you might equally have looked at the book itself, which will probably be more legible!

USING YOUR NOTES

You should remember, too, that a mass of closely written material is likely to be daunting when the time comes for revision.

It is therefore important that there should be **wide spacing**; and if all the notes are under **suitable headings and sub-headings** it will be easier to pick out relevant points in the future. In particular, **key words** and – where appropriate – **key sentences** can be written down.

Nearer examination time, you might transfer the key words onto postcards; you can then carry these around and refer to them at odd times, or leave them on the walls or on the mantelpiece where they can be easily looked at. If you leave spaces, you will be able to add more notes from a book or piece of research and you will also be leaving room for your own opinions and comments. Whenever you add extra points, we suggest you do so in a different colour.

In the case of diagrams, the actual physical act of copying them, if it is done with thought and not just mechanically, may help to fix the important details in the memory. Our students have often noticed that they remember what they have done themselves, be it diagrams or notes, better than they remember photocopies.

With any sort of note-taking it is important that as a dyslexic student you should **use your strengths** in order to offset your weaknesses. It may be difficult for you to write down what a lecturer has just said while at the same time paying attention to what he is now saying, and you may equally find difficulty in locating a passage in a book or in finding the right name in an index. If, however, you use skill and judgement in the selection of relevant material – which is something you can do well – then your relative limitations in the area of immediate memory and slow writing need not put you at too much of a disadvantage.

ORGANISING YOUR NOTES

The final piece of advice here might sound very tedious to you, but as tutors of dyslexic students we have quite often had to help them sort out a whole muddle of notes just before they are due to start revision. They may not even be sure which lecture or which module or which book the notes refer to: so at the start of each new lecture, write in: module number, topic, date, name of lecturer; when you are taking notes from books, label and reference them. And, if you have made a point of filing, topic by topic, all your lecture notes, handouts and notes from reading, you will later be very thankful.

READING WITH UNDERSTANDING

Many dyslexic students have reported that they find reading up a subject difficult and time-consuming. It is unlikely that, even with practice, you will be able to skim through a book, picking out the essentials, as quickly as a non-dyslexic student.

If you need extra time to complete reading, it may be that you will have been given a sum of money to buy your own copies of books, through your DSA. (Remember to keep all the receipts to send as proof if necessary.) Most college and university libraries allow dyslexic students to have a longer loan period, particularly for the restricted loan texts. You might also check whether your university has text-reading software installed on the intranet, or whether there are computer rooms with this specialist software, and scanners. Look too for CD-ROMs which convey information through text, sound and visual imagery – these are available in some (not all) subject areas – or texts which link up to websites.

All of these may give you easier access to texts, but you will still need to extract the information from them. There are various approaches and strategies that you can use. It helps to think about the whole process of reading.

- **Ask yourself why you are reading** and what you want to learn from it. You may sometimes be reading for background knowledge – to broaden your general awareness of the subject and to help you understand lectures; you may be reading to expand your lecture notes, or you may sometimes be reading up material for an essay or a tutorial. Identify your reason for reading: do not read vaguely – do not read without a purpose.

- **Think about what you already know** about the topic, ask yourself what you need to find out and try to predict what you will find in this text.

- **Read actively**. If you read with a pen or pencil in your hand, it may help to focus your attention. It may also help you if you place a piece of card under the line that you are reading.

ACTIVE READING

When you read, make sure that you **always make notes** of some kind (also see above for the section on note-taking from books). This forces you to think and may help your concentration. If you have books of your own, or photocopied journal articles, try using a highlighter or coloured felt pens to make important passages stand out. If you are writing down names and dates, they may be easier to remember if you highlight them or write them in a different colour.

- In the case of library books which of course cannot be marked, particular passages and diagrams can usefully be photocopied so that you can mark and underline the photocopy. You might even adopt an old Victorian habit and put key words, short summaries or comments in the margin of your text. If you photocopy onto A3 paper, so that you leave a wide blank margin around the text, you can use this space for adding your comments.

- You may consider using a scanner to get bulky information onto your computer – you can then work on it yourself.

- If you make a bookmark (of cardboard, not flimsy paper), you can jot notes onto it, or notes on a particular topic can usefully be put on cards or typed straight into your computer so that you do not have to return to the book over and over again.

- **Get into the habit early on of noting down all that you will need for referencing your sources:** this will save you a lot of time later on, as you will not then need to go back to the library to search for page numbers and publishers.

Use sound

Another aspect to active reading is that, as well as taking written notes, you should try to listen to the sounds of specific words and say them to yourself. In particular, you may find it useful to pay special attention to all relevant names and to make sure that you know how to pronounce them. It may also help if a friend reads them aloud so that they can be stored on a recorder, in which case the correct pronunciation may help you with the spelling. Sometimes reading a piece aloud helps you to get the sense of it and thus gain more from your reading.

You could also record yourself reading (do not worry about that feeling – we all have it – that you do not like the sound of your own voice); if you have a digital recorder, you can download the recording onto your computer and save it as a voice file so that you can listen to it again. You can add in your own comments as you read and listen to these later. Text-to-speech software can also be very useful (**see Chapter 16**) and you can save the sound files to listen to again.

Monitoring yourself as you read

The final strategy for you to think about is that you should monitor your reading: check on whether you understand by asking yourself what you have learnt from a particular reading task. You may also like to add a brief summary at the end of your notes. This will certainly help you to practise putting what you have read into your own words – something which is very important if you are to avoid the risk of being accused of plagiarism.

Meredeen gives a useful list of questions for checking your understanding (**see note 11.5**):

- How much do I remember?

- How well did I understand?

- How much can I explain in my own words?

As we have seen already, dyslexic students are likely to be weak at deciphering and strong at comprehension. If, therefore, you think of reading simply as deciphering – as translating marks on paper into spoken words – then your slowness and weak immediate memory may well be a severe handicap. If, however, you know what you are looking for and try to read with understanding, you are making better use of your strengths and, in the process, saving yourself a large amount of time and energy.

USE OF READING SERVICES

Some colleges run a reading service in which books and articles are recorded on tape. There are also national tape/listening libraries (**see note 11.6**). These services were intended primarily for visually impaired people, but there is no reason why a dyslexic student should not make use of them. Alternatively, you may be able to find a friend who is willing to read books and articles aloud so that they can be recorded on tape; and it is sometimes possible to reclaim the expenditure under the DSA. You would need to consult your support tutor or Student Services as to how to set this up.

Local libraries have a large stock of novels on tape, as well as some non-fiction books; and in some cases you will find tape-recorded guides to particular areas which can be a substitute for maps. You may find that you can use these for pleasure, particularly if you drive into college and can listen to them on your car radio.

READING LISTS

Most lecturers provide reading lists. Sometimes these are long and formidable, and a lecturer seldom intends that every book in the list should be read from cover to cover. An obvious step is for you to approach the lecturer for advice: which books are the important ones and which topics require most time? If you have an allowance through the DSA to buy books, you can explain this and say that you are keen to make the right buy. If you are in your first year, second- and third-year students can often give useful advice, though what they say should not be accepted uncritically. Mastering certain key texts as background reading is likely to be more valuable than ploughing dutifully through a list of books one by one.

GETTING THE BIG PICTURE

Let us now appeal to your imagination. It is possible to see reading or note-taking as being rather like a pyramid or a triangle. The point at the top is the theme or main subject of what you are reading, and, as you read, the topic broadens out into the dense mass underneath. Dyslexic students can get lost in this dense mass: the risk is that they may read large amounts of detailed material without knowing how it fits into the more general structure higher up.

In this connection we cannot resist quoting the disastrous instructions (from a dyslexic point of view) given to Alice by the King of Hearts in *Alice in Wonderland*: '"Begin at the beginning," the King said gravely, "and go on till you come to the end; then stop"' (**see note 11.7**). For a dyslexic student confronted with a book, we believe this to be the worst possible advice. We suggest that, instead, you work out for yourself as early as possible what you hope to get out of what you are reading. You can then approach the text with a clear purpose in mind.

If you still find the text too dense, it may be useful to go to an easier book which could help you to see an outline. One of our students did far too much reading for an essay and then could not sort her notes out. She was in her final year. We then looked at a GCSE sociology textbook that explained the whole topic in clear outline; as a result, she could then fit her detailed and very academic notes into this outline. She got an A! If the books on a particular topic seem extra difficult, you may like to consider an encyclopaedia or a CD-ROM as a starting point.

LOOKING FOR SIGNPOSTS

Once you have some general idea why you are reading and what you are looking for, you should then look in the text for more specific information. You can use certain parts of the text as signposts: the preface, the introduction, the table of contents (including the chapter headings and sub-headings) and the index. With practice, you will be able to learn to ignore irrelevancies, such as acknowledgements, and spend time on the points you have already decided are important.

The start of the book and the concluding chapter are often particularly useful in indicating its general direction, and the beginning and end paragraphs within a chapter can be a useful source of information as to the contents of the chapter as a whole. Some textbooks have brief abstracts (summaries) at the beginning of each chapter. It is important that you concentrate on important points and do not stray off into irrelevancies.

RAPID READING

Some of our students have experimented successfully with 'rapid reading' (**see note 11.8**). The main principles are that you focus on and absorb the first (topic) sentence and last (concluding) sentence of a paragraph, and that you should not read every word, still less every letter, but only groups of words or thought units. The reader has to develop a 'recognition span' in which he or she isolates and absorbs a phrase by its key words. Other students have found this too difficult to cope with.

We have already suggested that you should read with a pencil in your hand. If you then run it along the line, it will help to guide and focus your eyes. Tony Buzan (**see note 11.9**) illustrates how you can use a pencil (or a similar pointer) to guide your eyes in rapid sweeps across a page, so accustoming yourself to covering text at speed. This is worth experimenting with.

COLOURED OVERLAYS AND COLOURED LENSES

You may also like to consider the use of coloured overlays or coloured lenses. Some dyslexic students report that, when they read, they experience visual distortion: the letters on the page seem to blur, or wobble, or jump up and down. It is possible that they are being affected by the contrast between the white spaces on the page and the black letters. Some dyslexia assessors will also test for this (**see note 11.10**).

This distortion can sometimes be reduced or even eliminated if you use coloured overlays (sheets of transparent plastic) which are placed on the page. The most effective colour varies from person to person, and it is worth a support tutor or support service investing in a screening pack for the students to experiment with (**see note 11.11**). Quite a number of our students have reported that the use of coloured overlays (or coloured paper) has made their reading much easier: the colour gives an improvement in reading fluency and seems to reduce eyestrain so that they can read for longer stretches of time. Not all dyslexic students benefit, and there is still some controversy in the whole area (**see note 11.12**); but if you find reading tiring the use of colour is certainly worth your consideration.

If the overlays are used for about six weeks and appear to be successful, you may like to consider being tested by an optometrist for coloured lenses: you can have glasses made up in your particular colour (which may be different from the colour of the overlay that you have been using). Some students have tried using photochromatic sun glasses or, if they already wear glasses, having a tint put on them. We have, in fact, met students who did not know about the research in this area but who had, nevertheless, turned independently to coloured lenses to help with their reading and writing.

Even if you do not use coloured overlays or lenses, it is possible that using coloured paper, or working under a coloured light bulb, may help to reduce distortion and glare. You might also find a coloured plastic reading ruler useful: the range of colours available is limited at present but these make useful reading guides, and can double as book marks (**see note 11.13**). We also recommend that you experiment with the colour and contrast on the screen of your computer monitor.

Some students make a point of photocopying text onto pastel-coloured paper; this is worthwhile if you have difficulty reading high-contrast black-on-white text (see below) and it may also help you with organising and remembering your material. If you find some text, for example journal articles, very dense, it is also possible to enlarge it using a photocopier.

Lastly, whatever strategies and aids you use, we would like to repeat what we have said about study in general: read when your mind is fresh – do not try to read complicated material when you are tired or stressed – it is very hard to concentrate. Make sure you take breaks from reading as soon as your mind starts to wander.

CHECK POINTS FOR CHAPTER 11

To get the most from lectures:

- prepare for them beforehand so that you listen actively;
- listen for signposts;
- develop your note-taking style;
- consider recording lectures;
- organise and review your notes.

To cope with the reading:

- know why you are reading;
- before you read – remind yourself of what you already know about the topic;
- read actively;

- consider using reading aids and services;

- get the big picture first, for example by looking at basic texts or by flicking through a chapter for an overview;

- look for signposts;

- try out 'rapid reading' techniques;

- and finally – would coloured overlays or coloured lenses make reading easier for you?

Chapter 12

Essays and other written assignments

> This is a long chapter: students are advised to read it in small doses! It breaks down the work involved in a written assignment into its various stages; it also gives you strategies for tackling each stage and suggests how you can ensure that your writing flows logically from start to finish.

WHAT ARE YOUR DIFFICULTIES?

We would like you to suggest to your college tutors the following penance: they should imagine themselves cooking the breakfast and finding that the milk is boiling over, that the toast is burning, that the telephone is ringing, that there is a knock at the door and that several members of their family are simultaneously asking them questions. This may give tutors some idea of the problems confronting you as a dyslexic student when you have to write an essay or carry out an assignment: there are simply too many things to attend to, all at the same time.

Teachers will have told you to plan the essay as a whole, but there may be a dozen or more threads or separate topics which have to be thought about and arranged in order. In addition, no progress will be possible until you have found the right words for saying what you want to say, and even when you have found them there is the danger that in typing or writing them down your hand movements may get out of step with your thinking. Many students say to us, 'I can think faster than I can write.' As if all this were not enough, you then have to check whether the words are correctly spelled and whether there is correct paragraphing and punctuation. Our experience is that many students have not been taught punctuation; and since it involves learning to name and use yet another group of symbols – the full stop, the comma, the semicolon, the colon, the question mark etc. – it is easy to see why you failed to pick it up at a younger age, when all your energies were directed towards writing and spelling.

Many of the essay-writing skills are second nature to non-dyslexic students. If they wish to write a word, they do so; in most cases the word 'just comes' and they do not need to think about its spelling. There is no danger for them that words or phrases will come out jumbled up or in the wrong order; and even if they have not received individual teaching they may well have acquired the essentials of punctuation without conscious effort. As a result they are free to concentrate their energies on the subject matter of the essay and on the construction of fluent and easily readable sentences.

For you, as a dyslexic student, the process may be very different, and it is little wonder that your written style suffers in comparison. With so much else to think about you may forget what you wrote a moment earlier. The result may be a very staccato and jerky style as you struggle to express a large number of ideas briefly before you lose track of them. Alternatively, you may sometimes go to the opposite extreme and write long convoluted sentences as though you do not know when to stop. In general, so much is being demanded of you at the same moment that you cannot monitor all of it efficiently.

The result of all this is illustrated by a tutor's comment which criticised a dyslexic student's 'inability to sort out and organise his main ideas despite a keen understanding of the subject'. Sometimes, the essays of dyslexic students may appear to have a relatively low level of analysis or abstraction: they sometimes appear packed with detail which is not sufficiently related to key concepts or presented with adequate generalisations. This chapter offers some advice on how to minimise these problems.

STRATEGIES FOR WRITING – ONE THING AT A TIME

Most dyslexic students find it useful to break down complex material into its component parts and deal with these parts one at a time. It is widely agreed that, for many people, the best way to remember a six-digit telephone number is to break it down into two groups of three, or even three groups of two. The same principle applies if you need to remember items in series, such as the months of the year; and similarly if you need to spell or write longer words it is often helpful to break them up into smaller parts (compare the suggestions on spelling in **Chapter 14**).

Similar strategies will almost certainly be helpful in essay writing. The different components of the task need to be considered separately, one at a time. *Reading the question* is a different activity from *thinking about how to answer it*; and *planning the essay as a whole* is a different activity from *considering how best to get across what you want to say*, while *questions of paragraphing and punctuation* are different yet again. If you try to attend to all these things at once, the result may be chaos: you may well be told that you have failed to answer the question, that the essay lacks coherence, that the style is immature and that your punctuation is all wrong. If you have experienced such criticisms, we suggest that you work on them one at a time.

In what follows there will be sections concerned with:

- what is expected in a college essay;

- reading the question;

- reading for and planning the essay as a whole;

- getting across what you want to say;

- writing your first draft;

- paragraphs;

- setting out references;

- your final draft – and checking your work.

Questions of grammar and punctuation will be discussed in **Chapter 13** and strategies for improving spelling will be found in **Chapter 14**. We recommend that you read *this* chapter a little at a time.

WHAT IS EXPECTED IN A COLLEGE ESSAY?

Essays at college are not normally set with the purpose of making you 'write down all the facts'. Rather, you are being given the chance to examine a problem and to show that you can formulate ideas about that problem – thus presenting a debate or an argument. As an essay writer, therefore, your purpose will not normally simply be to describe things, concepts or events but to analyse, discuss and interpret them. This applies to scientific essays as well as to those written by students doing courses in arts and social sciences. Scientists may need to consider the implications of the topic, whether is it based on ground-breaking research and what further research might be done. It is useful in the case of any essay to ask, 'Why has this question been set?' You will therefore need to arrange your ideas in a logical order and to produce evidence from the relevant literature in support of your argument.

Some departments supply information as to how the assignment will be graded – a handout or, in some cases, a sheet at the head of the assignment. If they do, you should look at it carefully. It may say, for example, that marks will be given for your understanding of the subject, for the quality of your argument, for your use of evidence and for the way in which you express yourself.

READING THE QUESTION

The first essential, before you embark on an essay, is to read the question carefully. You should then spend time considering what the question means and what precisely you are being asked. This will ensure that all aspects of the question are covered in the answer.

If you ring or highlight key words in the question, you will be better able to focus on their meaning. A question set in a recent

English paper was: 'How successful is Wordsworth in integrating the various strands of philosophy and experience in *The Prelude, Book 1*?' All students discussed what was meant by 'strands of philosophy and experience', while many referred to the integration of the two; but there were very few who dealt with the key words 'how successful'. The question might in this case have been highlighted or ringed as follows:

> *How successful* is Wordsworth in *integrating* the various strands of *philosophy* and *experience*?

You would then be in a position to use the highlighted words to guide your answer. Thus, since 'How successful' is highlighted, you are immediately led to thinking about the notion of 'succeeding', while because 'integrating' is highlighted it reminds you that it is not enough to consider each of the components separately. Highlights on 'philosophy' and 'experience' are further reminders that the meanings of these two key terms are by no means self-evident.

In the case of many essays it may be helpful to experiment with changes in the wording (Does it mean this? or Might it mean that?), since such changes may help to clarify what is and is not relevant and may open up new ways of treating the topic. It is important, too, that you should make full use of the information which has been given in the title; this can be done in particular if you make sure that you pay attention to all the key words. Indeed there are some words which are likely to keep occurring both in essays and in examinations, for example 'compare', 'contrast', 'assess', 'analyse', 'discuss', 'outline', 'evaluate' and 'summarise' (**see note 12.1**). These words call for careful thought, and you should make sure that you completely understand their meaning.

Above all, you should spend time considering what is implied by the title of the essay and what are the important issues that it raises. Ask yourself: 'What exactly is the argument to be debated here?' 'What are all the implications?' 'What debate does it raise?' From these basic questions further questions will arise. Write these questions down on a sheet of paper – in the form of a mind-map if you wish – or on your computer screen. (An example of a mind-map is given in **Chapter 11**.) If you do this, there is a good chance that you will genuinely be answering what you were asked, and will not be sidetracked.

If you are still unsure about what the essay is about, then it may be helpful if you go to see your tutor. You should do so, however, only after you have gone through this initial stage of analysing the title, and have an outline of your plan written down, so that she can see that you have already given thought to the topic.

READING FOR AND PLANNING THE ESSAY AS A WHOLE

It is at this stage that you should be aware of your objectives; in particular you should ask yourself as far as you can:

- What are the main things that I want to say?

- How can I arrange them logically?

You will then need to do some preliminary reading. You may like to look again at the section on reading in this book (**Chapter 11**). It is a good idea to start by reading a short book or chapter that gives you an outline or overview of the topic; if you have lecture notes on the topic, look at these. It is also important that you should be clear as to what information you are looking for so that you are not wasting time on irrelevant material.

At the same time as you do your preliminary reading you should provide yourself with a master plan or page on the computer and develop the main outline of the essay on it. For this purpose you could use a mind-map, as you will be able to extend ideas across and down the page and then make the links between them. Many students prefer paper at this stage, but there is the useful mind-mapping software (**see Chapter 16**). Figure 3 is an example of a basic master plan. We have in fact chosen a topic from the history of education, but the same principles would of course apply to essays on most other subjects.

Let us suppose, then, that you have been given the following title for the essay: 'Assess the changes introduced into British state education by the comprehensive system.' Your first move should be to put the title in a central box from which arrows can flow in a variety of directions. You should then consider each key word in turn and write notes on each. 'In turn' is important: if you try to think of all the points at once, you may well forget some of them and become confused. (One advantage of a mind-map is that if a point does occur to you, you can put it down somewhere on the page and consider later where exactly it fits in.) The end product might look like that shown in Figure 3.

Once you have understood the central theme of the essay, it will be easier for you to ensure that all your reading is purposeful and that you select only material which is relevant.

Think about what you are reading. Try if you can to organise your material by giving it headings and sub-headings; these can then be linked to your master plan. Some students prefer to use cards rather than ordinary paper for this purpose: they are stiffer and therefore

Figure 3 Example of a master plan

easier to organise, and there is the advantage that cards of different colours can be used for different topics. If all cards are numbered, this will save time when you come to re-read them. Some students use A5 sheets (or A4 sheets torn in two) as they are smaller and therefore more manageable. You should write on one side of the page only; then, if necessary, you can cut pieces out or add them.

If you quote from the books which you have read, check that the quotation is relevant and makes the point that you wish to make – and for future reference make a note of the page number. Also make clear that it is a quote and that the words are not your own; otherwise it may seem that you are plagiarising (that is stealing other people's ideas and passing them off as your own). Either choose really apt quotes or paraphrase, using your notes as brief summaries.

There is a section on referencing later on in this chapter. In the meantime, when you take a book out from the library, make sure that you have recorded all the information which you need for your reference section – the full title of the book, the name and initials of its author and the book's publisher and place of publication (you could photocopy the page on which these details appear). We cannot stress too often the importance of noting down all references – on card or on the screen; either way you will be able to arrange them easily into alphabetical order when you have finished the assignment.

Some students prefer to plan as they read and put all their notes straight onto the computer, moving and editing at the same time. Others choose to put everything onto the screen and then move the material around. The difficulty in the second case is that you can see only a limited amount of material at a time and it can therefore take you quite a long time to search for relevant sections. However, you can use colour, bold or italics to indicate where certain parts belong. As already indicated, there is software which can help you to plan essays (**see Chapter 16**). You can also use a scanner; this allows printed text to be transferred onto your screen. You should be careful, however, that you do not put this material into your essay without analysing or paraphrasing it.

While you are reading, you may suddenly be struck by a new idea, and in that case you should be prepared to explore it. For this purpose, you may find it useful to keep a page where you write down notes for future use: these can include opinions, questions, agreements, disagreements etc. about which you will later need to examine all the relevant evidence. If you are working on the computer, you can scroll down to the end of your work and jot down the thoughts which pop into your mind, perhaps in colour, so that you can pick them up and use them later.

Keep your mind receptive and **keep asking questions**. Some of what you are reading may not fall easily under a particular heading, in which case it may be better to put off classifying it until you have read further and done the necessary planning. It does not matter at this stage if the pages are filled in a seemingly haphazard way as long as all relevant material is included (and you may need to refer back to the title in order to make a decision as to whether a particular topic is or is not relevant).

You can next look back at your master plan. This will help you to organise your notes and jottings into a coherent order. It is helpful to number each jotting as this will give you an order in which the different topics can usefully be discussed. Try using fluorescent markers or different coloured pens to circle related topics, and, as we have said, you can if you wish cut up your pages into strips so that the different topics can be clearly distinguished.

Before you start to write your rough draft, you should again look at your master plan, considering all the questions you have raised. You should then write them down in a logical order. **Check that each point follows on from the one before.** You may sometimes find that there is material that now seems irrelevant and that you can get rid of it. However, there may also be new ideas which you have learned from your reading, and these should be written down. You will probably end up with a series of questions or points arranged in a logical order. These can then be numbered, and you can sort out your notes into numbered piles which correspond. Then you will be able to expand in detail on each of the numbered points. One of our students put her points onto Post-it notes, which she arranged and re-arranged on her wall until she was satisfied with the sequence.

GETTING ACROSS WHAT YOU WANT TO SAY

Many dyslexic students can *talk* about difficult concepts with fluency and yet when they have to express themselves in writing they cannot get across what they wish to say with anything like the same level of sophistication. A group of dyslexic students had an interesting discussion of an essay written by a physics student on the theme of 'nuclear power stations'. What was particularly noticeable was the maturity and complexity of their spoken language in contrast with the level of language they used when they tried to summarise the argument in writing.

Having to write down the words seems in some cases to affect fluency and spontaneity. The extra effort needed adds an unwelcome complexity, and the result may be that some students come to doubt whether they will ever be able to find exactly the right word. If, in addition, they are worried about making spelling errors, they may conclude that the best response to all these pressures is to choose a simpler word, even though it may be a very much less effective one. To avoid this, it might be useful for some students to use a Dictaphone into which they can talk out their ideas.

Try talking through your ideas

This is the kind of situation where a tutor can be very helpful. He can discuss the use of alternative words and phrases and call attention to nuances of meaning. We often find that our students offer key words and phrases orally, which the tutor then writes down. (In fact, one of the most common comments made by our students – surprised by their fluency – is, 'Did I really say that?') Where appropriate this discussion can be recorded on tape and the student can be asked to summarise it in writing. The tutor can sometimes offer key words which trigger off further relevant phrases from the student.

A similar technique is that suggested by Dr Alex Main (**see note 12.2**). Main suggests that students struggling with written expression should select a passage written on a specialist topic. Main first read it with them, and they selected key words from each paragraph. The student then rewrote the passage using these key words as a basis for the reconstruction: 'This exercise, repeated several times with different passages, if necessary, builds up the student's critical awareness of her writing style, and increases her confidence in seeking different ways of expressing herself'.

Using diagrams and graphs

It may also be helpful if you consider the use of illustrations and diagrams as ways of getting across your argument, and in some contexts graphs, histograms, bar charts and pie charts can also be useful for this purpose. The great advantage of these is that they often convey information more succinctly and clearly than is possible by means of verbal explanations. If they are used, however, it is important that they should be well presented: it is best if they are drawn on a blank page which can then be mounted into the main text of the essay. Scanners and graphics packages are, of course, invaluable here. They should also be labelled and referenced if necessary.

Technical terms

Give careful thought to the question of whether and how to define technical or unfamiliar terms. In the first place, there are some situations where you can assume that the reader has the required knowledge. This is true, for example, of many mathematical or statistical terms, such as 'correlation coefficient', and of standard physical or biological terms such as 'impedance' or 'monozygotic'. Second, however, there may be terms which call for explanation, either because you cannot assume that the reader is familiar with them or sometimes because there is genuine doubt as to what they do mean, as in the case, for instance, of 'romanticism' or 'phenomenology'. When any unfamiliar term is explained, it is often useful to give one or more examples of situations where it is being correctly used. This shows that *you* understand what you are talking about. What is unsatisfactory is to introduce the word without explanation – which may baffle the reader – and then several lines later try to explain its meaning. Good examples can, in fact, be useful both in illustrating the meanings of words and in clarifying the intended argument.

Reading to improve your writing

Do plenty of reading, even though some of you find it hard work. One reason for this is that if you pay attention to the ways in which the writer is expressing himself you are likely to achieve a more mature written style yourself. It does not, in fact, take all that much effort to set yourself to read for, say, ten or 15 minutes each day, and the choice of material can be guided by your personal interests. As with other kinds of reading, it is important that this reading should be done purposefully, and we recommend that a dictionary is available for looking up unfamiliar words and that a notebook is available for writing them down.

Use a thesaurus

We have found that some students do not use a thesaurus. Once they have been shown how to use one, whether in book form or on a computer, they have found it a very valuable form of support in written work (**see note 12.3**). We have also found that students can be made more aware of style if they try to analyse some of their own work under the tutor's guidance. An exercise like this may demonstrate to you the greater powers of expression you can achieve if you examine shades of meaning with care (**see note 12.4**).

A DIALOGUE WITH THE READER

Part of developing a good style involves thinking about the reader. As we pointed out at the beginning of the chapter, some students write in a very jerky or abrupt style. It gives the impression that they have the knowledge but cannot be bothered, or are too impatient, to explain it thoroughly. They seem to assume that the reader knows what they are talking about. Thus, seemingly illogical leaps occur and it is not always easy to follow their train of thought.

We encourage students to see essays as a dialogue with the reader. This ties in with what we said earlier about the purpose of essay writing, namely to show that you can analyse and discuss the question set. The term 'intelligent layman' should help you to visualise the reader: you can picture your mum or your support tutor (indeed, a support tutor is often a layman, dealing with essays from every field of learning, most of which he knows little about). You should assume that the reader is unlikely to be aware in advance of how you are going to treat the subject, and therefore you should lead him through the essay step by step.

Now, a dialogue:

- introduces
- explains
- analyses
- assesses
- discusses
- links up
- summarises.

If you think in terms of a dialogue, it helps you to be clear as to your own train of thought and it also helps the reader to follow the chain or pattern of your ideas. This dialogue can comprise introductory or concluding sentences within paragraphs, or it could comprise whole linking paragraphs.

At each stage, therefore, it is important to check that the reader is being given a sense of direction. For this purpose, suitable signposting is very important – it makes explicit to your reader the logical links between one sentence or paragraph and the next.

Also, you should take special note of connecting words such as 'nevertheless', 'but', 'however', 'on the one hand … on the other hand', 'consequently', 'likewise', 'thus' etc. The function of these words is to mark a variety of relationships, including contrasts, similarities, alternatives and results. Even the use of the familiar words 'this' and 'that' can help the flow of ideas within an essay. To check that these connecting words are being correctly used is important for any writer, since such checking forces you to consider where exactly the argument is leading; without it there is serious risk that the essay will lack direction. We provide our students with a list of such words and an account of their functions.

WRITING YOUR FIRST DRAFT

This is the most important part of the writing stage. The rough draft is where you think, question, alter, move text, cross out, revise and edit. If all the work is done at this stage, the final writing-up should be a fairly mechanical copy of what has been done on the rough draft. You should take heart from the fact that almost all writers struggle with this stage of drafting – not just dyslexic writers.

If up to this point you have planned your essay by hand, you should now turn to the word processor. The advantages are that moving text, re-editing etc. all become very much easier. However, since there are some students who prefer to write their essays by hand we shall refer in this section to both ways of working.

If you are writing by hand, it is sensible to put the rough draft on one side of the paper only, since this means that passages can be re-written or re-ordered without other passages being thrown into disarray. You can cut sections off and add them on elsewhere (which is why this facility on your word processor is called 'cut and paste'). It is also a useful precaution to write the essay title in pencil at the top of each page; if this title is attended to, there will be less risk of writing things which are off the point. It may also be helpful to summarise the main points in the margin; and for this reason you should allow wide margins and plenty of space between lines and at the end of paragraphs. This will also enable you to make corrections. Trying to save paper can sometimes be a false economy.

If questions and problems crop up as you write, it is useful to have a piece of paper at hand so that you can make a note of them. Alternatively, you could put them in the margin of your script in pencil or a different coloured pen. The kind of comment you might write in could be: 'check reference', 'more needed here', 're-phrase', 'is this OK?' Some students may like to have a recorder handy into which they can speak their comments.

All this is easy on the word processor. If there are things you have queries about, you can write them in italics, in colour or in bold. You can do the same with your comments; it might be useful to put some stars (***) at the start and at the finish (***) of any comments that you make. If you move text, have some way of indicating where you are going to put it and where you have taken it from. It can involve some time searching through a document; stars are again useful. If you are not sure whether you want to move a piece or not, or if you want to move it somewhere to get it out of the way of the section you are working on, then, again, you can highlight it or put it in **bold** to indicate that it needs attention.

Getting started – and coming to the conclusion

Some students find it difficult to know *how to start an essay*. In fact, you do not need to write the introduction until you have written the body of the essay. In many ways the introduction is rather like the conclusion. There is no one set way of writing an introduction, and the suggestions which follow should not be adopted uncritically. However – depending on the topic – you may find some of the following suggestions useful.

- Say something about the key terms in the question.

- Indicate how you are interpreting them.

- Tell your reader what the essay is going to be about, i.e. how you are going to treat the topic and what will be your lines of argument.

Similar principles apply to the ending of the essay. This should be a brief summary in which you draw all your points together and make the overall position clear. It is useful when you write your last paragraph to look back to the introduction. There are a number of expressions which can usefully occur in it such as 'in conclusion', 'to sum up', 'it therefore follows' and 'finally'; and you will need to judge which of these is appropriate for the purposes of a particular essay. No writer of essays can afford to overlook the wise words attributed to a preacher who was asked for his advice on how to preach a good sermon: 'First,' he said, 'tell them what you are going to tell them; then tell them; then tell them what you have told them.'

PARAGRAPHING

When you are writing the essay, you should divide your topics into paragraphs. Every paragraph needs to be thought of as a unit, each in succession contributing to the unity of the essay as a whole. There need not necessarily be sub-headings at the start of each paragraph since this would be cumbersome; but you may like to 'think' or imagine them to be present or even write them in pencil for your own use. You will then be in a position to check that every sentence within the paragraph is relevant to its main theme and that the paragraph as a whole is relevant to the main theme of the essay and moves your argument or analysis forward. Once you have grasped the significance of paragraphing, you are likely to become clearer in your own mind as to what are the central points you wish to make in the essay, and as a result you will be better able to organise them in the most effective way (**see note 12.5**).

Although we do not recommend writing to a formula, the difficulties experienced by some students in shaping a paragraph led a group of us to devise a procedure which could be of help to others. A paragraph might contain:

- a general **opening** statement indicating the theme or topic of the paragraph – and perhaps its link with the previous paragraph; a **discussion** or elaboration of this;

- **evidence** to support the argument;

- **discussion** of evidence;

- **conclusion**.

The students worked out their own mnemonic for this – **ODEDC** – 'often dogs eat dirty carrots' (there was a reason for the carrots – someone's dog had just eaten some, and been sick). This formula has sometimes been found useful in writing answers to examination questions.

OTHER TYPES OF ASSIGNMENT

We are not going to discuss at any length the writing of laboratory reports, research projects or dissertations, since the guiding principles are, in general, the same as those for essay writing. Usually each department will issue its own guidelines for these more specialised types of writing, and if there is a rigid formula you can put it on your computer as a template. You should keep in mind your central objective and check that everything you write is relevant to it. If you are reporting on some research which you yourself have carried out, you should remember to include full details of your procedure; it is very easy to assume that the reader will know what you did – but he has not got second sight and you must *tell* him.

In the case of dissertations, it may be necessary for you to use more headings and sub-headings than in the case of essays, since a dissertation is in effect an essay writ large. The same kind of masterplan is likely to be useful, and it is particularly important that the logic of your argument should be clearly signposted (**see note 12.6**).

SETTING OUT REFERENCES

Projects and dissertations, and usually essays too, should include a list of references. Here you record the books and articles which you have used as sources or from which you have quoted. Do not, of course, make the piece simply a series of quotations otherwise the result will be what some tutors rudely call a 'scissors-and-paste' essay.

One of the most important functions of the list of references is to enable the reader to evaluate the credentials of claims made in the essay. For example, if you have used expressions such as, 'it has been shown that x', it is important to indicate how x was shown and who was responsible for doing so. You should imagine the marker writing, 'How do you know?' or 'Evidence?' over every statement that you make.

Some students find it difficult to know how to introduce references. To some extent this will depend on the style recommended by your department, but at many colleges the Harvard system is widely used. In this system the name of the author and date of publication are put in the text, and the full reference is given at the end of the essay or book. Books and names of journals are put in italics; in the case of books the town and publisher are given at the end, while the titles of journal articles are put in plain text, followed by the name of the journal in italics, followed by its volume, issue and page numbers. Thus in the case of a book you might write:

Bloggs, J. (2005) *My Friends the Owls*. London: Aviary Press.

while in the case of a journal you could write:

Bloggs, J. (2006) The Owl in ancient Egypt. *British Journal of Owl Behaviour*, 27, 1, 39–43 (**see note 12.7**).

We encourage our students to look in their books to see how writers present their references, and we have also drawn up a list of useful phrases such as:

- Brown (2004) states that ...

- Brown (2004) points out that ...

- Brown (2004) describes how ...

- This has been shown by Brown (2004), who ...

If you refer in the reference section to a book or article, this is, in effect, an undertaking that you have read the work in question. If, as sometimes happens, you have to rely on secondary sources – for example a textbook which asserts that Brown pointed out such and such in an article in an untraceable journal dated 1870 – the correct procedure is to quote the textbook, since this carries no claim that you have read the original paper.

It is also important to check that the style of the reference list is consistent. What is irritating to the reader is to find that the year or place of publication is given in some cases and not in others, or that some references to journal articles carry page numbers and some do not. Advice on the most appropriate style for the references should readily be obtained from the department. We must emphasise again how important it is when you are doing the initial research to keep a record of all the references which you consult. Students can spend many tedious hours trying to find them again.

YOUR FINAL DRAFT – AND CHECKING YOUR WORK

When writing your first drafts, there is no need to spell out each word in full, since nobody has to recognise what is written except you yourself. If you are doubtful about some grammar or spelling, you can always mark or highlight the words in question and return to them at leisure. Similarly, if you are not immediately able to produce the exact wording that you want, you can again indicate this and return to the passage when your mind is fresher. If you start worrying about such things at the time, there is a serious risk that you will lose track of your arguments and forget what you were trying to say. As we noted, the advantage of writing on a computer is that you can use bold or colour or italics to indicate places where you would like to make changes.

When you have completed your rough draft, you will need to give time to checking it. The crucial point in such checking is that you should make sure that what you have said reflects adequately what you *meant* to say (compare also what is said in **Chapter 19** when you come to sit your examinations). As we have already indicated, there is a tendency on the part of dyslexic students to take too much for granted on the part of the reader: they may not appreciate that the details of their argument need to be 'spelled out' (an interesting and significant metaphor) if someone else is to understand it. They may, in fact, genuinely believe that they have made themselves clear when all that the reader finds is some cryptic utterances which in themselves do not amount to an argument at all.

A useful device is to read aloud and record what you have written and then play it back. This will provide the opportunity for *listening* rather than *looking*, and the result may be that inadequacies in logic, presentation or style are easier to detect. Many students who write onto a computer which has text-to-speech software say that they find it really useful to listen to their work being read out to them, especially if they leave some time before coming back to listen to it (see below).

The following are some further points which need to be checked:

- Does the essay answer the question?

- Does it contain irrelevancies which should be excluded?

- Does it maintain a logical sequence, and does the use of 'connecting' words or expressions such as 'therefore' or 'in contrast' contribute to showing the direction of the argument?

- What is the point of each paragraph, and does it form part of the flow of the essay?

- Are the sentences complete and are they of the most suitable length?

- Can the things which you have learned about style, grammar, punctuation and spelling (**see this chapter and Chapter 13**) be put to good use?

This checking or editing will need to be done at least three times, as it is extremely difficult to read for sense and style, for punctuation and for spelling simultaneously. We suggest one check for sense and style (which should include a check that the essay reads coherently), one for punctuation and one for spelling.

It is often helpful if you can allow a gap of several days between the completion of your rough draft and its re-reading. After this interval, you can come to what you have written with a fresh mind, and it is easier to imagine yourself as someone who is looking at the essay for the first time. You may find it helpful to think of yourself as a tutor whose task is to make critical comments. You can then mark these in pencil or with a coloured pen. We ourselves, wearing our hats as tutors, have often found it helpful to say to students, 'From now on you do not need me to make these critical comments.'

Students should redraft their written work in the way that suits them best. A few students will want to handwrite their first and even second drafts. They may not yet feel confident about typing out their work to begin with, especially if they have been used to handwriting work in school. It is not a good use of time to handwrite many drafts: it is better to get the work onto a computer as soon as possible and then print out drafts so that they can be more easily read through, highlighted, annotated or cut up and rearranged if necessary. Alterations can then be typed in straight away.

It will help the person grading your script if your work is well presented. It is best, therefore, if you type with double spacing or use wide-lined paper, writing on one side only. Remember to number all your pages. On the front cover you may need to include:

- your name
- the name of your course
- the year or module number
- the name of your tutor
- a clearly written title.

You should follow your department's guidelines here, and with respect to page headings and numbering if this is required. Again, a bibliography or reference list needs to be in the department's style, and it is useful if you package your essay in a plastic envelope or folder. (Do not put every page in a separate envelope, as this means the marker has to pull each one out in order to read it, and this is very time-consuming.)

And – finally – do not forget to hand the work in!

CHECK POINTS FOR CHAPTER 12

You will be more successful if you tackle essays and other written assignments in stages – and try to concentrate on one thing at a time.

- Ask yourself why the question has been set; what are the issues and ideas that you need to explore?

- Give time to reading the question; highlight and focus on the key words.

- If you develop a rough outline or master plan, it will be easier to focus your reading on relevant material.

- Be careful to note down details for references.

- If you think of your writing as a dialogue with the reader, this will help you to make your points clearly and in a logical order.

- Make sure that each paragraph carries the essay forward.

- Follow your department's guidelines for referencing.

- You may need to write several drafts before you are happy with your work.

- Check your writing in separate stages for sense and style, punctuation and spelling.

- Don't forget to hand your work in.

Chapter 13

Grammar and punctuation

This chapter is mainly addressed to the support tutor: we have found that it is difficult for students, dyslexic or otherwise, to teach themselves grammar. Computer grammar checks vary in their complexity, and students often work better with a support tutor who can explain the terms that come up. As many tutors who work with dyslexic students are language-trained, we have simply indicated the type of approach needed and the main difficulties faced by dyslexic students.

INTRODUCTION

Some dyslexic students have improved their written language considerably as a result of help with grammar. In the past students were taught parsing and clause analysis (learning about the parts of a sentence and how they fit together); but until recently these had largely gone out of fashion. We believe, however, that their importance has been underestimated. They may, in fact, be coming back into the classroom as a more grammatical approach to language develops through the National Curriculum. Training in grammar may also help dyslexic students to understand the grammar check on the computer.

Words are precision tools, and the person who has a thorough knowledge of how they function may be compared to a craftsman who has a wide repertoire of skills, or to a cricketer or tennis player who has a wide range of strokes. In our view all students – and dyslexic students in particular – are likely to benefit if they are made aware of the rules of basic grammar; without good writing skills it can be difficult to express ideas clearly and effectively.

It is important to go slowly, since it is impossible to study grammar without using at least a few technical terms, and these may be somewhat daunting. A tutor who, without adequate explanation, introduces words such as 'adverb' or 'conjunction' may confuse the students. It is possible, however, to make clear to them that in learning about grammar and punctuation they are embarking on an intellectually challenging discipline, namely a systematic study of certain aspects of human verbal communication.

Some of our students ask specifically for 'grammar lessons' and seem to find them stimulating. Once they recognise that technical terms are unavoidable in such a study they are likely to feel happier about trying to learn them.

If students come forward asking for help with grammar, it is a good idea to look in advance at some of their written work and analyse their errors before you actually meet them in a tutorial. This is likely to be less demoralising for them than having to listen to criticism the moment they arrive.

We also ask students to develop their own awareness by noting down any difficulties which arise when they are writing.

In general, a 30- to 40-minute session is enough. Over a period of time the tutor can collate the points that are discussed in the tutorials and give them to the student as a personal grammar book. This can be supplemented by relevant texts and exercises (**see note 13.1**).

THE SIMPLE SENTENCE

The most useful way to start is to introduce the idea of a simple sentence. This is the basic unit from which, eventually, to expand into more complex sentences. It can also be used to introduce key grammatical terms. We try to make the teaching a joint exercise as far as possible and we also try to keep it subject-related; we therefore extract a sentence or two from the student's work or ask them to give us one orally. Here are two examples of such sentences:

> Three sorts of grass grow abundantly on Bird Island.

and

> We marked out the same number of plots in each sward. (**see note 13.2**)

SOME KEY GRAMMATICAL TERMS

From such sentences certain key grammatical terms can be introduced (**see note 13.3**), while at the same time you can make the student aware of the implications for spelling.

These grammatical terms are:

- subject, object, noun, pronoun;
- verb, tense;
- adjective, adverb.

An understanding of tense will help the dyslexic student with the *-ed* ending. Using 'marked', you can show the student that most past tenses end in *-ed*. The effect on sound can be discussed: in some cases the *e* which comes before the *d* is sounded ('acted', 'hurried' etc.), while in other cases it is not ('groaned', 'crammed' etc.). As in 'marked', the ending may have a t-sound, and though in most cases the *-ed* spelling is retained, there are a few words where the letter *t* actually appears in the spelling, as in 'wept', 'crept' and 'smelt'. We have often met misspellings such as 'happend', 'determind' and 'gatherd'. Although these represent what is heard, the writing of *d* in place of *-ed* is evidence that the writer has not fully appreciated the past tense ending (**see note 13.4**). Indeed, students may well be generally confused about the concept and use of tense, and this is sometimes evidenced in written work by tense-switching.

Learning about adverbs helps students to understand the *-ly* ending. They can then see the function of *-ly*, work out the original word and add -*ly*. This helps with the spellings of words such as 'likely' and 'safely'. We have been surprised how few of our students knew this rule. Several students have made their own cards with examples as reminders, for example they might have a card with '-*ly*: badly' on it to show how the rule works.

A tutor should take care not to introduce too many of these terms in any one session and not to use any of them without indicating the job which each one does. For example, you would not simply introduce the word 'adjective' out of the blue; rather, you would ask the student to think about '*green* grass', 'a *large* island' and '*different* sorts' and then to consider what job is being done by the words 'green', 'large' and 'different'. The logic of class membership is perfectly intelligible to a dyslexic student, and in this context the need for the word 'adjective' becomes obvious.

If you expand the simple sentence, you can then introduce the comma and perhaps provide a checklist of its uses. The student might add more adjectives, using commas to separate them, or add a separate phrase:

- The grass was long, green, red and salty.

- In a study of Bird Island, for example, three sorts of grass were identified.

WRITING COMPLETE SENTENCES

'But how do I know whether or not it is a sentence?' Many students – not only dyslexic students – write combinations of words which do not form a complete sentence, such as:

- To analyse this topic.

- Starting with the first example.

- Attlee, a Labour Prime Minister.

- In a very short time.

- Who served under Elizabeth I.

- Whereas the temperature was lower.

When these non-sentences are seen out of context, it may seem clear that none of them is complete, but this may be far from clear to dyslexic students who are struggling to put their ideas down on paper.

One way of getting a student to recognise a non-sentence is to provide combinations of words, some of which do *not* form sentences. Thus it will be easy for him to recognise that

on Bird Island grass

is not a sentence since the words in that order do not make sense. Moreover, even if the word order is changed and we say or write

grass on Bird Island

the result is still not a sentence. A useful way of explaining why this is so is to point out that a sentence should answer a particular question, for instance the question, 'What kinds of grasses are there on Bird Island?', but that these words fail to do so. The student might then come to recognise for himself that there is no verb in the sentence.

Another useful way of helping dyslexic students to see that a combination of words is not a sentence is to get them to realise that a sentence is a 'stand alone' unit. Sometimes their minds race ahead of what they are writing: they mentally link one 'sentence' up to another without realising that the full stop is a complete break. For example, the following combinations are wrong because there should not be the breaks that are suggested by the use of the full stops:

Because many conifers grow on mountain sides. Drainage is easy. There being many natural streams. Which flow downhill.

It is useful to have strips of card to isolate the non-sentences and to highlight the real unit of sense; this enables the student to realise what is happening. It should then be possible for you to work out jointly the criteria for a complete sentence. These are:

• It must make sense.

• It must answer questions such as 'who', 'what' or 'when'.

- It should have a subject and a verb.

- It must start with a capital letter and end with a full stop.

All this can be quite difficult for dyslexic students. It can be good training for them to learn to read their work aloud, seeing each sentence as a separate unit. They may sometimes be able to recognise the non-sentences from their own intonation.

PUNCTUATION

Once the simple sentence is understood, it is useful to look at punctuation. A common error is to end a sentence with a comma, not a full stop; as a result, the student strings would-be 'sentences' together separated only by commas. This is a fault among many students, dyslexic and non-dyslexic alike. It should be made clear to them that the full stop is used to mark boundaries between sentences; if they are careless about the use of this particular mark, the sense of their work can be affected:

> We studied the marshland, although it was raining, there were many geese there.

(Where does 'although it was raining' fit?)

It could again be that the dyslexic student's mind is moving on to the next sentence. In this case the important thing is to know that after a complete sentence there has to be a full stop. Faulty punctuation may reflect faulty logic.

If students are encouraged to listen carefully to passages which are read aloud to them, they may notice that when the reader's voice falls and he makes an appreciable pause he is almost certainly indicating a full stop; in contrast, if there are minor pauses these will be represented in the written version by commas. We have found that students can detect faulty punctuation fairly well when they read their work aloud or when it is read aloud to them; sometimes we work off two photocopies: the tutor reads the work aloud while the student follows with a pencil in his hand and marks what he now recognises as punctuation errors. Students also find text-reading software useful in this respect as it is possible to recognise when the 'reader' has spoken for too long without the fall in the voice that is prompted by a full stop.

The colon and semicolon can next be introduced: these are particularly important for academic writing. They are useful for those dyslexic students who tend to write long involved sentences, since these sentences can then be broken up.

The colon can be regarded as a sign that some kind of expanding statement or list is about to be introduced, as in: 'There are various ways in which this can be done: ...' (followed by an indication of what these ways are) or in 'You should take with you the following: ...' (with an indication of specific items). We have asked students to visualise the colon as two gateposts: the gate opens onto a wider 'field' to expand or illustrate the meaning.

In contrast, the semicolon simply divides the full sentence into two distinct sub-sentences with a closely related meaning, for example:

> The Saxons invaded the south of England; the Danes invaded the north.

With some of our students, we have quite successfully made small leaflets with the punctuation mark clearly on the front, and on the two pages inside a list of its uses on one side and examples of usage on the other.

COMPLEX SENTENCES

In the case of complex sentences dyslexic students in particular often have difficulty in writing clearly and succinctly. They can often be helped if they are shown ways in which sentences can be expanded. It is important therefore to explain what job is done by a conjunction. Discussing the meaning of the word 'junction' helps here, and the whole idea is easier to grasp once the student understands what a complete sentence is. We have found it helpful to start with 'and' and 'but' and build up from there.

It will be necessary to explain that a conjunction can occur at the start of a sentence but that a full sentence needs to follow. Students who start a sentence with words such as 'because', 'although' or 'whereas' can often fail to complete it. This point can more easily be detected if the sentence is read aloud.

SENTENCE LENGTH

In general, dyslexic students tend to make errors of two opposite kinds. The first is to write what comes out as a series of sharp staccato sentences. The second is to go to the opposite extreme and write long, involved sentences that try to compress too many ideas within too short a space. In that case the student does not see the sentence as a pattern; each new idea is added as it occurs to him, and the sentence becomes unconnected and disjointed. As a result it is difficult for the reader to understand the overall meaning.

Golden rule 1

Keep to one main idea per sentence.

Golden rule 2

Never start a sentence without knowing how you are going to end it.

A sentence which rambles on should be broken down into shorter sentences, with the logical links between each being made clear. If sentences are too short, however, the student should consider how they can be made to flow more easily; in particular, the introduction of longer sentences containing words such as 'when', 'because' etc. may convert what seemed like isolated and unexamined ideas into a coherent logical argument. We suggest that if students are prone to writing very long sentences they make a physical check on the page and mark where the full stops occur. We have had some fun colouring in sentences with different highlighters to indicate varying sentence length; this can be done in study groups. We have also found it useful to invite students to comment on each other's work from the point of view of sentence construction and length, though this should be done only if there is good rapport between members of the group. Third, there is:

Golden rule 3

Think of your reader.

Students should be reminded of the fact that this person needs to understand what the student has written – *but yet cannot ask them questions.*

In our experience teaching sentence structure in a fairly formal way can be beneficial for a number of reasons: not only can students be taught a more fluent style but also, perhaps more importantly, they are made aware of the sentence as a unit, which can be shaped and modified so that it expresses as effectively as possible the writer's message.

SOME COMMON FAULTS

One reason, we suspect, why the written style of some dyslexic students seems cramped or stilted is that they produce these short, staccato-like combinations of words without making explicit the logical links between their different ideas. Thus, what the writer may have meant in the 'Attlee, a Labour Prime Minister' example was: 'My next topic is to discuss the achievements of Prime Ministers since the Second World War, and I shall therefore begin with Mr Attlee.' In this sentence the word 'therefore' has an important job to perform and should not have been omitted. There are plenty of occasions where, implicitly, the arguments in the script of a dyslexic student are perfectly logical; where he may need help is in making them explicit. Once again he should remember 'Golden rule 3': think of the reader.

Another common error is to write sentences with unrelated parts. Thus, if a student were to write:

Working on the marshland it was raining.

it can be pointed out to him that this is a clumsy sentence and in particular that it fails to indicate *who* was working on the marshland.

Even worse, it is sometimes possible to present a distorted picture which implies something that one does not mean. Thus:

Walking down the road my hat blew off.

suggests by implication that my hat was walking down the road. One can avoid this kind of mistake by working out who is the subject of the sentence and adjusting the verb form accordingly. Thus:

Walking down the road, I was overtaken by John.

is correct, since the sentence makes clear that I was the person walking down the road.

Alternatively one can put things right by the use of conjunctions. For example:

While I was walking down the road, my hat blew off.

is also correct.

In addition, there are times when the presentation can be made more logical simply by changing the order of the words. Thus in the case of:

We will be pleased to see you, if you will call together about your problems.

the movement of the words 'about your problems', so that they follow 'pleased to see you', is clearly an improvement. The wording then becomes:

We will be pleased to see you about your problems if you will call together.

Similarly:

He remembered that he had forgotten his girlfriend's birthday while shaving.

can be corrected if the words 'while shaving' are put after the word 'remembered'. This example can also be used to illustrate the correct placing of commas. Thus:

> He remembered, while shaving, that he had forgotten his girlfriend's birthday.

is acceptable, as is:

> He remembered while shaving that he had forgotten his girlfriend's birthday.

What is unacceptable is:

> He remembered while shaving, that he had forgotten his girlfriend's birthday.

This violates the 'two-commas-or-none' rule: there are many sentences which are acceptable both when there are two commas and when there is *no comma* but not (as in the last example) where there is *one* comma (**see note 13.5**).

Subject/verb agreement can be confusing in some contexts. Thus, if one is being strict:

> a group of scientists are working on this theory,

is wrong; the subject of the sentence is 'a group', but it is easy to be misled by the word 'scientists'. The sentence should read: 'a group of scientists *is* working on this theory.' Similarly:

> many studies of this topic has shown …

is wrong since 'studies' is the subject of the sentence and therefore needs the plural verb 'have'. Dyslexic students (and others) need to remember, too, that 'data' is a Latin plural: thus 'these data show …' is correct; 'this data shows …' is wrong. There are also two words derived from Greek where there is a danger of a similar mistake. The following are all grammatically correct: 'this phenomenon', 'these phenomena'; 'this criterion', 'these criteria'. In contrast, 'this criteria' and 'this phenomena' are both incorrect.

Another common difficulty arises over the use of the possessive adjective 'their' with singular reference, thus:

The child was asked to raise their hand.

A patient may have difficulty with their mobility.

One way around this, avoiding the use of the clumsy his/her, is to pluralise to:

The children were asked to raise their hands.

Patients may have difficulty with their mobility.

For the sake of logical accuracy the student should be encouraged to think of the correct placing of words such as 'only' or 'even'. These should be put immediately before the word or phrase they refer to. Thus:

This is only allowed if ...

is wrong, while

This is allowed only if ...

is correct. Similarly:

He only discovered some old rubbish

is wrong, while

He discovered only some old rubbish

is correct.

In the case of 'even', 'He could even do it better than Smith' is wrong, while 'He could do it better even than Smith' is correct. Mistakes over commas and over the words 'data', 'only' and 'even' are, of course, not limited to dyslexic students.

SCIENTIFIC WRITING

In a scientific paper it has been normal practice up to now to write impersonally, and some departments do not allow the use of 'I' or 'we' in scientific papers. In that case one cannot say, 'I did this' or 'We did that'; instead the passive form has to be used and one says that this or that *was done* or that *it was decided* to do this or that.

However, writing in an impersonal scientific style can be very difficult for dyslexic students since it involves the construction of longer sentences. Simple exercises converting active to passive can be helpful, and there are some useful books on scientific writing, with some telling examples which the student may like to consult (**see note 13.6**). It is possible that in the future the impersonal style will no longer be insisted upon (**see note 13.7**).

CHECK POINTS FOR CHAPTER 13

Support tutors can help students to develop the accuracy of their written expression by focusing, for short periods, on grammar and punctuation.

- Topics should be based on the needs demonstrated in a student's written work.

- Students can also be encouraged to discuss any areas of uncertainty they experience as they write.

- Go slowly and do not introduce too much terminology too quickly.

- A notebook can be built gradually, based on the topics covered.

- The simple sentence is a good starting point to develop awareness of what constitutes a complete sentence.

- Simple sentences can be expanded little by little until complex sentences are developed and the role of conjunctions is understood.

- At the same time, punctuation can be considered, and its use expanded.

- Three 'golden rules' will help students to monitor their written expression:

  1. Keep to one main idea per sentence.

  2. Never start a sentence until you know how you will end it.

  3. Think of your reader.

- Students' mistakes are often common faults which can be explained with reference to basic grammar.

- Scientific writing – in particular the use of the passive voice – is difficult for some dyslexic students, and again a gradual approach is needed.

Chapter 14

Spelling

Here is some encouragement for dyslexic students. The
English spelling system *does* have some regularities and it *is*
possible to see some logic in what may have seemed random
patterns. There is discussion, with detailed examples, about
strategies for successfully learning spellings, about the origins
of technical terms and about the usefulness of the word
processor.

WOULD TUITION BE HELPFUL?

Not all dyslexic students wish for help with spelling, but in our
experience quite a number of them worry about it. It is important
that help is available for those of you who feel the need for it (**see
note 14.1**).

Spellcheckers on word processors are, of course, useful, but
they have their difficulties, which can sometimes contribute to
extra stress. For example, they are of value only if you know the
approximate spelling; they may throw up a bewildering list of
alternatives. Also, ordinary spellcheckers cannot detect a correctly
spelled word used in the wrong situation, such as 'there' in place of
'their' or 'they're', or 'college' in place of 'colleague'.

We have found that quite a few students benefit from spelling
help and that if you become more aware of spelling patterns real
improvement is possible with relatively little expenditure of effort.
For example – and this, of course, depends on the individual – we

would expect a well-motivated student to benefit from about three or four sessions of suitable tuition in spelling.

WHERE TO FIND HELP

The first step is for you to find someone who can help. In some colleges this could be a support tutor. Otherwise, you can make enquiries through the college Disability Service or Learning Support section, through the local Dyslexia Association (if there is one) or sometimes through your own department. Institutions vary in the structure of support. It is sometimes possible to use postgraduate students, particularly from departments such as Linguistics and Education, where there may be an interest in dyslexia. You might be able to tap into a 'buddy' or student mentor scheme, and, if payment is required, it may be possible to draw on the Disabled Students' Allowance (DSA).

At this level of spelling, willingness to cooperate is a more important qualification than formal training; so it is always possible to ask for help from a sympathetic friend. Indeed, one student we taught was lucky enough to become engaged to a fellow student whom he described as 'an excellent speller'. We are tempted to adapt the saying about 'marrying money' to: 'Do not marry good spelling, but love where good spelling is.'

The kind of help you receive from a friend or tutor will depend to some extent on what form of spelling training you have had in the past and on your particular needs. It is likely that volunteer tutors may be uncertain where to start. In what follows we make some suggestions which can be adapted according to individual needs.

It is probably best, in the first place, if you – the student – give your tutor a sample of your uncorrected written work in advance of any teaching session. The tutor can then examine and group the types of mistake that you are making and afterwards discuss them with you. There may also be helpful suggestions in your assessment report.

You may also like to consider whether you have any preferred method that makes spellings easier to remember. For example, some students actually close their eyes and **picture the spelling**; others try to **say the letters aloud**, while others again will **write the word down and look at it**. A combination of all these methods may be helpful for many people.

We recommend that the tutorial sessions on spelling should be kept short, perhaps half an hour at most, and that not more than two or three spelling patterns should be taught at a time.

REGULAR PATTERNS IN THE ENGLISH SPELLING SYSTEM

A particularly effective way of helping is for the tutor to demonstrate the regularities, or patterns, in the English spelling system. For example, it is regularly the case that past tenses end in -*ed* and if you are made aware of this it is a principle which you can apply in many different contexts.

Although it is possible for the tutor simply to correct words that are misspelled, this is unlikely to produce any result of permanent value unless both you and he think about the correction and try to work out where you have gone wrong. It is often useful if you work together on a laptop or word processor, since this means that parts of words can be moved around on the screen and combined and recombined to form the correct spelling. This can sometimes be an exercise in proofreading, that is in detecting spelling errors. It is possible, in that case, to discuss the spellings as you make the corrections, and in some cases it may be helpful if you note down the correct spellings in categories or groups as you have gone along.

As was pointed out in **Chapter 1**, it is a basic difficulty for most dyslexics to hold simultaneously in mind more than a limited number of disconnected symbols or to remember the order in which they have to be arranged. Moreover it is obvious that for all of us a combination such as 12-12-12-12 is much easier to remember than a succession of eight isolated digits; and the reason why some dyslexic youngsters have trouble with series such as the months of the year is undoubtedly because there is no special logic to them – the components are isolated units which simply have to be remembered in a particular order (**see note 14.2**).

In the case of spelling, however, there are all kinds of regularities; indeed, the English spelling system is far more logical than many people realise. This means that if you can identify particular patterns you will be able to *deduce* what letter to put next instead of having to rely on your uncertain memory. It follows that, if you have not been taught this already, you should be made aware of the correspondence between the letters which we write and the sounds which we make in speech. This will immediately give you a way of deducing spellings instead of having to remember them. In that case even your misspellings will be intelligible from the phonic point of view, and in most cases your reader will be left in no doubt as to what word you intended.

Long and short vowels

There are certain regularities that it will reward you to learn. You should notice in the first place the difference between long and short vowels: thus 'hat' has a short vowel sound while 'hate' has a long vowel sound. (This long sound, in fact, coincides with the name of the letter; see 'bit', 'bite'; 'hop', 'hope'; 'cut', 'cute'.) Let us now suppose that letters are added so as to make longer words, for example 'hatter' – one who makes hats – and 'hated' (strongly disliked). You will notice that where there is a *short* vowel, the consonant which comes next is *doubled* and that where there is a *long* vowel the consonant which comes next remains *single*. Here are some examples:

- saddle–cradle
- letter–Peter
- hopping–hoping
- written–writing
- supper–super.

Similarly, one normally writes *-tch* or *-dge* after a short vowel (as in 'fetch', 'ledge' etc.) and *-ch* or *-ge* after a long vowel or pair of vowels (as in 'teach', 'sage' etc.). There are a few exceptions to this rule, the most important of which are 'which', 'much', 'such' and 'rich'. When there is a k-sound one writes *-ck* after a short vowel (as in 'back', 'luck' etc.) and *k* on its own after a long vowel sound (as in 'make', 'speak' etc.). There are exceptions to the doubling rule; in particular, it does not hold in the case of words derived from Latin or Greek, such as 'pedometer' and 'monozygotic'.

Hard and soft c and g

There is a further rule which states that the letters *c* and *g* are hard before *a*, *o* and *u* and soft before *e* and *i*. There are exceptions to these rules but they are rare.

The logic behind 'their'

There is even a logic in some of the easily confusable short words if you look for it. Thus, if we wish to say 'belonging to *you*' we add the letter *r* to the word 'you' so that it changes to 'your'. It follows that if we wish to say 'belonging to *them*' we start with the word 'they' and again add the letter *r*. Since, however, the letter *y* often changes to *i* in the middle of a word, we write not 'theyr' but 'their'. There is therefore no need to confuse the word with 'there', which has the same pattern as the other two 'place' words, 'where' and 'here'. This may help you to remember:

OWNE R

OU R

YOU R

THEI R

A sketch of an ear may also be of help to students who are liable to confuse 'hear' with 'here'.

If you continue to have difficulty with these short words, then they can be written out on cards or posters and placed above your desk. Some of our students keep recurring spellings on cards in a filing box and get the relevant ones out when they need them, or have a little notebook handy. It is useful to highlight the difficult parts in colour, so that they stand out.

MNEMONICS AND OTHER STRATEGIES

Mnemonics, even though they may seem childish or silly, can sometimes be helpful. For example, a student who is confused between 'piece' and 'peace' can think of 'a **pie**ce of **pie**'. There are similar mnemonics for longer words; for example, those who have difficulty over the spelling of the word 'necessary' should remember the maxim: 'Never Eat Cake: Eat Salmon Sandwiches And Remain Youthful.' Students who wonder how to start the word 'psychology' may like to remember the words: 'Please Say Yes', while those unsure of how to start the word 'physics' may like to remember that 'Pete Hates You'. If 'because' is a problem, try: 'Big elephants can always understand small elephants.'

Separate out parts of words

It is always possible to separate out the difficult parts of words. To return again to 'necessary', the hardest part is likely to be -*cess*-. (If it helps, you can think of -*cess*- as '1 Collar and 2 Sleeves' – *css*). Once you have isolated -*cess*-, you can try:

acCESS

proCESS

sucCESS

It may also be useful if you isolate – or get someone to isolate for you – the part of a word which is difficult to spell, and use colour to highlight this difficult part. For example, in the case of 'stimuli' you would isolate $i – u – i$; in the case of 'colour' you would isolate $o – l – o$, while in the case of 'conscious' you would isolate $s – c – i$.

Similarly, you may like to think of certain letters going in *pairs*:

-nm

-ly

wh-

-oo

In the case of *-nm* you may like to put them together on a poster as the core of 'enviro*nm*ent' or 'gover*nm*ent'; *-ly* is a useful combination because adverbs end in these two letters; the two letters *wh-* start words which ask questions, for instance when?, where?, why?, which? and what?, and in the case of *-oo* you might say to yourself, 'The two *o*s in too are too many' or 'There is one *o* and another *too*'.

You may also like to note the combinations *sci-* and *-ology*. *Sci-* is the start of the words 'science' and 'scientific', and the same root occurs in 'conscience' and 'conscious' – the original Latin word means knowledge or awareness. An ending for a large number of words is *-ology*, for example 'biology', 'ecology', 'palaeontology' etc. The *-log-* part comes from the Greek and means 'study of'; thus, since *bios* means 'life', biology is the study of things which are alive (**see note 14.3**).

The sounds of words

In the case of long words we suggest that you say them carefully aloud before trying to write them. Some students benefit from listening to words being spelled out. One possibility is to speak them into a recorder and then play them back, while another is to ask a friend to say them for you. It is important that you should pay attention to small differences in sound between different words, since, if you are not clear as to what sounds you are trying to represent, the chances of representing them accurately in your spelling will be very much less. You could ask your tutor to go over the pronunciation very carefully with you, particularly in the case of technical or scientific terms.

A possible exercise is for the tutor to listen to the pronunciation of her students. This needs to be done carefully and tactfully, or perhaps as a light-hearted exercise, as was possible in the case of the psychology student who confused 'Bradley' and 'Baddeley' – both eminent psychologists. One student whom we knew continually used to say 'persific' in place of 'specific' ('persific gravity'), while another confused 'conscious' and 'conscience'. We have, in fact, been surprised at the number of mispronunciations which we have noticed over the years, and sometimes it is possible as a result to recognise the reason why particular words have been misspelled (**see note 14.4**). Students should be encouraged to say very carefully – and even exaggerate – the sounds of the words which they misspell, for example: 'enviro*n*-*m*ent'.

Breaking words down

It is also a good idea to break longer words down into segments or syllables (this can be done effectively on the word processor) and, if possible, to recognise the *root* of a word. For example, the word 'contemporary' has the same root as the word 'temporal' – the basic idea being that of 'time'. We regularly give our students a list of prefixes and suffixes with their meanings. Thus 'recrimination' contains the familiar prefix *re-*, the familiar suffix *-ation* and two straightforward middle syllables, *-crim-* and *-in-*. Provided you do not feel under pressure of time, you need have no difficulty in writing these segments separately and then arranging them in the correct order. It may also help if you say the word carefully and then tap out the number of syllables.

Another possibility is to use a pencil to mark the boundaries between syllables or to use pencils of different colours to mark familiar prefixes and suffixes, or again to use the word processor, selecting colour, different fonts and spacing in order to break up the words. Let us take as an example the word 'readily'. If you inspect this word, you will probably recognise both its connection with 'ready' and its *-ly* adverbial ending. You may also recognise the *-ea-* pattern, which also occurs in 'bread', 'instead' and the like, and we have already mentioned how *y* usually changes to *i* in the middle of a word. The *read-* will then take care of itself; the *-ly* adverbial ending is already familiar, and all that remains is to change the *y* in 'ready' to *i*. To take a few extra seconds to work out the spelling logically is far better than making a wild guess, and what is involved is a succession of deductions and not the memorising of these different points simultaneously.

Using a word processor

As noted earlier, we have found that using the word processor to teach spelling can be very effective. The tutor and student can develop a multisensory approach – so that they **look** at the details of what is on the screen, **listen** to the word's sound and **pay attention** to the finger movements which they make on the keyboard. Some students find that they begin to type certain letter combinations, such as *-tion*, *-ly* and *psych-* from automatic hand movement. The use of read-back software can also be very helpful. Students can also store a bank of vocabulary on their computers, using the autocorrect function (see below) and scan in book indexes to access difficult spellings (see also next section).

TECHNICAL TERMS

A strategy which may be helpful for some students is to make a list of technical terms and then obtain information, either from a tutor or with help from a dictionary, about their derivations. Here are some examples:

- *ped-* (Latin) and *pod-* (Greek) mean 'foot'; hence 'biped' = two-footed and 'tripod' = three-footed;

- *gaster* is the Greek for 'stomach'; hence a 'gastropod' is an animal whose stomach also serves as a foot, like a snail;

- 'zygote' is derived from the Greek word meaning a 'yoke' and thus implies two cells yoked together; and if you know this it will be easy for you to make sense of a derivative term such as 'monozygotic', where two cells linked together come from a single (*mono-*) egg, like identical twins.

The doubling rule does not apply to prefixes. Sometimes there are double consonants, as in 'symmetrical' and 'commit'; but here there always were two consonants and the end consonant of the prefix has been changed to match the beginning one of the root word.

For prefixes, too, there is no rule as to whether the vowel is long or short; this varies even with the same prefix. Thus there is 'prefix' but also 'preface', and both have a single consonant.

We are not giving you a comprehensive list of useful technical terms here. However, you may well find it gives you a greater understanding of a word if you look up its derivation in a dictionary. You may also benefit from learning about the history of the language and the changes in it as it has developed. Look at textbooks, glossaries and indexes before you write an essay and then compile a list of the most needed words (or they can be entered into your computer spellchecker – see below).

AIDS AND REFERENCE BOOKS

Apart from offering assistance with actual spelling, your tutor can guide you towards self-help.

There are many books and manuals on spelling which you may find helpful (**see note 14.5**), and you and your tutor may like to discuss together which one best meets your needs.

Whether or not you set about trying systematically to improve your spelling, we strongly recommend that you buy your own good-quality dictionary and get into the habit of referring to it as a matter of course. You can look not only at derivations but also at stress marks and other indicators of pronunciation. If you are unsure of the order of the letters of the alphabet, write the alphabet along a 'bookmark' card which you can keep in the dictionary.

We have found that dictionaries designed for those learning English as a second language are often very useful to dyslexic students (**see note 14.6**) since both types of learner need the same structured and patterned approach. These dictionaries often give the spellings when new parts are added to a word. For example:

run, running

dine, dining, dined, diner, dinner

Other dictionaries containing specialist technical vocabulary may also be useful to students concerned with that particular specialisation (**see note 14.7**).

Besides a full-scale desk dictionary you may also find pocket spelling dictionaries very useful, since they provide a quick and easy way of checking spellings (**see note 14.8**).

What many dyslexic students find invaluable are the pocket electronic spellmasters. They contain spell checks, offer alternatives based on sound and meaning and are very easy to use. There are various types of these, including those with specialist dictionaries (a medical one, for example) and you can usually can find one to suit your needs (**see note 14.9**).

Build your own dictionary

In addition, you may like to build up what is in effect your own dictionary. For this purpose an alphabetically divided index book is probably best, but you can use an address book. In it you can enter specialist vocabulary, important names, short words which cause difficulty, confusing letter combinations and the like. Many students have found these personal dictionaries very easy to use and very helpful, and in many cases they have taken pride both in adapting them to their needs and in giving them an artistic appearance. You may occasionally find it difficult to look up a word in a dictionary because you are unsure of its first letter, and once these words have been identified they can be placed in a separate section at the front. Words you are likely to need regularly in an essay or dissertation can be put on cards, which can be kept ready for consultation during the editing stage.

Use AutoCorrect

Another useful strategy is to add difficult spellings to your word processor's 'AutoCorrect' function (on the Microsoft Word 'Tools' menu). This is especially useful for long scientific or technical words. For example, if you have trouble spelling 'pulmonary thrombosis', you can enter 'pt' into the 'Replace' box, and then 'pulmonary thrombosis' into the 'With' box. Then every time you need to use the full term, simply type 'pt', and the computer should replace it for you. (Tip: press the space bar before and after you type 'pt' into the 'Replace' box, otherwise every word that has 'pt' in it will suddenly have a heart attack too!)

Finally, we should like to emphasise once again that the priority in most writing is the flow of ideas. For this reason, it is important that you do not worry too much over problems of spelling. If you are not sure of a spelling, you can always write something in pencil and carry out a check later or use your spellchecker. Meanwhile you are free to concentrate on the important thing, namely the writing of the essay, with this particular source of anxiety removed. One of the advantages of spending time on spelling during the early months in college is that you may reach a level where worries over spelling no longer divert you from the subject matter of the essay.

ADVICE TO A TRAINEE NURSE

A few years ago we were approached by someone wishing to obtain help for a dyslexic trainee nurse who was having major difficulty with her spelling. Not only did the nurse herself feel uncomfortable about this; more seriously, those in charge of her training course took the view that spelling as poor as hers would cause patients and their families to doubt her competence and perhaps, by association, the competence of the hospital where she worked.

We began by asking her for a list of the words which she found particularly difficult. Some of these were non-technical words, for instance 'unnecessary', 'insufficient' and 'acclimatisation'; however, her particular problem lay in the long technical terms used in her job. With the aid of a friend she gave us a list, which included the following:

carbenoxolone

sucralfate

dicyclomine

peroxisome

arginine

acinar

reticulocyte

megakaryoblast

sarcolemma

oligodendroglia

thalamencephalon

telencephalon

cimetidine

bretylium

mebeverine

disopyramide

zymogen

osteoclasts

agglutinogen

agglutinine

myelogenous

aneurysm

syncytium

cholinergic

synchronisation.

These particular words are highly specialised, and few readers of this book will need them. However, they illustrate *general principles*, and if readers *generalise* from what we say here they may be able to use similar principles in devising ways of remembering *any* complex word.

The advice we gave was divided into six sections, as follows:

1 general principles: dividing longer words up into smaller units and using a multisensory approach;

2 some common letter combinations;

3 the 'c and g' rule;

4 words derived from Latin and Greek;

5 silly mnemonics;

6 going through the list.

1 General principles: dividing longer words into smaller units and using a multisensory approach

The words on your list will be very hard to remember if you try to write them all at one go. Sub-divide them and concentrate on the parts separately. Do not try to remember more than about four letters at a time. We will try to give some guidance in section 6 as to how to divide them up. This can often be done in a logical way; and if there is a logic in the way one letter follows another you will not be in the difficult position of having to learn all the letters separately. (In what follows we will refer to these bits of words as 'word parts'.) When you are sufficiently familiar with the word parts on their own try, very slowly, to say them one after the other so as to make up the whole word, for instance *di – cyclo – mine*. When you hear a long word, tap out the number of syllables, and if possible get someone to check that you have done so correctly.

It is widely agreed that 'multisensory' methods are most effective in helping dyslexic learners with spelling. This means: **listen** to the word carefully; **say** it carefully, paying attention to your mouth movements as you do so; **look** carefully at what is on the page, and try to **visualise** the word in your mind; pay attention to your **hand movements** as you write. **Take plenty of time**, and do not fudge by slurring over the word as you say it.

2 Some common letter combinations

You will have come across many of these in your normal reading, but we would like to remind you of some. Some words end in -*ine* ('arginine' is like 'mine' and 'fine') and some in -*ium* (for instance 'valium'). In breaking words down look out for common letter combinations.

3 The 'c and g' rule

The letter *c* has a hard sound (like *k*) if it is followed by *a, o* or *u* (as in 'cat', 'cot' and 'cut'); it has a soft sound (like *s*) if it is followed by *e, i* or *y* (as in 'centride', 'cimetidine' or '*di – cy – clomine*'). The letter *g*, with a few exceptions, also has a hard sound before *a, o* and *u* (as in 'gap', 'gorgon' and 'gut') and a soft sound before *e, i* and *y* (as in 'gem', 'gym' and 'gypsy') (compare 'arginine').

4 Words derived from Latin or Greek

(This section is optional, but you may find it interesting, and it may help you to remember certain combinations of letters.)

- *sucr* – connected with sweetness
- *ethyl* – connected with ethane
- *acinus* – grape
- *gen* – producing (note the soft *g*)
- *zyme* – ferment
- *clast* – breaking (compare 'iconoclast')
- *reticulum* – a net (network of fibres)
- *cyte* – a cell (note the soft *c*)
- *myelo*s – marrow or soft white substance
- *mega* – large

- *karyon* – nut

- *sarx* – flesh

- *lemma* – sheath

- *syn* – together

- *oligo* – little

- *dendron* – tree

- *encephalon* – brain*

- *choie* – bile**

- *chron* – timer**

* there was no *f* in classical Greek; therefore when the f-sound occurs in words derived from the Greek it is written as *ph*.

** in words derived from the Greek, *ch* has a hard sound, as in 'chemistry', 'Christmas' etc., not a soft sound, as in 'chain'.

5 Silly mnemonics

Although dyslexic students can do much to help their memory by noting logical patterns, it may also be useful, at least as a fall-back, to invent silly mnemonics. These, oddly enough, are memorable precisely because they are silly! You will be able to invent your own, but there are a few suggestions in the next section.

6 Going through the list

Here are some suggestions, based on the points which we have been making. In particular:

- break the word up;

- tap out the number of syllables;

- bring in speech and writing as well as looking and listening;

- learn to identify common combinations of letters (for instance -*zyme*).

We strongly suggest you take this list in small doses!

- *carbenoxolone*: car – ben – oxo lone: Ben is a lonely person in a car and wants some oxo.

- *sucralfate*: sucr (common combination) and Alf ate some!

- *dicyclomine*: di – cyclo – mine (*cyclo-* starts with soft *c*; -*mine* is a common combination of letters. Or think of Princess Di on a cycle that is mine).

- *peroxisome*: we suggest per – ox – I – some (with long *o*, as in 'dome') – again phonetically regular.

- *arginine*: ar – gin – ine (or ar – gi – nine).

- *acinar*: affecting the acinus. The Latin *acinus* means 'grape'; presumably it is thought to be like a grape in shape. The *c* is soft.

- *reticulocyte*: *reticulo* = net + *cyte* a cell (note the soft *c*).

- *megakaryoblast*: we suggest *mega* (= big, as in megaphone), then *caryo* (which means nut), then *blast* (which means grow or sprout).

- *sarcolemma*: sarco – lemma. *Sarx* means 'flesh'; *lemma* means a 'husk' or 'membrane'.

- *oligodendroglia*: oligo – dendro – glia.

- *thalamencephalon*: thalam – encephalon. As a nurse, you will already know that 'thalamus' refers to a part of the brain and that 'encephalon' means 'brain' (see above). So it is really quite logical – and where there is a logic, it will save you having to rely on your memory.

- *telencephalon*: tel – encephalon (encephalon again).

- *cimetidine*: cim (soft *c*) – eti – dine. You can dine on it!

- *Bretylium*: I suggest bret (which is regular) – yl – ium (which is a familiar combination of letters).

- *mebeverine*: meb – ever – ine. All the parts are phonetically regular.

- *disopyramide*: we suggest di – so – pyra – mide (five syllables). By the way, you use *dys-* with a *y* only when it means 'difficulty with' something, as in 'dyslexia'; *dis-* often means 'not', as in 'disquiet', and sometimes *di-* implies cutting into two, as in 'dissect'.

- *zymogen*: *zyme* = a ferment; *gen* = producing.

- *osteoclasts*: osteo – clasts (*osteo* = bone; *clast* = breaking).

- *agglutinogen*: perhaps start with *glutin* (= antibody). As with many words, such as 'abbot' and 'attend', the consonant doubles after the *a*. Note that in some words, such as 'alexia' and 'ataxia', where the *a* implies some failure or difficulty, the next consonant does *not* double.

- *agglutinine*: take out *glutin* as before – and the rest is straightforward.

- *myelogenous*: *myelo* = marrow; *gen* = producing.

- *aneurysm*: according to our dictionary, 'aneurism' is also OK; *-ism* is easy to remember and *eurys* is the Greek for 'broad' – hence the word means a widening or broadening.

- *syncytium*: most of the words that you will meet with the sound *sin* will, in fact, be spelt *syn-*. The Greek *syn-* means 'together', as in 'synthesis', 'synopsis' etc. If in doubt, put *y* rather than *i*. The *c* before the *y* in *cyt-* is soft, as usual; and you know the combination – *-ium*. Take these points separately, one by one – say the word slowly and carefully, as it will be more difficult to say – and spell – if you go too quickly.

- *cholinergic*: cholin – ergic (with the *g* soft before *i*).

- *synchronisation*: *syn-* as usual; you know words such as 'chronic' (another example of the hard *ch*, as in 'chemistry' etc.) and then there is the *-ation* ending.

In the case of 'unnecessary' we gave the student the silly mnemonic (see above). In the case of 'acclimatisation', the student knew *-ation*, in this case with *-is* before it. She also knew the word 'climate'. With the short *a* at the start, the *c* must double; so it is *acc-* then the rest of 'climate', dropping the *e* before *-isation*.

This story has a happy ending: the student passed her exams and is now a qualified nurse.

CHECK POINTS FOR CHAPTER 14

The first priority in most writing is the expression and flow of ideas. So, it is important that you do not let spelling uncertainties stop you saying what you want to say, in the way you want to say it.

Consider having **a few** sessions on spelling with a support tutor. You may be surprised at how useful this will be in learning about:

- regular patterns in the English spelling system;

- mnemonics and other strategies for learning spellings;

- the origins of technical terms;

- useful reference books and spelling aids.

In particular, students have found it helpful to:

- build their own notebook of useful spellings;

- use the AutoCorrect facility in Microsoft Word.

Chapter 15

Mathematics and statistics

After briefly considering the types of difficulties that dyslexic students may have experienced with maths in the past, this chapter goes on to provide encouragement, examples and general strategies which may be helpful to any students who are anxious about the maths or statistics they meet on their courses.

DYSLEXIA AND MATHEMATICS

Most dyslexic students are likely to have struggled with certain aspects of mathematics. The difficulties are basically of two kinds.

In the first place there are problems over calculation. In particular, a very high percentage of dyslexic students have found it difficult to learn times tables and quite a number are slow in carrying out simple addition, subtraction and division (**see note 15.1**). It seems that they have fewer immediately available 'number facts' than do non-dyslexics, for example they may not know 'in one' that $8 \times 7 = 56$ or that $15 - 8 = 7$, and if no calculator is available they may need to spend considerable time in working out the answer. This is not normally due to a lack of understanding of how the number system works – they know what working needs to be done. The trouble appears to be that these basic number facts do not easily become automatic (**see note 15.2**).

In the second place, it often takes dyslexic learners longer to become fully aware of the significance of a mathematical symbol. Any symbol such as '+' or '−' is difficult, at least for younger learners;

and often it is helpful if the teacher can introduce concepts not by writing a lot of symbols on the board but by *doing things* (physically adding two blocks to three blocks, for instance). Symbols such as '+' can then be introduced as descriptions of what is happening. This kind of introduction to mathematical symbols may be of help even to older students. Even after such an introduction, however, many dyslexic students will most probably need more exposures to the concept and its symbol than non-dyslexics before the learning is well established.

Careful attention to basics is particularly important in the teaching of algebra. There are many dyslexic people who find algebra difficult – and there is a personal friend of one of the authors who teaches other branches of mathematics but refuses to teach algebra because he 'finds it impossible'. The point is that if a symbol conveys nothing, then even a person with high reasoning powers will have nothing for these reasoning powers to work on, and he may mistakenly conclude that mathematics in general is too difficult for him.

However, once the function of the various symbols has been grasped, his reasoning powers will have the chance to show themselves, and tiresome 'chores' such as carrying out calculations can be done by calculator. It is important for dyslexic students to know enough about the number system to enable them to tell approximately what the answer should be – and, when they use a calculator, they need to be careful not to press the wrong button! Otherwise, however, the calculator can be a great time-saver (**see note 15.3**).

If you wish to take a course which has some mathematical content, for instance physics, engineering or a course which requires statistics, you should not be deterred by the fear that you are 'no good at maths'. If you really feel that weakness at mathematics is going to be a problem, it might be wise to get some training in the basics before your course actually starts – so that if the worst happens you could consider a change of course. However, we have found in many cases that dyslexic students have simply overlooked the significance of a particular piece of notation and that this is something that they can learn. We suspect that the dyslexic

mathematics teacher mentioned above, who said that he found
algebra impossible, was never taught it properly.

DO NOT BE PUT OFF BY SYMBOLS

Many different symbols are used in mathematics, and the important
thing from your point of view is that you should learn the function
of the symbols that you need. (Some dyslexic students have reported
difficulty in learning the symbols used in chemistry, but these, too,
can be learned if you go slowly enough.)

There are plenty of symbols which you already know, for example
the symbols '1', '2', '3' etc. which stand for particular numbers. You
probably also know quite a few of the symbols which tell you what
to *do* with numbers, for instance '+' which means *add*, and '×' which
means *times* or *multiply*. (If 3 children have 2 oranges each, then there
are 3 × 2, that is 6, oranges altogether; one can therefore speak of
'three *times* two', or 'three *multiplied by* two'.) In general, if there is
a symbol whose meaning you do not know, ask someone to explain
it or go to a book (**see note 15.4**). If you learn statistics, there will be
various new symbols whose meaning you will need to know – but
once you have learned what job they do you will be quite as good as
anyone else at operating with them.

You may find it interesting to think about numbers in general.
There are all sorts of situations where we use numbers: in particular,
we use them for *counting* things and for *measuring* things. For
example, we may need to count the number of children in a class,
the number of cars that go past a particular road junction in a three-
hour period, the number of potatoes that you have planted in your
garden and so on. Similarly you may need to *measure* the length of
carpeting needed in a room or, if you suspect you are ill, your body
temperature. In the first case you would use a tape measure; in
the second, a thermometer. In all such cases the result is expressed
numerically, and once you have learned the symbols, '1', '2', '3' etc.,
you will be able to understand what this result means.

SOME MORE SYMBOLS: ALGEBRA

To make things easier for you we should now like to introduce you to some further symbols. If they are already familiar to you, you may like to skip this section; but the important thing is that **if you are confronted with any unfamiliar symbol it should not be too difficult to make yourself familiar with its meaning**.

You have probably already met the algebraic symbol x. If someone has difficulty with this symbol, it may be helpful to show him a simple subtraction sum with the aid of bricks. If you have five bricks and take away three bricks, you will have two bricks. This operation can then be written down as '5 – 3 = 2' – and it applies to bricks, pencils, paper clips and all kinds of other things.

Let us now ask the question, 'Five take away *how many* leaves two?' Let us suppose that this 'how many' refers to an *unknown* number – but one whose value we can work out. We then write this unknown number as 'x', and this means we can then write '$5 - x = 2$'.

This group of symbols, which contains the *equals* sign, is called an 'equation', and if we then work out the value of x this is *solving the equation*. The equation $5 - x = 2$ is an easy one to solve – the answer, of course, is that $x = 3$. However, once you have solved a few easy equations, there is no need to be terrified by the more difficult ones: they will take you longer and you will need to proceed carefully step by step, but the symbols x, '=' etc. need not themselves be off-putting. Remember, of course, that x in a sense means '*any* number' and that in different equations its value will be different.

In some cases you may have two unknown numbers, in which case it is customary to use the symbols x and y, whilst if you need a third unknown number you would write it as z.

STATISTICS

As was indicated in **Chapter 4**, a knowledge of statistics is necessary for a number of different disciplines, including psychology, education, economics, biology and agriculture. It would be a great pity if any students were deterred from these courses because of fears over their competence at statistics.

If you are doing statistics you will need the symbol X – that is, capital X, as opposed to the lower-case x, which is used in equations. Suppose John has scored 10 points on a test, Mary 8 points, Elizabeth 11 points and Tom 9 points. We can then say that these four numbers, 8, 9, 10 and 11, are different values of X. We could put them in a column, like this:

10

8

11

9

and we might say that X_1 is 10, X_2 is 8, X_3 is 11 and X_4 is 9. We can also note that the average score in this case is 9.5, that is the *sum* of the different Xs divided by the *number* of Xs. This average is known more technically as the 'mean'; it can be written as:

$$\overline{X}$$

(pronounced X-bar). The sum of the different Xs is written as ΣX (pronounced as 'sigma-X'). Then, if the number of Xs in the sample is written as 'N', we can describe the working out of the average by means of the following notation:

$$\overline{X} = \frac{\Sigma X}{N}$$

or, in words, X-bar equals sigma-X over N.

In due course, if you continue in your study of statistics, you will be introduced to further symbols. These include χ^2 (pronounced 'chi-squared') and the alphabetic letters t, r and F. It is beyond the purpose of this chapter to explain these different symbols to you, but there is no reason to think that learning their different functions will be any more difficult for you than was the learning, say, of the '=' sign.

You may still feel alarmed by symbols; but, once again, if you **think positive** you will be able to understand the ones that you need. They are merely ways of describing what you are doing – which in the above example was adding numbers together and taking the average. Our advice is simply that when you come across new symbols you go slowly and make sure you fully understand what each symbol stands for.

Many students are taught to use statistics software in large classes in computer laboratories. For various reasons some dyslexic students may find it hard to keep pace with the operations being demonstrated and may easily become panicked into thinking that they cannot do statistics. Panic is the enemy here, and again thinking positive is essential. If you find yourself in this situation:

- take action early;

- take advantage of any 'shadow classes', or statistics support on offer; often such sessions will go at a slower pace than that of more formal classes and there will be more individual help available;

- do not be afraid to ask questions if you do not understand something;

- you might find it valuable to work with fellow students who also feel unsure;

- look at some of the very basic guide books (there are several available, **see note 15.5**) which explain the operations carefully, step by step.

Here are some of the strategies that our students have found helpful when they have been struggling with maths and statistics:

- identify what you know;

- work forward from this in **small steps**;

- keep checking back to ensure that you understand;

- relate numbers to real things: if you are dealing with statistical information about people, try to visualise those people; if the statistics come from your research about fish, picture those fish, and so on;

- remember what it is that you are trying to find out about these real things: statistics are a means to an end, not an end in themselves;

- use diagrams, flow charts and pictures if they help you;

- use colour where it helps, e.g. in remembering symbols or formulae or for separating out lines of figures in tables and spreadsheets.

USING COMMON SENSE

We indicated earlier that you might have difficulty in adding up a column of figures. The interesting thing about statistics, however, is not that it involves adding up but that we need to use our **reasoning** in deciding **how to interpret the results**.

As an example let us take the following column of figures:

45 +
49 +
46 +
 4
—

In this case it would be possible in principle to carry out the same procedure as we did in the case of the test scores of John and his friends, that is we could take the average. But, if four children earn respectively 45p, 49p, 46p and 4p, one does not have to be good at addition to recognise the absurdity of saying that the *average* earning is 36p. The skill called for here is that of statistical reasoning, and we have met many dyslexics who are brilliant at this even though adding columns of numbers at speed may be difficult for them.

If you want to do a course which requires a knowledge of statistics, do not be put off by the fear that you are no good at maths. If you proceed systematically and slowly, you will find that statistics is not all that difficult.

CHECK POINTS FOR CHAPTER 15

On some courses students are expected to understand and use a certain level of maths and statistics. Those dyslexic students who are not confident about using numbers may panic when they are faced with these demands. If you are such a student, our advice is 'try not to let anxiety get in the way of your learning'.

- Stay calm and use your reasoning powers.

- Do not be put off by symbols.

- Take advantage of any support on offer.

- Identify what you know and work forward from this in **small steps**.

- Keep checking back to ensure that you understand.

- Relate numbers to real things.

- Use diagrams, flow charts, pictures and colour to help you learn.

- Do not be afraid to ask questions if you do not understand something.

Chapter 16

Information technology

This chapter provides an overview of the equipment and software that many dyslexic students find invaluable: portable equipment, word processors and software.

WHAT DO YOU NEED?

Since the first edition of this book appeared in 1986, there have been tremendous advances in technology and you can be sure that there are many more yet to come. Although at times we refer to various types of software, we do not name individual items or computers. This is for three reasons.

In the first place, changes are occurring extremely rapidly and any information presented may therefore soon be out of date. Second, there are specialist groups who regularly produce updated information bulletins and hold conferences (**see note 16.1**). Third, there is no point in recommending equipment if it is incompatible with what is already used in a particular college or department.

Many of the new developments are likely to be of particular benefit to dyslexic students; those who receive the Disabled Students' Allowance (DSA; **see Chapter 3**) will be in a position, within limits, to obtain much of what they need. They will usually be offered training too so that they can make the most of their equipment and software. We strongly recommend students to take up this training.

There may also be equipment and other facilities provided by your college. Some of the equipment which is used by hearing-impaired or visually impaired students can be of help to dyslexic students – and vice versa. We suggest that you find out what information technology facilities are available for use within your department and in the college generally. Ask, too, if there is dyslexia-friendly software networked on the college intranet.

PORTABLE EQUIPMENT

First, however, you may like to consider some of the small portable electronic pieces of equipment we referred to in earlier chapters. These are usually available in large stores or in electrical suppliers.

There are **personal digital assistants (PDAs)** which were originally designed simply as personal organisers but have become much more versatile over the years. They are handheld devices which can be linked up with a personal computer and printer. PDAs have many functions, the main ones being their schedule and diary facility (which can often be set to bleep at appointed times). Many also include a selection of the following functions: a calculator, an address book, a spreadsheet, a radio or stereo, the facility to access the Internet, send and receive emails and play computer games.

Information is added to PDAs by writing on the touch screen – the writing is turned into type – or by downloading the information from the personal computer when the two are connected. These could be very useful for a new student having to cope with the complexities of the early days at college. Another solution used by many students is the diary facility of their mobile phone, as many phones can be set to give reminders if needed.

Many students carry **calculators** around with them, and there are now talking calculators and large-digit calculators (**see note 16.2**). For spelling, there are various pocket-sized spelling aids, such as the whole Franklin range, with *Spellcheckers*, *Language Master* and *Thesaurus*. There are now **speaking spellcheckers (see note 16.3)**. Many students find these indispensable; this is because they are easy to use and carry around and are much simpler than computer spellcheckers. They have a 'sound alike' and thesaurus program, which means that you can tell the difference between words which sound alike, such as 'they're', 'there' and 'their', by being given the various meanings.

We have referred to **Dictaphones** throughout the book and have indicated, in particular, how useful they are for recording lectures or what you read into them. They might also be useful for recording important sessions with a tutor, if you are worried that you will not be able to remember all the advice that is given, or simply for recording your own ideas on an essay, or information on a field trip; some students use them for revision. Mostly, the Dictaphones used by dyslexic students nowadays are digital: it is possible to 'mark' points in the recording so that you can find them again quickly, and recordings can be downloaded and stored on a computer, to be listened to later (**see Chapter 11**).

WORD PROCESSING

The majority of dyslexic students nowadays use a computer of some kind for word processing. Some students, however, still find computers difficult or intimidating. Colin Wilsher, one of the dyslexic contributors to the first edition of this book, was clear at the time (1986) about the benefits of word processing for dyslexic writers. Although the position with regard to word processors has changed considerably since then, his points are still relevant:

Technical advantages

- Mistakes can be corrected immediately and will never be seen by the outside world: the student does not have to print out until he is satisfied with his work. Dyslexic writers can therefore present to the world written material of a first-class standard. This is particularly useful for those with very poor handwriting. This ability to produce a polished, finished article is extremely rewarding.

- Word processing allows revision of ideas: whole pages can be seen and revised. This includes not just retyping words but moving sentences and paragraphs about the document. This is particularly useful to a dyslexic writer who may initially put down ideas out of order, and after re-reading may wish to change the sequence.

- Editing of your work can be done by others, or you can edit the input of others. This allows dyslexic writers to use other people as mediators between themselves and the written word. A proofreader can correct a student's mistakes directly onto the disk; using the 'track changes' and 'comment' facilities; any changes or suggestions can then be reviewed and discussed.

- Software packages come with basic spelling and grammar checkers.

- It is possible to enter particular words that you use a lot, which may have tricky spellings, into the computer's 'AutoCorrect' list of words; you can arrange this so that just by typing in a few letters of a word (for example *qual*), the computer will immediately produce the whole word – 'qualitative' (and **see Chapter 14**).

- Word processor programs can be commanded to search for a word or phrase in the text – to correct every instance of a particular misspelling in one go, for example.

- You can use parts of existing documents to create new documents without entering any new material. For instance, a series of personal letters (with similar content) to several different people can be rewritten by the computer by changing only a few words for each recipient.

- If you become proficient with working straight onto the word processor, you can skip the pencil and paper stage, and go straight to entering ideas directly onto the computer.

- Many dyslexic students feel that practice with a word processor helps their spelling ability. This is because every word has to be spelled out and it gives practice at phonetic breakdown of words.

However, if you use a word processor, it is important to consider the physical effects of long hours spent working on the keyboard and in front of the screen. We recommend that you think carefully about what type of chair to use and about the way in which you use your hands and forearms (we know two students who suffered from repetitive strain injury); for the sake of your eyes, you should take a ten-minute break from the screen every hour. You can also dull it down, change the colour of the background and the colour, style and size of the font, or put something in front of the screen so that you are not always looking at it.

In general, therefore, you should plan your time on the computer carefully. You will need not only to use the keyboard but to follow the various menus. If you become physically or mentally tired, mistakes can very easily occur and you can do silly things. This happened when a student pulled a plug out to boil a kettle late at night – a moment's thoughtless action, and she lost everything that she had done over several hours.

You should make a habit of saving your material each time you pause for a break, and make sure that you keep a back-up copy on a memory stick or disk. Another good idea is to email your work back to yourself – then it is always 'out there' for you.

If you have not learnt computer skills at school or college, you will need some training to help you to get going. Computer manuals are dense and very difficult to access and it is better to be taught personally. Your college will probably run courses and, in addition, there may be local evening classes which cater for people with different levels of word-processing ability. If you go on a short course, you will find that you will be given simplified handouts for each stage. There are also some advantages in learning to touch type (so that you can type without looking at the keyboard), but this is not essential, and many dyslexic students say that they spell better if they look at the keys. If you are interested, however, it is possible to obtain software for touch typing; and there is even talking software which helps people to become more familiar with the keyboard. There are also simplified, clearly set out manuals that explain all the necessary processes for basic computing and word processing (**see note 16.4**).

It is interesting that some students actually perform worse on a keyboard than when they write by hand. It seems that they are somehow *drawing* the words when they write and can therefore perceive the spelling patterns more clearly than when they type. Some students also make many typing errors which, if they are not confident spellers, may go unnoticed.

Notebook (often called **laptop**) **computers** are small portable computers which vary in capacity. It is possible that you may need a small straightforward notebook for taking notes wherever you go (on extended field trips or practice placements). Most notebook computers on the market are just slightly bigger than an A4 pad, and less than two inches thick. If you plan to carry one around, it is important to consider its weight – and also consider how long it can run on a set of batteries. You will need a carrying case too. You will obviously need to have a notebook which is compatible with an easily accessible printer.

Portable computers are likely to be useful for note-taking in lectures; they can also be taken into the library and, indeed, can be used wherever you decide to work. They are also handy because they allow you to work side by side with a tutor or a scribe, since together you can move text around and alter spellings, and they are easier to take home for the holidays. It is, of course, important to look after them carefully to ensure that they are not damaged or stolen: if you are the owner of any expensive piece of equipment, you should take out an insurance policy. (If you are eligible for the DSA, this will generally meet the cost of insurance.)

SPELLCHECKERS AND OTHER SOFTWARE

If you need a spellchecker (as most dyslexic students do), we suggest that you look at the type of program which is provided, how the spellchecking is presented on the menu and how easy it is to use. For students with poor spelling, spellcheckers are by no means easy – they may not be sensitive enough to recognise the word that is being attempted (even if spelled phonetically), and if a list of rather similar-looking words is offered, it is easy to pick the wrong one.

Sometimes, a good thesaurus facility can be of more use than a spellchecker: if you cannot find the right alternative on the spellchecker, one possibility is to choose a simpler word and then use the thesaurus to find a better one. In that case, hopefully, the word which you originally intended will come up. For example, if you wanted to say 'manufacture' and could not spell it, you could write 'make' and then look up the alternatives – and with any luck you would find 'manufacture'.

It has been suggested that students get on better if they build their own spellcheckers from scratch (**see note 16.5**). It is possible to scan in your own subject-specific words and names. A read-back facility can help to indicate incorrect spelling and poor sentence construction and punctuation. This seems to work more effectively than just reading through work on a print-out, as you can then listen with a pencil in your hand to mark the errors.

Grammar programs are useful to a limited extent. A disadvantage is that their advice is given using grammatical terms, which means that a tutor is usually needed to provide explanations. However, they also show the sentence with the mistake highlighted and they will detect non-sentences, faulty agreements (for example a singular subject with a plural verb) and incorrect endings to a sentence. They may even pick up the wrong use of 'their', 'there' and 'they're'.

New software which may be of help to dyslexic students is increasingly being produced. What you choose is very much an individual matter. Thus, there are some students who prefer to work out their thoughts on paper and use a word processor only when they are ready to write the rough draft, whereas others are happy to do their thinking at the keyboard. A particular piece of software may be suitable for some students and not for others – and, if there is sufficient computer capacity in the college or support unit, a tutor could keep a suitable supply of software for students to borrow or try out.

There is software for all of the following:

- **Planning essays:** there is, for example, a 'think sheet'. This is a planning program which enables students to organise notes under topic headings, as if they had a pile of note-cards; the ideas can then be rearranged to form a mind-map; there is also software which can help the student to brain-storm ideas and then arrange and sequence it in the form of a concept map (like a spidergram), or a more ordered flow chart.

- **Spelling practice and tuition.**

- **Grammar practice.** (As we noted above, some programs use grammatical terms and are best used with a tutor.)

- **Mathematics packages.**

- **Graphics packages:** draw package; quick sketch, autosketch.

- **PAL (predictive adaptive spellcheck):** this predicts from context; you type in the beginning of a word and your word will be predicted.

There have also been considerable advances in **text-to-speech software**: the voice can be modified, and its speed increased or decreased. The use of sound obviously makes text accessible to people with reading difficulties and it can alert you to the use of the wrong word and quite often to the wrong grammar in your own work.

This text-to-speech software is an obvious help with proofreading. Also, some students may benefit from listening to text that they have found through the Internet, or from scanning in text from books and listening to it through the text-to-speech software. In that case they will need a scanner with optical character-recognition software and a text-to-speech system. Scanning a lot of text can take time – but you can also save time by scanning photographs and diagrams into the text. The main danger is that students are liable to incorporate chunks of text into their essays instead of summarising or paraphrasing. There is the same danger with information found on the Internet; however, students will find that institutions now routinely ask them to submit assignments electronically as well as on paper so that all work can be scanned by software designed to detect plagiarism, whether intended or not.

There have been tremendous advances in the use of the **voice-recognition systems**: when you speak, your words are entered into a word-processing program which you can then edit and print out. This technology has been much improved over the last few years, although it still does not suit everybody (**see note 16.6**). Dyslexic students who use this system may need help to ensure the correct input of vocabulary: if this software is provided through the DSA, help and further training will usually be provided too.

Computers, along with the use of resources on disk and the Internet, are providing vital resources for dyslexic students, where learning can be accessible, individually paced and, above all, multisensory with the combination of visual image and sound. Thomas West (**see note 16.7**) celebrates the power of the computer in enabling dyslexic people to be freed from the hard graft of writing. It seems that the developments in computers are moving towards the greater use of a multimedia approach, and we can expect dyslexic students to derive immense benefit from this.

CHECK POINTS FOR CHAPTER 16

Which technology students use, and how and when they use it, will depend on individual preferences and the demands of the course they are taking. However, there is no doubt that the equipment and software described here have been liberating for many dyslexic students. This includes:

- portable equipment: spellcheckers, calculators, PDAs (organisers);

- desktop and portable computers;

- word-processing packages and refined spelling and grammar checkers;

- software for planning and organising documents;

- text-to-speech software;

- voice-recognition systems;

- resources on disk.

Students – do take advantage of any training you are offered – in computer skills in general, and on the specialist software in particular.

Chapter 17

Examination arrangements

This chapter reviews the adjustments that are commonly made to the way in which students are examined, and briefly covers some further adjustments to traditional examinations. We also discuss administrative arrangements and some of the less straightforward issues which may arise for staff and students.

ADMINISTRATIVE ARRANGEMENTS

If dyslexic students are to have extra arrangements in a way which is fair and is seen to be fair, a number of administrative issues arise.

Ideally, each student's case should be treated individually and based on her specific needs. These should have been pinpointed in either her dyslexia assessment or the Assessment of Study Needs for the Disabled Students' Allowance (DSA), with the report indicating which aspects of assessment by examination are likely to put her at an unfair disadvantage, for instance because of her speed of writing.

A support tutor or academic tutor might also make recommendations for adjustments to the method of assessment, but in some institutions these might have to be ratified by a psychologist. The means by which a candidate normally presents her work should be taken into account, as should any provision which she has previously had, for example at GCSE or A level. The learning outcomes of the student's course must also be considered in the process of implementing reasonable adjustments, that is departments need to be very clear and specific about what they are looking for in examination answers.

As far as dyslexic students are concerned, the examining board will almost certainly require a dyslexia assessment report, perhaps supported by relevant facts from the student's tutor. Many students will already have had examination arrangements at school and will therefore have a fairly clear idea of what they can expect at college.

In some cases the dyslexia assessment report will set out clearly the recommended adjustments; the psychologist or specialist teacher will have based these upon the student's performance in the various tests and upon the measure of the speed and accuracy of her reading and writing. He may have discussed them with the student. Sometimes a tutor who has gained an extra insight into the student's performance, or who is aware of the different nature of varying assessment methods used at the college, may then submit a recommendation for adjustments not already mentioned in the assessment report.

Setting up extra arrangements for examinations is time-consuming from the college's point of view, and colleges vary in their procedure. Most have a clear code of practice, which should be set out in writing and available for students to see (**see note 17.1**). In some institutions students go to the examinations office with their list of courses or modules and their assessment reports, and they then check with the Examinations Officer what arrangements have been agreed. In other places, a Learning Support Plan may be agreed with the student, and this may include details of reasonable adjustments to the assessment process.

Whatever the system in place in your college, do find out about it and be sure to **make arrangements in good time**. If students leave their request for adjustments, or even dyslexia assessment, until the very last minute, they will probably find that the examinations office is working under extreme pressure and there is the risk that they will not be able to deal with all the requests. Students should bear in mind, too, that there are many other students who need adjustments in examination arrangements – not only dyslexic students (**see note 17.2**).

Finally, it is easy to understand how the examination period is a time of tension not only for students but for tutors and administrators also. Whatever reassurances have been given, some dyslexic students may still feel that if they receive adjustments they are being treated differently in some uncomfortable sense, and tutors and administrators should realise that to find themselves in this position may not be easy for them. Quite a number of our students have in fact found themselves torn in two directions: on the one hand they want to be assessed in the same way as everyone else, yet on the other they know that they will not do themselves justice unless they allow themselves to be treated as 'special cases'. Examination officers should be aware both of the tensions that the students feel in these circumstances and of the need for confidentiality.

We have occasionally found, too, that there are tutors or administrative staff within a department who react with hostility, for example by accusing the student of looking for an easy way through the system. This may well be because they themselves are under pressure and do not want any extra hassle with complicated or time-consuming arrangements. Things are made worse if dyslexic students do not realise the general pressures that there are on academic and administrative staff at examination times and become overdemanding of their 'rights'. Empathy on both sides is very important.

COMMON PRACTICE

At present the most common adjustments to examinations are:

- giving candidates extra time;
- providing a word processor (and software) for students to use;
- allowing candidates during the examination to dictate their written answers either into a recorder or to a scribe (amanuensis) or to a typist;
- dictation taking place shortly after the completion of the examination (transcription);
- providing someone to read the questions aloud to the candidate or allowing questions to be read on tape;

- oral examination;

- allowing a candidate to sit the examination in a separate room;

- giving (untimed) breaks during the examination.

We comment briefly on these procedures and on the ways in which students can make the best use of them.

Extra time

It is common policy nowadays to allow extra time to dyslexic candidates. As has been pointed out already (**Chapter 1**), there is good evidence that slowness in dealing with symbolic material is an inherent characteristic of the dyslexic adult and that speeding up is possible only to a very limited extent. Someone who is slow in this way is therefore at a disadvantage, which is irrelevant from the Examining Board's point of view (**see also Chapter 20**).

It is usual to offer ten to 15 minutes per hour. This can be adjusted, however, in the light of the candidate's assessment. If, for instance, a candidate has a particularly slow handwriting or reading speed, it may be possible for more time than this to be allowed. Some students report that they may not use all of their extra time in an examination, but the knowledge that it is there makes a great deal of difference to their ability to stay calm and minimise the effect of their dyslexia.

Whenever extra time is offered, it is sensible that the candidates in question should enter the examination room early rather than leave it late, since the noise of other candidates leaving the room is likely to be a serious distraction, whereas the chance to look at the questions in detail before other candidates have arrived may lessen the sense of being under pressure of time. There is the further advantage that early starters will be less noticeable to the other candidates. Some institutions may provide a separate room for extra-time candidates, though not all dyslexic students will wish to use it.

Use of word processing

There are some dyslexic students who have problems with handwriting: they may be slow and they may be unable to write legibly. Their spelling uncertainties may further affect the speed at which they can write. Examining Boards will almost certainly recognise that it is unfair to expect such a student, who has been using a word processor for his written coursework, suddenly to change to handwriting during an examination; indeed, the handwriting of the student may even have deteriorated through lack of practice. It is clearly proper that such a student should be permitted to use a word processor during examinations.

We advise students who have not used a word processor in examinations before to do a dry run beforehand, typing an essay under time constraint. At Bangor the cut-and-paste and spellchecker facilities are normally available, although we advise students to switch off the spellchecker until they have completed their written answers so that time is not lost making corrections as they write. Here, too, and in other institutions concept-mapping, text-to-speech and dictation software are available for use by certain students.

Dictating answers during the examination

If a scribe (amanuensis) is used, it is very important to practise well before the examination and to establish a correct code of practice. Only certain kinds of communication between candidate and scribe are permitted. Guidelines are usually available which set out what these are, for example the candidate has to make clear when he is thinking aloud and when he wants the scribe to write something down. A postgraduate student in the candidate's department is sometimes employed as scribe, and it is good practice for the scribe and candidate to do a trial run before the actual examination.

Dictating answers after the examination

The same principles will apply as those mentioned above.

Using a reader

Not all dyslexic candidates need this or would ask for it. However, as has already been pointed out, a dyslexic candidate may easily misread the examination paper, and the risk of error is minimised if someone else does the reading.

Oral examination

If the rules of the examining board allow it, this can often be a useful source of additional information for the examiners, though, as will be seen in **Chapter 20** (p. 233), it is not invariably the right answer. If a candidate is to be examined orally, then, as with interviews, it is important that he should practise in advance.

Separate room

This may be a room in which all the students who are given extra time sit the examination. However, some students, especially those with attentional difficulties or for whom examinations are particularly stressful, may need to have a room to themselves, although there will of course be an invigilator present.

Untimed breaks

In the case of a student for whom *extra* extra time has been recommended, breaks should be considered, as no candidate can reasonably be expected to sit and concentrate for extended periods.

SUGGESTIONS FOR FURTHER ADJUSTMENTS

There are various extra adjustments that Examining Boards may wish to consider. Not all dyslexic candidates will need them, but the case for agreeing to them is that *some* candidates may do themselves better justice as a result, without there being any risk of endangering relevant standards.

These suggested adjustments are:

- coloured examination papers, coloured answer papers and coloured filters should be made available;

- densely printed or complicated examination papers might be magnified or enlarged;

- duplicate copies of the question paper should be available;

- the layout and wording of exam papers should be as clear as possible;

- a spare answer book should be permitted for rough work.

With regard to coloured paper, the cost would be minimal, and even if only a small number of candidates found reading easier the measure would be justified. The same is true for enlarged papers. Clearly, the ability to read without eye strain is not something on which a college Examining Board would wish to grade its candidates.

Duplicate copies of examination papers enable the student to have both sides of the question paper in front of him at once. The point here is that a dyslexic student can very easily lose his place when moving from one question to another in a complicated exam paper (or, indeed, forget to turn the paper over – this has happened).

The advantages of clear layout and wording are self-evident. In meetings with academic staff we have discussed the importance of layout and wording of exam papers (this is especially true in the case of multiple-choice question papers) and have occasionally been pleased to be asked to check an exam paper for its dyslexia-friendliness.

It is not always appreciated how much time dyslexic students have to spend looking for rough notes which they have written in a different place in their answer book. Having a spare answer book ensures that such rough notes are easily accessible. Examining boards which ask for all rough work to be handed in could continue to do so.

A final word: some dyslexic students have told us that they think they produce better essays in written examinations than they do in coursework, explaining that this is because they are forced to keep to the point when they know that time is limited, whereas they tend to digress too much and lose their way in longer coursework assignments. However, these students are in the minority, and most students have welcomed the forms of assessment offered by a growing number of courses (**see Chapter 5**) as an alternative to a formal written examination.

CHECK POINTS FOR CHAPTER 17

Adjustments are made to the way in which examinations are delivered on the basis of a student's individual needs, as recommended by her dyslexia assessment report, her Assessment of Study Needs or after discussion with tutors.

Common adjustments for dyslexic students are:

- giving candidates extra time;

- providing a word processor (and appropriate software);

- allowing candidates during the examination to dictate answers either into a computer, recorder, to a scribe (amanuensis) or to a typist;

- dictation of a student's written answer, to a scribe/typist shortly after the completion of an exam (transcription);

- provision of a reader, or allowing questions to be read on tape;

- oral examination;

- allowing a candidate to sit the examination in a separate room;

- giving (untimed) breaks during the examination.

Further adjustments might be considered, including coloured or enlarged exam papers, provision of duplicate copies of the question paper and spare answer books for rough work.

Students need to be clear about what they need to do – and when – to ensure that the exam adjustments they need will be in place. It is also important for staff to realise that many students may feel ambivalent about appearing to be 'special cases'.

Chapter 18

Preparing for examinations, revision and memorisation

Here is another chapter of practical advice for students: there are guidelines on planning and organising yourself and your notes for effective revision. We describe a range of memorisation strategies which have been used successfully by our students in Bangor. There are also suggestions on making the most of the pre-exam revision period.

A WORD OF ENCOURAGEMENT

Yes, of course many students find examinations a strain – and this is certainly not limited to dyslexic students. However, our evidence shows that you should expect to succeed.

Statistics were collected on the performance of dyslexic students at Bangor during a three-year period (**note 18.1**). They numbered 196, though this figure does not include the 22 who left college before their final year or took time out: 188 successfully obtained degrees; five sat the examination and failed, while three left college during their final year. This represents a 95.9 per cent success rate. During this three-year period, one dyslexic student obtained first-class honours while 74 obtained upper-seconds.

If any dyslexic students feel apprehensive at the prospect of examinations, this figure of 95 per cent success rate should give them some encouragement, as should knowing that in 2002–03, in British universities overall, 7.4 per cent of students with dyslexia were awarded first-class degrees – while only 6.4 per cent of other students achieved firsts (**see note 18.2**). Whatever result you achieve, though, to study for – and to achieve – a degree should be regarded as a triumph in itself.

For all students, if they want to do justice to themselves, careful preparation for examinations is essential. In particular, many mature students may never have done any exams for 20 years or more and they will seem to them a big hurdle. The right approach and the right kind of planning can help to make the whole process of preparing for and taking the examination much less stressful. In this chapter we look at ways in which you can make the best use of your memory and we discuss this in relation to long-term planning and to the intensive period of revision and practice just before the examination. The next chapter (**Chapter 19**) takes a closer look at examination techniques.

LONG-TERM PLANNING

One final-year student told a group of fresher students, **'Start thinking about the exams in the first week of term.'** They were quite shocked, but the advice was good. A dyslexic student needs to plan well ahead for examinations, and if possible start this planning at the very beginning of the course. You cannot afford to find yourself in a position where a large amount of revision is needed and there is only a short time to do it in and your notes are all jumbled together.

It is most important to look at a copy of the syllabus or module outline early in the course so that eventually you can plan your revision around it. In addition, lecturers who have mentioned large numbers of books and articles during their lectures are usually willing to provide guidance as to which are the most important ones. We suggest that you look at these as early as possible: if they are library books, they are more likely to be available when other students are not competing for them and, more importantly, it will save you from trying to find them for last-minute skimming.

It is also useful if, as early as possible, you can look at copies of previous examination papers. These are often kept in the library or may be available for downloading from the college intranet.

They will give you an idea of what lies ahead. You may be able to detect themes which crop up over and over again and to work out how closely the questions set are related to the material given in lectures. You will also become familiar with the layout and rubric (instructions) of the papers.

You should be working on your notes throughout the year. Regularly review lecture notes and any notes that you have taken from books and, if you have time, expand them so that you have a coherent body of material to revise from. As a dyslexic student, you will find it very difficult if you try *both* to read up new material *and* to revise – all in the last few weeks before the exams. You need to prepare your notes so that you can learn from them: it is best if you do this preparation as you build up your notes over the year, rather than when you start to revise (**see Chapter 11**).

USING YOUR MEMORY

To help you with your revision, here is a simple analogy (**see note 18.3**).

Imagine your memory is like a food cupboard. You put food into it and store it until it is needed. If you put your food into the cupboard in a certain order, keep the shelves organised so that the different tins and packets are in separate parts, label them clearly and every now and then check to see that they are there, it should be fairly easy to find whatever food you want when you open the cupboard. In contrast, if the cupboard is all jumbled up, it is much harder to find the food – you have to rummage around for it and often cannot find it.

When you revise you are, as it were, putting everything you learn into the food store – large amounts of it. You need, therefore, to organise your material and ideas so that they are easily found when you want them. You need to label them so that you can retrieve them quickly and efficiently. It is important to work out what helps you to remember things so that, while you are building up the memory store, you are also ensuring that things are easy to find again.

STRATEGIES TO HELP YOU REMEMBER

Most dyslexic students have difficulty in learning things by heart: they cannot easily get things off pat (**see note 18.4**) or recite them mechanically. Memorising can be made much easier if the right *strategies* are used.

The discussion that follows makes use of *strengths* of dyslexic people, and in particular recognises the fact that many of you are good at logical reasoning. We are going to suggest ways in which you can organise your notes so that, like the things in the food cupboard, they will be easy to use. The techniques may in some ways be similar to those you have already used in learning to spell.

Make sure you understand your material

Before you try to memorise anything, be sure that you *understand* it. If you find a section of your notes to be really difficult, do not just memorise the words: try to work out what the words mean or ask someone else to explain them to you. We remember things much better if we really understand them – and much worse if we do not. Seemingly separate ideas will become easier to remember if you look for logical links between them and indicate these links in your notes.

Feeding your memory

You need to think about how you best remember material that you have learnt. Do you see a picture of it? Do you remember the lecturer's voice? Do key words stay in your mind? Do you remember posters pinned up in your room? There is evidence which suggests that we vary in this respect (**see note 18.5**); so it is important that you should work out what suits you best personally. However, it is likely that things will stick better in your memory if several different sensory channels work in combination – vision, hearing, movement and so on – and the more sensory pathways you create to a memory, the more likely you are to be able to find it when you need it. Here are some suggestions:

- **Use colour and pictures to help you remember your notes:**
  write introductions in one colour, main points in another. Use
  coloured pens for underlining things. If it helps, draw pictures
  in your notes.

- **Add shape**: one student we know set out her revision points
  for one topic in the shape of a six-pointed star, while she used
  a clock diagram for another topic with 12 key points. If you use
  mind-maps, you can make them interesting and lively by colour
  coding different aspects of the topic.

- **Summarise important points** on postcards or posters: these
  will be key words which will trigger your memory. (For an
  example of a revision card, see the end of this section.) You
  can develop a set of cards that you can carry around with you.
  Or make large, eye-catching posters (not too many) and put
  them on your wall and on your ceiling. Keep looking at them
  – think how we subconsciously absorb the material displayed
  in advertisements.

- **Number your points**: you may well find that numbers trigger
  the memory. If you know, for example, that a gas has six
  properties you can use 'six' as a memory jogger and will not
  feel that you are confronted with an indefinite list.

- **Create mnemonics**. These can be really silly, or very rude. (We
  know that medical students specialise in very rude mnemonics.
  We have a list of them but they are not fit for publication!) If
  you are studying English and need a mnemonic for the four
  'big' Shakespeare tragedies, you have HMOL – 'Her Majesty's
  Off Licence' (*Hamlet, Macbeth, Othello* and *Lear*). Initial letters
  are good memory joggers (**see note 18.6**). We took up this idea
  by asking our students the capital cities of various European
  countries; few knew any of them, but when we supplied the
  first letters they were able to recall them quite easily.

- A very helpful way of learning, if it suits you, is to **record your
  notes**. Many of our students listen to their notes as they walk
  or drive around. Some of them get their friends to read parts of
  their notes so that their own voice does not become too tedious.

Several have put music onto their recordings as a background and have found that it is an aid to memorising. Others revise to the sound of music, always using the same tunes for the same topic. Eventually, what you hear can be linked with its visual equivalents on the cards and on the posters.

- You may like to **try 'pegging'**. According to Buzan (**see note 18.7**), 'a peg system can be thought of much like a wardrobe containing a certain definite number of hangers on which you hang your clothes'. Basically, pegging involves making associations or links, so that what you want to learn is linked (or 'pegged') to something. For example, you could visualise a room and 'peg' your notes about the Industrial Revolution to different features of the room:
  - *door* – machinery
  - *fireplace* – raw materials
  - *rug* – factories
  - *lamp* – transport
  - *bookcase* – coal
  - *armchair* – steam
  - *settee* – cities
  - *coffee table* – population.

The best way to do this kind of thing is to create your own system.

- **Visualise what you want to remember**. The more dramatic and surprising you make your mental images, the easier it will be to remember them. Using the example of the Industrial Revolution, you might have pictures in your mind of something like Figure 4.

Figure 4 Mental images are more memorable if they are unusual

- Another way to visualise ideas – especially if there is a sequence involved – is to **make up a mental video film**. You can then 'add' movement and sound to your images. Again, the more dramatic and exaggerated this is, the more effectively you will remember it.

- You may also like to try a technique usually associated with aromatherapy and **try memorising things by associating them with particular aromas or smells** which you carry with you into the examination room: at the very least there may be a certain perfume which makes you feel relaxed and confident! One of our students suggests that **taste can be used like this too**: if you always suck a certain sort of sweet when you are revising a certain topic, you could take these with you on the day of the examination. You will have to decide for yourself if this works for *you*.

Some time ago one of us (DEG) was confronted with a tearful student facing page after page of narrow-lined A4 paper, packed with closely written words. There was a solution! The notes were worked on with coloured pens and fluorescent markers, headings were transferred to postcards and to posters, which were pinned onto walls, names and lists were read into the tape recorder, mnemonics were devised and diagrams and flow charts with cartoons, pictures, stars etc. were created.

What we need to remember is this: written material on its own, particularly when it is closely packed, can be very daunting. Just 'reading through and trying to remember' is not a reliable revision strategy. In contrast, a 'multisensory' approach using some of the strategies we have suggested (*looking* at colours, *listening* to sounds, *writing* with a felt pen and *moving* about the room) may make things much easier. A student who had created diagrams for all the topics in a module commented afterwards that 'it was the doing of it – the being active – that helped me to remember' rather than the finished product.

Try putting key words onto small cards. These key words may then trigger off other points. You may well be amazed at how much you can remember. Here is an example of such a card.

```
Industrial Revolution
1      Machinery
2      Raw materials
3      Factories
4      Transport
5      Coal
6      Steam
7      Cities
8      Population
8: M R F T C S C P
```

Figure 5 A revision card

There are eight points here, which can be represented by the eight letters; and here is a sentence for remembering them: 'My Red Fat Tom Cat Soon Catches Parrots'.

THE PRE-EXAMINATION REVISION PERIOD

It is not possible to specify an ideal time for starting revision. If you are in a modular system, you may have lectures almost up to the exam period, with no free weeks for revision. This is the case if you have mid-semester exams. Much depends on how well you have done your background reading and sorted your notes out. This revision period is under *your* control.

When, where and how to revise

Try to **get yourself organised** before you start. Buy plenty of coloured pens and get hold of as much scrap paper as you can. Some cardboard, postcards and A3 size paper are also useful. Check that you have a recorder onto which you can talk your notes if this strategy works for you. Think, even, about your food – some students plan out their meals for the week ahead. Decide where the best place to work is.

If you are living with people who are not doing exams at this time, make sure that they do not disrupt your revision. If you live away from college, it may be worth finding out when the local library is open, as it will probably have a reading room where you can study. Plan your time off – you will need breaks.

Back to one of our previous adages – **think positive**! There is a good probability that you will pass your exams for the simple reason that most people *do* pass. If you approach the exam period negatively, this may discourage you from studying. The obvious thing, in any case, is that you should try to do as well as you can.

Structure your work. If you have not done so, you should organise your notes in such a way that you will be able to learn from them. You will probably find that you have to start working in more detail on them by making condensed notes, producing short summaries and drawing up lists of relevant points as introductions to a subject. By writing summaries and lists you are in effect reconstructing the subject matter of your course.

Even though some examining boards may not penalise poor spelling, there will probably be essential words which it will pay you to learn. You could isolate two or three a day and work out ways of remembering them; you should then consolidate your learning by writing them down and saying them over to yourself. Be careful, too, of words that are similar to each other in both sound and appearance, such as 'hypothermia' and 'hyperthermia' – the difference is important!

Make sure your revision time is suitably planned. Try writing a list of topics and making a revision timetable. Make plans for the revision period as a whole, and then break them down into weekly plans and daily plans. Think back to what was said about organising your study time in **Chapter 10** – allow plenty of time off and do not set yourself impossible tasks. Some time off is necessary each day, and there should be one day a week when you have a complete break. As we said – you need breaks. Watch out for the habit of putting off work by constantly revising your timetable – but be prepared to revise it without feeling that you have failed to meet your targets. Even if your timetable is eventually abandoned, the initial making of it is valuable as it forces you to consider what you need to do.

Check at this stage that you have plenty of old examination papers to work from. You should make a detailed list of topics – rather than questions – that are likely to come up. **We do not recommend deliberate question-spotting** since this encourages the view that to every examination question there is a single right answer. In many examinations the obtaining of a high grade almost invariably depends on the ability to think and criticise. If you develop a topic bank, you can work on the material for these topics, and once you know this material you can then apply it to any question that may come up. How you are graded will often depend on how you handle it.

Another method of examining, used mainly in science departments, is to set very short questions which demand rapid recall. For these questions you will need to use the memorisation techniques which have already been discussed. It is particularly important to **practise multiple-choice questions** as these can be quite difficult to work out. Some of our students have worked together in groups on this type of examination paper and pooled their ideas on how to approach it.

If you know at this stage how long each examination paper lasts, how many questions you have to answer and what marks or grades are allocated for each question, you can then plan a time schedule. In the case of marks it is worth calculating how many minutes are available for each mark to be earned, how much time should be spent on the first question, at what point you should have answered half the questions and so on.

YOU ARE NOW GOING INTO THE LEARNING PHASE

As we pointed out, it is very important that you should not find yourself in a position where you have to carry out a large amount of rote learning in a short time. You may see some of your non-dyslexic friends flinging themselves into all-night revision sessions, but you will almost certainly find it difficult to speed up more than a limited amount. If you work against time, the stress of fighting for precious minutes may cause you to go blank or be unable to think clearly. Your writing and spelling may deteriorate and you may find that you cannot concentrate.

Without proper sleep and rest periods you may find the situation worsening. For these reasons we have constantly advised dyslexic students to work slowly and steadily. The tortoise gets to the winning post eventually even if he does not run as fast as the hare; and if other students try to behave like hares, that is no reason for trying to imitate them.

You should plan your schedule in such a way that at some times in the day you are doing really hard memory work, while at other times you are reading or practising examination papers. If you **vary the type of revision**, this may help to prevent you from becoming stale.

Work actively

Do not just read it through without thinking about it. Always have a pen or pencil in your hand so that you are continually writing down relevant points. If it suits you, talk to yourself – sing – walk around the room – do anything as long as you are *active*:

- ask yourself questions and write down your answers;

- make a question bank and use it every day;

- take your cards or tapes out with you and use them if you have to wait for a bus or have some spare time;

- in a group of friends, test each other.

Learning is most effective if it is continually being tested. In other words, you learn more by going over what you have learned.

> Above all, practise, be active.
>
> Revise
>
> Recall
>
> Review

Recall and review are very important. As you get nearer the time of the examination, think of yourself as going into training so that you are in the best possible shape for answering the questions.

Using old exam papers

When you return to previous exam papers and use them for practice, your first step could be to take a question and map out an answer in the form of notes. These notes should contain an effective introduction that brings in the *key* words; they should indicate the way in which the answer is to be presented and the way in which the different threads are to be gathered together in a conclusion.

You should remember that tutors are normally very willing to give help both when you are revising and at other times; and you may like at some stage to check whether the notes which you have produced seem to the tutor to be along the right lines. One lecturer gives the following useful tip to his students: when they write a practice essay, they should do so not on every line but on every alternate line. Then, when they come to check what they have written, they will be able to write in on the blank lines the details that they had missed out.

Attention to what you are writing may also be an aid to memorising. Eventually you might feel it would help you to attempt a full-length answer in timed conditions (without coffee breaks and the like!) and, after that, a full-length paper.

If the exam is one in which you have to write short answers on the printed paper, make a photocopy first and use it for practice; you may like to check, for instance, whether you can fit your answer in the space provided. It is also a good idea to practise diagrams, again trying to fit them into the space.

Working on previous exam papers not only helps you to get your timing right but also enables you to get used to different rubrics ('Answer two questions from Section A and two from either Section B or Section C') so that you are not bewildered by these when you meet them in the actual examination.

Check your exam arrangements – and put in some practice

If you have any adjustments to the way you take the examination, such as a scribe or the use of a Dictaphone, or if you are doing your exam on a word processor, you will need to check that the arrangements have been completed and to practise the necessary techniques.

If you are using a word processor, it will be worth going into training on the keyboard to improve your speed and to enable you to work out how much you can type in a restricted amount of time. If a word processor is not permitted, make sure that you practise your handwriting, particularly under timed conditions. A small number of dyslexic candidates dictate their answers to a scribe. If you are planning to do so, it is wise to check that you are familiar with the correct pronunciation of scientific terms and the like.

LOOKING AFTER YOURSELF

Finally, you are unlikely to do yourself justice in examinations if you are tired or under pressure. **It is therefore particularly important that you should have plenty of sleep and plenty of fresh air and that you should eat properly.** We have already said that it is more important to relax if you cannot sleep than to become tense worrying about the fact. It is also worthwhile thinking about possible ways of combating stress, for example you may like to practise relaxation or deep breathing.

Bear in mind also that stress can be catching. Do not allow yourself to be misled by the horror stories which you hear around the time of the examinations as to how much or how little revision your friends have done. Remember, too, that at examination times there may be all kinds of rumours circulating and that it is usually best to ignore them. All these things are matters of common sense, but we have found that if a student is under stress common sense is sometimes forgotten.

CHECK POINTS FOR CHAPTER 18

You should expect to succeed – dyslexia need not stand in the way of your getting a good degree – but you also need to expect to work hard to get there.

- Plan ahead and do not leave things until the last minute.

- The first step to doing well is to make sure you understand your material. Make your revision **active**: do more than read through your notes.

- Work on your notes to identify key points to remember.

- Use multisensory techniques to reinforce your memory.

- Practise **recall** – test yourself.

- Look at old examination papers.

- Work slowly and steadily – and **look after yourself**.

Chapter 19

Sitting the examinations

This chapter gives guidance for students on sitting various kinds of exams: there are suggestions on practical preparation before the exam, how to tackle the question paper, what to do if you 'go blank' and strategies for managing time during the exam itself.

SUGGESTIONS FOR THOSE WHO FEEL ANXIOUS

Sitting an examination is quite a different experience from revising. The revision period may have seemed like an endless jog along a long road; the exam, in contrast, is like a short intensive race, run at sprint speed. If you can, you will do better if you approach your exams methodically and with a positive outlook.

To some extent exams are a test of nerves. There are students – not just those who are dyslexic – who are highly skilled and highly intelligent but who nevertheless seize up when faced with a written exam paper. It is therefore not surprising if you feel anxious. If, however, you prepare yourself for exam conditions and practise exam techniques during the run-up period, you will be better able to take the examination itself in your stride.

If it seems like a real ordeal, you might discuss the whole examination process with your tutor or your fellow students. It could be of help if you try a technique used effectively by athletes preparing for competition: visualise what lies ahead – by imagining yourself waiting to start, looking at the paper and coping with the students around you (**see note 19.1**). It might be worth going to see the room where the exam is being held if you have not already done so; then you will know what sort of a room it is and may even be able to visualise where you will sit. Some colleges arrange for candidates who have extra time to sit their examinations in a separate room; if this applies in your case, it really is worth finding out where this room is so as to avoid last-minute panic.

Remind yourself of this: examiners want you to pass!

CHECK ON WHAT PAPERS YOU ARE TAKING, WHERE AND WHEN

An obvious point – but one worth mentioning – is that you should make sure that you turn up in the right place at the right time. Although all students make such mistakes from time to time, a dyslexic student is likely to be more at risk on such matters, for example it is not all that difficult to mistake 'Tuesday' for 'Thursday' or to mistake 14.00 (i.e. 2 o'clock) for 4.00 (i.e. 4 o'clock). If you have problems over punctuality, you need to make a special point of not being late: none of us can produce our best work if we are feeling flustered.

Check that you know:

- the name of each paper that you are taking;
- its reference or code number;
- where the exam will be held;
- what time you need to be there.

This is especially important if it has been arranged that you sit the exam in a separate room, as there will not be complete sets of papers there, but only the papers for the candidates who have been allotted to the room, and maybe you will not be with anyone else from your course.

DO NOT BE PUT OFF BY WHAT OTHERS SAY

At the time of the examination you may come across students who tell you in detail about every topic which they have revised. There may be some who say that they have learned everything – and others who claim to have done no work at all. Comparing notes on the way to the exam room is unhelpful, and you may find it better to keep to yourself in the moments before the exam starts. It is important to approach the exam in a calm frame of mind, and this means avoiding any situations which could give rise to panic.

Many students have asked us about last-minute revision. This depends on you: you should not be trying to learn *new* material immediately before an examination, but if you feel easier in your mind you could refresh your memory by looking over your condensed notes, revision cards and posters or, if you have them, listening to your revision tapes.

MAKE A CHECKLIST OF WHAT TO TAKE INTO EACH EXAM

It's a good idea to make a checklist of what you need for each examination paper. You are likely to need some of the following: pens, highlighter pen, rulers, pencils, pencil sharpener and rubber (for multiple-choice questions) and – for some subjects – a calculator (make sure that there is a spare battery). If you have 'slips' to put onto your exam scripts, don't forget these, and have a little stapler to secure them to your work. As a precaution, put everything in a pencil case. (We know of one student who washed his jeans with his calculator in the pocket the night before a mathematics paper!)

If the examination is being held first thing in the morning, then, to avoid panic, you should organise all these things on the previous evening – and check, too, that your alarm clock is working. Try to make sure that you have a good night's sleep before an exam: your brain needs sleep to function at its best.

Writing examination answers takes up energy. It may therefore help if you have a good breakfast on the day of the examination, and, if it is allowed, why not consider taking glucose sweets, barley sugar or chewing gum into the examination room? (However, make sure they do not have crackly paper, or the other students will not thank you.) You may also want to take a bottle of water, especially if the exam is a long one.

IN THE EXAMINATION ROOM

In the examination room, again keep calm. If you have to sit and wait for people to settle, try deep breathing as a way of helping you to relax. If you go in early for your extra time, be prepared for some disturbance when the others come in – but if possible continue writing. It is also important that you should train yourself not to be distracted by what other people are doing in the examination room. Your concerns are yourself, the exam paper and the clock. The other students may appear to be writing faster; they may even leave the examination room early. However, if you as a dyslexic student try to write too fast, your mistakes may increase dramatically. If others leave early, there is not the slightest reason for you to feel under pressure to do the same.

The first few minutes of an examination are perhaps the most stressful. Be aware that this could be when you will panic and make silly mistakes. Take plenty of time and care over reading the instructions at the top of the paper. Highlight the key instructions, or ring them with a pencil. If there is more than one section, make sure that you have checked how many questions need to be answered from each and which questions are compulsory. Turn the paper over to make sure you do not miss any questions on the back of the sheet.

TIMING YOURSELF

Where this applies, look at the marks awarded for each answer and work out how long you should spend in proportion to the total time allocated. In some science papers the first section is of the 'short-answer' variety, whilst the 'heaviest' section usually involves the writing of an essay; and since this second section is likely to carry most marks make sure that you allow yourself sufficient time to write it.

It is also very important to work out the timing per section and per question. For example, if you are sitting a three-hour paper in which you are required to answer four questions, it is probably wise to allow at least 20 minutes for reading the instructions and deciding which questions to answer; this will leave 160 minutes, that is 40 minutes per question. If you have been allowed extra time, you can adjust your calculations accordingly. As a precaution, you should check your arithmetic and make sure that you do not misread your watch. One of our students always sets her watch to '12 o'clock' at the start of exams, as she can then work out more easily how much time she has left; you need to be sure, if you do this, that you will not get confused about the *real* time.

Be careful not to spend more than your allotted time on one or two questions to the neglect of the others. If you really run into trouble over time, most examining boards will give you some marks for brief outline notes (perhaps with key words, names etc.) in place of a full answer. You should make it clear that you could have written at greater length if you had had the time (see below). But we suggest you use this remedy only as a last resort.

THE QUESTIONS

It is important to **read through the whole paper at the start**. If there is a choice of questions, decide immediately, if you can, which ones you are going to answer. If you put a tick against these, it will save you having to re-read the paper later. You may like to write down at any stage things which you think you will need for answering other questions, for instance names or formulae; and, if an idea for a different question occurs to you while you are writing, it is worthwhile jotting it down somewhere so that you do not forget it. Rough work should eventually be crossed out, as most examining boards expect this.

We suggest that you **start with the question which you think you can do best**. This will give you confidence and ease you into the exam. When you have chosen a question, read it carefully again several times, ringing the key words. Errors may creep in, and it is essential, for example, that you do not overlook the word 'not' or misread 'greater than' for 'less than', 'important' for 'unimportant', or, like one examination candidate, 'Henry IV' for 'Henry VI'. In some subjects the questions will probably require very careful analysis; for this reason it is essential to be on the lookout for shades of meaning which must be recognised if you are to grasp the full significance of the wording.

When you underline or ring the key words, look out in particular for the 'logical' words: 'necessary', 'possible', 'always' and the like – and check after every paragraph that what you are writing is still relevant. Thus, if you are asked if something is *always* the case this may be an invitation to explore situations where seemingly it is *not* the case. You should also think carefully about the words with which the question starts – words such as 'discuss', 'examine', 'explain', 'compare' and 'analyse'. These words help you to understand what you are expected to do (**see Chapter 12, note 12.1**).

In most exam questions there will almost certainly be more than one key word. Indeed, there is a risk that if the student relies on a single key word – for example the word 'intelligence' in a psychology paper – he may produce the kind of answer which tutors rudely call a 'write-all-you-know-about' answer, and this is scarcely likely to gain high marks. To think to oneself, 'Wow! Here's the question on "intelligence": off we go!' is no way to proceed if some highly specific question about intelligence has been asked. In general, the examiner is asking you to discuss a particular issue – **attempt the question only if you are clear about what this issue is and have something to say about it**.

YOUR ANSWERS

It is also very important to think before you write and to **plan each answer** carefully. Your plan need not be long, but it will be your guide through the question. Many students have found it useful to take two answer books (if this is allowed) or at least two separate sheets of paper so that they can plan their answer on a sheet which 'travels with them'. If this is done, the plan is still available when they turn over a page and they need not waste time or become confused in having to look back for it.

Try jotting down your points in a basic spidergram. Then number them so that they show the order you want to tackle them in. If you find that you are absolutely stuck for something to write, you can at least take the question, discuss it and analyse its implications.

This might help if you 'blank out'. This is something that everyone dreads – it happens to most of us at times. If this happens to you, try to write *something*, even if it is not very good: you can always cross it out and at least it will keep you writing. And try to relax. Another possibility is to leave the question that you were working on and move on to another one about which you know you have something to say. We have seen students sit for many minutes not writing, and it is possible that the longer you sit, the harder it is to get going again.

Most dyslexic students are given *extra time*. This is unlikely to be much in a short exam but could be as much as 45 minutes in a three-hour paper. You will probably find it very tiring, and quite difficult, to write solidly for almost four hours. Take time off between questions to allow yourself to think, to clear your mind and perhaps to check what you have written. We knew a student who would put her head down on the desk and relax for five minutes between questions – rather a risk to take, but she found it worked (and she got an upper-second class honours in history).

If you are dictating your answers to a scribe, it is best to make some written notes before starting to speak and to have a pen and paper handy in case you wish to stop and organise your thoughts in the middle of an answer. You will need to indicate to your scribe when you want her to write, when you want her to stop and when you are thinking aloud but do not want her to write. As we pointed out earlier, you will need to be able to pronounce accurately any names or technical terms with which she may be unfamiliar.

DO NOT WORRY TOO MUCH ABOUT CORRECT SPELLING

It is important that you do not let any uncertainties you have about spelling become a major concern. If you do, you may lose track of where you have got to in your answer. If you find yourself worrying about a word, remember that some misspelled words are relatively unimportant, whereas a rambling answer matters a great deal. There may be scientific words which have to be exact, for example 'chlorine', 'chloride', 'chlorate', and you should be particularly careful over words which sound similar but have a different meaning, such as 'clarify' and 'classify'. Your best plan will probably be to leave some words misspelled and perhaps mark them with a query so that if you have time you can return to them. Above all, make sure that the flow of your argument is maintained.

SHORT-ANSWER QUESTIONS

Particularly if you are doing science, it is likely that you will be given some short-answer questions, involving only a small number of words. In most exams the requirement is that you have to answer *all* of these, usually by writing on the exam paper itself. If there is a blank space for your answer, as there normally is, you will be able to deduce from it how long your answer should be, and as the marks awarded for each question are usually shown you will also have an idea how many specific points need to be made if you are to get the maximum mark. These sorts of question call for immediate recall rather than discussion and you need to move rapidly. We suggest:

- you answer first the questions that you know you can do – in any order;

- if you cannot do a question, you do not waste time worrying about it but move on to one that you *can* do;

- you do not spend time rewriting the question; you should simply give the answer;

- you bear in mind that sometimes three words may get you three marks (but check in advance with your tutor whether full sentences are required).

It is quite useful to imagine the examiner marking relevant points tick by tick: ask yourself if you have provided enough points to enable him to make the right number of ticks.

MULTIPLE-CHOICE QUESTION PAPERS

In the case of multiple-choice examinations you are given a set of questions and a choice of possible answers from which you have to select the correct one. For this you normally require an HB pencil, and you will need to find out from the instructions if answers may be rubbed out.

There are advantages for some dyslexic students in this type of examination in so far as it saves writing and avoids problems over spelling. Nevertheless, you should take care because some of the words may well have fine shades of meaning which have to be distinguished; in addition, there may be complications such as double negatives – 'it is *not* the case that such and such *never* happens'. It is sensible to ring or underline words like these.

As the questions can be answered in any order, we suggest you start by looking through all of them at a reasonable speed: reading right through the paper may trigger your memory for particular questions. Then do at once all those to which you know the answer. If you are in doubt, you may find it helpful to cross out the options which you are sure are wrong, and then study carefully the ones which are left. As in other types of exam, make sure that you watch the time: it may sound obvious, but if you have to do 50 questions in an hour it follows that you will need to have done 25 in half an hour.

ORAL EXAMINATIONS

If you are given an oral examination (or 'viva') you should remember that **the examiners are on your side** and are not there for the purpose of catching you out. Memories of unsympathetic questioning during school days may return, and if this happens in your case it is understandable. However, it would be totally unprofessional for any member of an examining board to try to victimise a candidate, nor would other members of the board permit it. It is important in this connection that you should not mistake friendly or neutral questions for hostile ones.

You should take the first two or three questions very cautiously; that is when you are likely to be at your most nervous and when you could rush into an answer and say something inappropriate.

Examining Boards may wish to use oral examinations for a variety of reasons. One of the most common is that if they examine you orally they are giving you the chance to clarify or expand on points which you have made in your written papers. It may simply be that the written answer was somewhat cryptic and that the board wishes to check that you have genuinely understood the point of what you have written, or it may sometimes be that they wish to check further on your originality or creativity.

A great advantage of the oral examination, from the point of view of many dyslexic students, is that it gives them the chance to display the quality of their thinking without the effort of having to write things down on paper. Also it is generally understood that whatever a candidate does in an oral examination he cannot actually be marked *down*. If you are able to relax and to recognise that the examiners are on your side, there is a good opportunity, whatever the standard of your written work, for you to show the high quality of your thinking.

AFTER THE EXAM

We said that comparing notes with other students, before an exam, might be unhelpful; the same may be true after the exam. There is a danger that chatting to others will make you start to think about what you did not do and should have done, and what you missed out and it is too easy to forget all the things you did right, especially when you are feeling tired after an exam. Now is the time to look forwards, not back.

CHECK POINTS FOR CHAPTER 19

Remember, above all, that the examiners want you to pass!

- Check – well before the exam – that you know when and where it is, and have ready everything that you need to take in with you.

- If you want to do last-minute revision, look at your revision notes rather than trying to cram new material.

- Try not to listen to pre-exam chat.

- Timing is important; so work out how long you will have for each question.

- Read questions several times; ring or highlight key words.

- Use a spare answer book for plans and notes.

- Start with the answer(s) you feel most confident about.

- If you begin to run out of time for writing, give an outline plan of what your answer would be.

- Don't spend time worrying too much about correct spelling (unless spelling is being examined).

- Think about the best strategy for you to use if you 'go blank'.

- After an exam, put it behind you – look forwards not back.

Chapter 20

Discussion points for moderators and Examining Boards

This chapter is addressed to those who are concerned with the design and assessment of courses: it provides points for reflection and discussion relating to the fairness of assessing the achievement of dyslexic students by traditional methods.

REASONABLE ADJUSTMENTS

The earlier editions of this book were concerned to urge 'that as a matter of policy all Examining Boards will be willing to treat dyslexic candidates as "special cases"'. Dyslexic students now have the protection of the law to ensure that reasonable adjustments are made to the learning and assessment processes (**see Chapter 5**). The most commonly arranged adjustments for examinations are described in **Chapter 17**. A dyslexic student arriving at college with an up-to-date and relevant assessment report will not usually find that there are any problems with the implementation of the report's recommendations for examination adjustments.

However, there are still areas where understanding of the issues is scanty, and where discussion is needed. As was pointed out in **Chapter 17**, when an Examining Board is considering an individual candidate it will normally be informed by his assessment report, coupled perhaps with a recommendation from his tutor, suggesting certain types of adjustment. The Board is then empowered, if it so wishes, to provide these adjustments or, if the application is retrospective, to revise the grades which were originally allotted. The disadvantage of not operating some such system is that without it there is serious risk that some dyslexic students will be incorrectly graded.

We have sometimes asked ourselves whether, as a matter of logic, a statement that the candidate is dyslexic can have any relevance to the awarding of a grade or degree class. Thus, if one were examining candidates on the ability to run 100 metres in quick time, one might feel sorry for a candidate with mobility difficulties who failed the test, but that would be no reason for pretending that he had passed; and it is arguable that there is a comparable problem over a dyslexic candidate: if he possesses the requisite skills, he should be graded accordingly; if he does not, no amount of 'sympathy' over his dyslexia can justify giving him a higher grade than he merits.

We have met not only examiners but, indeed, candidates who have been troubled over this point. Only a very unscrupulous candidate would want 'concessions' (**see note 20.1**) in the sense of extra marks over and above what he had earned, and many students have emphasised to us that they are anxious not to seek any kind of 'favour' from the Examining Board. As we saw in **Chapter 1**, to say that a candidate is dyslexic is to imply a constitutional limitation which is not his fault. However, if the candidate lacks certain skills, it might be argued that a causal theory as to how he came to lack them is in no way relevant.

We have put this case as strongly as we could, but we believe it to be flawed and that it is most important to re-emphasise that the adjustments made for dyslexic candidates are not ' favours' but are necessary steps for securing a level playing field for all candidates. The following seem to us to be the arguments in favour of making adjustments.

- In the first place, if the fact that a candidate is dyslexic is not known or not taken into account there is serious risk that he will be marked down for lack of skills which, from the Examining Board's point of view, are *irrelevant*. This is a point to which we shall return shortly.

- Second, a large amount is now known about what to expect from dyslexic candidates, for example that clumsiness of expression may conceal all sorts of good ideas. At Bangor, students are issued with 'slips' which highlight their individual difficulties and suggest guidelines for marking. They also act as a warning against overhasty grading: as has been pointed out, the script of a dyslexic student may contain some original and creative ideas although he has difficulties in expressing them in writing (see Chapter 12).

The difficulties in providing fair assessment for dyslexic candidates in examinations have been highlighted by the *Singleton Report* (see note 20.2):

> For people with dyslexia, written examinations present a situation in which they are required to demonstrate their talents and learned capabilities using a medium (recall and written expression under conditions of extreme time pressure) which impinge directly on the core of their disability (memory and written language). Without some special arrangements, such candidates would be disadvantaged in comparison with other candidates who do not have this disability.

For these reasons it is proper for Examining Boards to take a candidate's dyslexia into account and it is proper for dyslexic candidates to request this; in doing so they are not asking for any favour but simply collaborating with the Board in trying to bring about the fairest possible assessment.

THINGS WHICH CAN GO WRONG

The essential point for an Examining Board to bear in mind is that in a written examination the dyslexic candidate is being asked to respond via a medium – the written word – which creates special difficulty for him. It is possible, therefore, that he may have plenty of good ideas which in the conditions of the examination fail to appear in his script. He may be a brilliant computer programmer, for instance; he may devise a new technique for zoological or botanical research or have grasped some new principle in economics; he may show in discussion that he is a brilliant creative chemist or may make a highly original contribution to the appreciation of *Macbeth*. In the script which he presents to his examiners, however, none of these things may come through.

This was summarised for us a few years ago by a science student who said to one of us (TRM), 'When we had the practical classes during the year, I always had to explain to my partner what we had to do. Yet after the examination she was offered honours and I was not.' It must be that in this case the student's exam script did not demonstrate that he had the necessary knowledge and that his Examining Board did not check by other means whether this knowledge was present. Examples such as this, of course, strengthen the case for basing part of a student's overall grade on coursework – a policy that is now common practice.

One of the curious things we have noticed over the years is that many dyslexic students often assume that they have made points clearly and logically and that the reader will immediately pick up what they wanted to convey. In tutorials one can sometimes say, 'I think what you mean is …', wishing to help a student with his expression; sometimes the student replies, with genuine surprise, 'But isn't that what I have said?' when he is very far from having said it! In the stress of examination conditions all such weaknesses become exaggerated and, because of his difficulty in expressing himself in writing, a student's thoughts may fail to keep pace with the words he is writing. Potentially, there may be a valid and interesting argument, but because of his difficulties with the written word the force of this argument may not come through to the reader. If he then decides to slow down, he may panic because he finds he does not have enough time to complete the paper.

This brings us to a problem which regularly confronts the dyslexic candidate in examinations – the problem of determining the best trade-off between speed and accuracy. If time were unlimited, and he did not feel under pressure, there would be the chance to check whether what he wrote in his script was really what he wanted to say. If such checking takes him a long time, however, he will find himself in danger of leaving much of the paper unfinished, and for this reason he may decide to forfeit accuracy in the interests of speed.

A student we met some years ago said his tutor had noticed that he tended to attempt those questions which had the shortest wording, rather than those which on other grounds might have been easier. We will return to the issue of giving extra time later in the chapter.

A further difficulty for an Examining Board is that the performance of dyslexic students may vary from one day to another. On a good day, the putting of ideas on paper may be very much easier than on a bad day; there appears therefore to be an element of chance in their performance which adds to the difficulties of correct assessment (**see note 20.3**). It is, of course, true that any of us may seize up or go blank on occasions, but a dyslexic student is particularly at risk in this respect; and if he goes totally blank during one examination and has a good day during another, the spread of his marks is likely to be considerable.

There is also a problem of awarding a suitable grade if the student misreads one of the key words (as in our earlier example of 'clarify' for 'classify'). It is also possible for a student to misread the instructions and fail to answer the appropriate number of questions from each section. There is often no easy answer to these problems. In the next section, however, we shall make some suggestions which Examining Boards may like to consider.

ON WHAT IS THE CANDIDATE BEING EXAMINED?

The fact that one has to examine a candidate who is dyslexic – in the words of Dr Johnson – 'concentrates [the] mind wonderfully'. It forces one to consider what precisely are the things for which the candidates are being awarded a high or a low grade. Examining Boards are, of course, right to insist on their own autonomy. For that reason it would be inappropriate to say simply that, for instance, poor spelling or poor handwriting should be disregarded. What we can do, however, is to help Boards to ensure that they do not unwittingly mark a candidate down for lack of skills which they would agree on reflection to be irrelevant. Thus if a Board is concerned to determine a candidate's knowledge, his ability to reason logically and his powers of creativity and originality, one can point out that, as a matter of logic, it is bad examining if the marker of the script allows himself to be influenced by poor spelling or poor handwriting.

When this matter is considered, it will probably be found that in some contexts a particular grade in an examination is simply a certificate of achievement. In that case the Examining Board is saying that, no matter what the candidate does in the future, he has at this moment reached a particular level of competence. In other contexts, however, and particularly in the case of qualifying examinations, achievement is taken into account only because it is assumed to be a good predictor of whether the person will display and maintain certain standards in the future.

For most examination candidates this assumption is justified. Thus, it is perfectly proper to argue that a person who lacks knowledge in certain areas should not become a dentist, a nurse, a teacher or whatever it may be. There are, in fact, further safeguards in the system – in particular interviewing and the taking up of references – by which unsuitable people are excluded from such jobs even though they have passed the requisite examinations. What is needed, as far as dyslexic candidates are concerned, is that there should be safeguards in the other direction. If they are downgraded in their examinations for lack of skills which are not relevant to dentistry, nursing, teaching etc., then they are deprived of the opportunity of doing such jobs even though they would in fact be entirely suitable. In view of what is now known about dyslexia this could be a tragic waste.

Similarly, when Boards are examining for honours and need to make a decision as to the candidate's degree class, they will probably decide that their primary concern is to indicate the candidate's achievement, not to try to predict his future progress (**note 20.4**).

In this connection there is a serious risk that an examiner, particularly if he has large numbers of scripts to mark, may unwittingly be misled into awarding a dyslexic candidate a lower grade than he deserves; after all, it is very easy to suppose if a person cannot spell and has immature handwriting that his thinking is therefore immature. As was indicated above, a slip reminding the Examining Board that a candidate is dyslexic is a useful safeguard.

In the case of non-dyslexic candidates there are certain things which can be taken for granted – for example that they will have no difficulty in reading the question, in writing the answer or in carrying out a simple subtraction sum. These skills may be components of the end product which is required of all candidates, but it is for the Board to decide which of these components are to be regarded as important. If the ability to read print at speed is not thought important, for example, then, as a matter of logic, candidates who do not possess this skill should not be penalised. Indeed, if they were so penalised, the Board would be committed to explaining why the same penalties are not exacted from candidates with visual impairment.

Difficult problems of marking can sometimes arise if a candidate has written enough to lead the examiner to suspect the presence of some good ideas but insufficient to show that he has fully grasped the point of what he has said. Since, as we have seen, the style of a dyslexic student may be stilted and his script may contain some awkward and ungainly expressions, the examiner sometimes has to make some kind of guess as to how the candidate might have elaborated his argument had he been given the chance. Has he, for instance, simply dropped in one or two names or mentioned one or two key concepts without having understood them, or has he understood them perfectly well and simply expressed himself somewhat awkwardly? And at what point does stylistic inelegance – a relatively unimportant matter – turn into failure to explain oneself – a weakness which clearly an Examining Board must take seriously?

The use of technology in examinations was noted in **Chapter 17**. In his book, *In the Mind's Eye*, Thomas West (1997) suggests that many of the traditional literacy skills – those, in his words, of the 'medieval clerk' – can now be performed by computer, and he suggests that when those who are dyslexic are free of these 'chores', there will now be a greater opportunity for their talents to flourish. This certainly raises important issues for Examining Boards. In particular, they should perhaps reconsider what value they place on memorisation skills. If these are regarded as important, then those dyslexic candidates who find memorisation difficult, as most of them do, will obtain lower grades. As against this, it is arguable that nothing is gained by insisting that candidates should hold in mind information which for the remainder of their lives they will be able to obtain by pressing a button on a computer. Similarly, it is arguable that coloured paper and the like should be provided for any candidate on request, as suggested in **Chapter 17**, since few Examining Boards would regard themselves as being in the business of giving higher grades to candidates who are unaffected by dazzle.

SOME SUGGESTIONS

Although it is for Examining Boards – and not for us – to decide what is and is not important, we should like to offer the following formula as a possible guide for those marking the scripts of dyslexic candidates: **it is important to look for evidence of creativity, knowledge and reasoning powers which are not apparent at first glance**. An untidy and seemingly scrappy presentation can sometimes conceal important and original ideas.

There may also be difficulties if the candidate's performance is uneven; for example, if the examination comprises four papers she may do well on three of them and perform disastrously on the fourth. When confronted with her pattern of marks, the Board needs to determine whether the performance on the weak paper is genuinely due to lack of knowledge or whether she has failed to show the knowledge which she possesses. It will also need to decide whether failure to show such knowledge (a failure which may be repeated in the future) merits any appreciable penalty when the knowledge was in fact present.

Similar problems arise, as we have already noted, if the candidate goes off the rails as a result of not following the rubric or misreading the question. Presumably, the intention behind a rubric such as 'Answer two questions from Section A and two from either Section B or Section C' is to ensure that the student's knowledge covers a sufficiently wide area. It follows that if the Board can be satisfied on other grounds, for example on the basis of an oral examination, that the student's knowledge is sufficiently wide, then mistakes over rubric need not be too severely penalised. The same principle can sometimes apply when the question itself has been misread, as in the case of the candidate in a history examination who wrote on Henry IV instead of Henry VI. If the candidate *could have* written about Henry VI, this is highly relevant. It is unsatisfactory, in our view, to award no marks at all if the candidate misreads the rubric or answers the wrong question, since this places her on a level with those having no knowledge at all in this area; and if one argues that she should receive a zero mark 'because she ought to have been more careful' this assumes that such misreadings are serious academic faults.

In this connection it is worth noting that the mean (or what is popularly known as the 'average') can sometimes be a very misleading statistic. In the case of a dyslexic candidate the spread of the results may be unusually wide: there may be high marks in some papers while in others something may have gone seriously wrong. When this happens it need not imply that the candidate is simply 'weak' without qualification. Uncritical averaging of marks will almost certainly give a distorted picture.

One of the adjustments made by most Examining Boards (see Chapter 17) is to allow dyslexic candidates extra time. There may still be situations, however, where, with or without extra time, the student fails to complete the paper. One possibility here is that the Board should compare the work of such a candidate in timed examination conditions with his performance in dissertations, projects etc. for which unlimited time has been allowed. If the marks are higher in the latter situation, it is reasonable to infer that what he can do in timed conditions may not fully reflect what he can do in untimed conditions, and this is clearly relevant to the issue of grading. Not long ago a dyslexic student said to one of us, 'They thought that by allowing me extra time they had done all that was needed to ensure me a level playing field, but they didn't understand how my dyslexia affected my performance.'

In **Chapter 17** we also mentioned the possibility that Examining Boards should allow dyslexic candidates to be examined orally. This procedure can be used either on its own or as a supplement to the information obtained from the written papers, and it can sometimes provide the Board with very useful information about a candidate. We have in fact met many dyslexics who are fluent orally and are therefore glad to be examined in this way. However, this is not an ideal solution for *all* dyslexic candidates, since on a bad day some of them may become tongue-tied or unable to find the right words for expressing their argument.

We believe it could sometimes be of help to an examiner to consider what a good copy editor might have made of the script. A copy editor is in no position to query the ideas which an author wishes to express but he may well be able to help the author to make his points in a better or more telling way. We suggest therefore that candidates should not be penalised for something which a good copy editor could have put right. The Examining Board is in that case saying that it prefers a well-informed candidate with creative ideas and good reasoning powers but whose script shows such blemishes to a candidate with fewer such skills whose spelling and sentence construction are adequate. This seems to us a judgement that most Boards would find acceptable.

In our experience there is greater risk of underestimating the dyslexic candidate than of overestimating him. The central question which needs to be asked, in our view, is this: has the candidate lost out through lack of skills which from the point of view of the Examining Board are irrelevant? If so, then there is a case for adjusting or revising his grade. Detailed thought is needed, therefore, as to what knowledge and skills the examiners should be looking for, and how, as discussed in **Chapter 5**, these might most fairly and efficiently be assessed.

CHECK POINTS FOR CHAPTER 20

Reasonable adjustments to the traditional ways in which students are examined go some way towards providing dyslexic candidates with a fairer opportunity to demonstrate their knowledge and understanding. However:

- the issue remains that if these are being assessed by timed written examination dyslexic students remain at a disadvantage – significantly more so than with other students;

- their ability to express themselves in writing at speed is compromised by their disability, and the provision of extra time does not eliminate this problem;

- this is exacerbated by pressure and anxiety, and the problem may be particularly acute at times;

- as a direct result of their dyslexic difficulties, the scripts of dyslexic candidates may not do justice to their learning and understanding;

- there is a danger that their scripts will be marked down for apparent lack of skills which, on reflection, are seen to be irrelevant;

- an 'average' of a dyslexic student's marks across a course may be misleading.

It is easier, therefore, to underestimate than to overestimate the achievement of a dyslexic candidate, and serious consideration should be given to forms of assessment alternative to the timed written examination.

Chapter 21

Out of college and into work

This chapter is mainly for students – but has something for tutors too. We consider the protection and support available to dyslexic employees. There is advice on applying for work, on how and when to disclose and discuss dyslexia and on the challenges in the workplace. For tutors there is advice on writing references for dyslexic students.

INTRODUCTION

This book was originally written to suggest ways in which dyslexic students could make the most of their college careers. College careers will hopefully lead on to professional careers – for many students, including in particular those studying for medical, teaching and social work degrees, their courses will include compulsory professional placements (**see note 21.1**). This book therefore closes with some brief guidelines for the student on applying for jobs and on dyslexia in the workplace. There is also some advice for tutors on writing references for their students.

This is a general chapter. There have been many books written for dyslexic adults (**see note 21.2**) and there is increasing understanding generally about the challenges that the workplace can pose for them and the people they work with, along with a growing appreciation of the qualities and abilities that they may bring to their work (**see note 21.3**).

The number of dyslexic graduates has risen massively since 1986, when the first edition of *Dyslexia at College* was published (**see Chapter 5**), and it is very likely therefore that many employers will come across dyslexic employees. DEG recently met someone who, on hearing that she worked with dyslexic students, said, 'really good people to have on a team ... they very often come up with good ideas ... they seem to have a different insight and can offer a different perspective on problem solving'. Another employer we know has a small business and he has taken on a recent graduate who is dyslexic: he describes this employee as, 'very methodical; he always carries a notebook and writes everything down; he uses coloured papers, and plastic overlays, and often supplements his notes with sketches'.

Most encouragingly, there are statistics which suggest that there is very little difference between the success of graduates with dyslexia in the job market – or in continuing with their studies at master's or PhD level – and that of their non-dyslexic colleagues (**see note 21.4**). What is even more encouraging, both for potential employees and their employers, is that there is now much more support available. This comes in many forms – not least of which is the protection of the law.

THE LAW

We have already talked about the Disability Discrimination Act (DDA) as it affects education (**see Chapter 5**). The DDA (1995) was first introduced to give rights to disabled people in work or when applying for a job. Those with dyslexia have protection under the Act (**see note 21.5**), and it is now unlawful for an employer to discriminate against people who are disabled by:

- treating them less favourably because they are disabled (so, for example, it would be unlawful for your job application to be rejected simply on the grounds that you are dyslexic);

- failing to make reasonable adjustments to remove barriers in the way of their doing the job if they would be substantially disadvantaged without the adjustments.

So, protection is there. Although the chances are that you will never need to resort to the law, you will benefit from the increased awareness and creation of opportunities that have come along with these changes as more employers become aware of their duties under the Act.

EMPLOYERS

Some employers display a 'disability symbol' (a green circle with two ticks and the slogan 'positive about disabled people', **see note 21.6**) to show they have made certain commitments to employing disabled people: one of these is to interview all disabled job applicants, so long as they meet the minimum criteria for the job. Many of these employers belong to the Employers' Forum on Disability, whose members are looking for ways to improve opportunities in work for disabled people (**see note 21.7**). They may have benefited from specialist input about dyslexia in the workplace from training consultants who can offer training and advice, both to employers and employees, about making adjustments which will not only be dyslexia-friendly but also often make good sense for everyone in the workforce (**see note 21.8**).

ACCESS TO WORK

Further and very practical support may come through a scheme called Access to Work (AtW). Through this, workplace assessments can be arranged so that recommendations can be made for helpful strategies and adjustments. The scheme can fund the purchase of equipment and specialist software, as well as a range of other support that might be recommended to enable you to carry out your work to the best of your ability (**see note 21.9**).

An example of someone who benefited from AtW is one of our ex-students. She had a workplace assessment when she started a new job which involved interviewing people and recording data on a computer: through the AtW scheme, money was given to her employers to pay for a digital recorder (so that she did not need to worry about taking notes when she was interviewing people) and a flat screen for her computer (she found a shiny screen was more difficult to read from). **(See Fiona Zinovieff's experience of AtW in Appendix IV.)**

There is a huge amount of advice and information available now in this area; the websites of Skill (the National Bureau for Students with Disabilities) and the British Dyslexia Association (BDA) carry links to further useful sites. The information we have given you here is intended as a brief overview or starting point so that you are aware of the support that is available. However, even before all this becomes relevant, students need to start thinking about what they want to do; this is not always easy when you are thinking about final exams, but it is just as important.

THINKING AHEAD

Some of you will already be certain about what career you are aiming for; you are the lucky ones as you will be clearer than your fellow students about what to do next to achieve your goal. More of you, though, will still be wondering about what to do and where to go next. This can be a difficult time for any graduating student and, like all students, you have to think hard about what career will suit you best. There are several questions that you can ask yourself:

- What interests and motivates me?

- Where do my strengths lie?

- What sort of tasks do I find most difficult and stressful?

- What has my experience so far taught me about the work I might be happiest doing?

- Where can I go for advice?

Everyone will have their own answers to these questions; but one thing that is important for all students to think about is that they will be likely to be happiest in a job that neither over-challenges nor under-challenges them.

Take every opportunity to look around and ask for advice. If the Careers Advisory Service in your college has not already contacted you by the end of your second year, take the initiative and contact them. You will be surprised by the help they can offer and the careers they might suggest – and it will be made clear to you that this service will still be available to you for a number of years after you have graduated. Be prepared, though, to explain to advisers how your dyslexia affects you, so that they are clear from the start what sort of work would enable you to make the most of your abilities.

MAKING APPLICATIONS

The Careers Adviser will also be able to help you with making applications and putting together a CV (**see note 21.10**). As a student you will have developed strategies for managing dyslexia and you will have shown the determination and organisational skills needed to take a degree. Before you fill in an application form, you should list the positive qualities and skills that you have gained through your time at college. Your CV should cover anything positive related to job applications and skills developed, from course requirements, work placements, social responsibilities, holiday jobs and so on. You should adapt, or tweak, each application – and maybe also your CV – so that it presents you in the best light with respect to the particular job you are applying for.

Most application forms will be electronically submitted, but some employers still prefer personally written versions. In that case it is essential to have the application form photocopied; do practice drafts to see how much you can fit into the spaces provided, and get them checked and checked again. Do check the instructions for filling in the form: you may be asked to use black ink, for example, so that it can be clearly photocopied. Keep a copy of your application form and CV to read over before any interview so that you can cover any questions which may arise in connection with what you have written. There may be some stringent questions that you have to answer in front of an interview panel.

DISCLOSING DYSLEXIA

Some application forms ask you directly if you have a disability; others may refer to specific learning difficulties, for example dyslexia; others again may ask questions, perhaps confusingly, about health issues; there may also be application forms that give you no opportunity at all to disclose dyslexia.

If there is a direct question about disability, you will need to think hard if you are reluctant to disclose dyslexia. If you believe that your dyslexia will in no way affect your work, you may be tempted not to mention it. However, you cannot predict with total certainty how your job will develop, and if you do not disclose your dyslexia at the start, you may find yourself in a very difficult situation if you later, for some reason, need to disclose it; and of course, at this stage, your employer may find it difficult to consider any adjustments which might benefit you.

If there is no space on an application form to disclose dyslexia, you could include a reference to it in your CV or in the covering letter, or you may decide to wait until you have an interview. Do remember that some employers guarantee an interview for any applicant who has disclosed a disability.

The important thing is that you should not assume that potential employers will react unfavourably if you tell them about your dyslexia. If you really feel strongly that you do not want others to know that you are dyslexic, you can ask for the information to be kept confidential so that it is not passed on without your permission.

Most importantly, the earlier you disclose, the more control you have over the way that this information is presented (**see note 21.11**). We advise students to practise using the wording 'I am dyslexic, *and* ...' rather than thinking in terms of 'I am dyslexic, *but*...'. Remembering that everyone is different, think how many positive ways *you* can complete the sentence 'I am dyslexic, and ...'. You can:

Stress your abilities:

- I am dyslexic and I have an unusual/original approach to solving problems.

- I am dyslexic and this means I am very good at thinking about 'the big picture' and seeing the overall pattern of a project or scheme.

- I am dyslexic and I have strong visual skills (**see note 21.12**).

Stress how your experience of being dyslexic has shaped you:

- I am dyslexic and because of this I have needed really to think about and develop strategies to overcome any difficulties I meet.

- I am dyslexic and I have learned to be very determined and persistent in terms of tackling my workload at college.

- I am dyslexic and this means that I have needed to be extra-organised with my work and with time management.

- I am dyslexic and so I am very experienced in using computers

- I am dyslexic and I have had to develop effective people-management skills.

- I am dyslexic and I have therefore had to get used to working very hard to achieve my aims!

As we have emphasised, it is important to think positively about your skills and what you have achieved. Gerber *et al.* (1992) compare two groups of dyslexic adults in terms of their success in employment. The major factor determining success was the ability of an individual to take control of their life. This involved having clear goals, knowing how to bring them about and being adaptable if a problem arises. This was illustrated by one of our ex-students, now a junior trainee in a large company, who found that he was drowning in paperwork: he designed his own briefcase with colour coding and trained himself in filing his paperwork every night. He thus began to feel that he was back in control.

INTERVIEWS

Again, your university Careers Advisers or dyslexia tutors will be able to give you advice here, and there is plenty of general guidance available **(see note 21.13)**. **You need to spend some time preparing for an interview.**

- Think about possible questions and ask someone to give you some practice in answering them.

- If you are asked to give a short presentation – these are increasingly part of job interviews – prepare carefully and get in plenty of practice.

- If you are very nervous (and most of us have interview nerves), think of the presentation positively as something that you can control and which gives you the opportunity to highlight your strengths.

- Be prepared to talk about your dyslexia (you can make this interesting – do not assume that the interviewers will be well informed), and show that you have thought through what your strengths and weaknesses are, what they will mean for this job, what strategies you think you will use, what strategies you have developed in the past and what adjustments you may need.

CHALLENGES IN THE WORKPLACE

How much can we generalise here? Just as every dyslexic person is different, so are jobs, and even the same job may be more or less challenging depending on the nature of the workplace, the expectations and attitudes of colleagues, the support available and so on.

What can be said with some certainty is that as you move into the workplace the picture will have changed again for you, just as it did when you moved from school to college. Only a few occupations involve exams – *that* particular pressure will be behind you – but the expectations of others regarding your day-to-day performance, along with your own expectations of yourself, may mean that you are under a different sort of pressure for much of the time. As a student you are mostly free to manage your work in your own time, at your own pace and in your own space; the workplace does not usually afford you that freedom.

Of course, this is something that faces all new graduates, whether dyslexic or not. We do know from talking to our ex-students, however, that, for many of them, anxieties about failing may be heightened by issues with learning to manage new workloads under what seems like constant pressure. This is especially so in environments where there may be interruptions, distractions, changes and unexpected new demands on your time.

Not surprisingly, therefore, cracking the issue of 'organisation and time management' may be critical. Our experience confirms what McLoughlin *et al.* (2002, p. 205) have to say concerning such challenges facing dyslexic people in the workplace. They list that the main challenges are:

- organisation

- overload of work

- time management and work prioritisation.

It is not the intention here to frighten you – but to be forewarned is to be forearmed, and there are plenty of strategies that you can use to meet these and other challenges, including those strategies suggested by McLoughlin and his colleagues (2002). As one of our ex-students told us: 'I'm at an advantage over many non-dyslexics – I've had to develop strategies in the past, I'm not afraid of hard work and I'm not afraid to look for advice when I need it.'

Turn to the back of this book and look at what some of our ex-students have written about their experiences since leaving

Bangor. In particular, Fiona Zinovieff and Emily Newbury have some very practical advice about managing dyslexia in the workplace.

FOR THE TUTOR: WRITING REFERENCES FOR DYSLEXIC STUDENTS

This section is mainly directed at tutors who may be asked to write references for their dyslexic students. However, it may also be of interest to the students themselves.

In a reference, referees have a duty to be both honest and fair. They may be asked *specific* questions, in which case they must obviously answer truthfully to the best of their knowledge. They may also be asked *general* questions, in which case they should do their best to give as fair and balanced a view of the student as possible; this should demonstrate the student's strengths and achievements, while also indicating any limitations that are relevant to the job being applied for.

Applicants are not obliged to reveal a disability to their employer or potential employer unless they are asked a specific question. In this sense, disability is private and the individual may refuse permission for the referee to disclose any information. However, employers, in order to meet their obligations under the DDA, may decide that they need to know whether an employee has any disability, and are thus entitled to take appropriate steps to encourage (not force) a disclosure.

At college, dyslexic students have the right to confidentiality, and must give permission before their dyslexia is revealed to any third party. At the same time, those providing references have a duty to be truthful and not to mislead prospective employers or those making selection for further training. In general, referees should not disclose any disability without the student's agreement. The only way that this situation can be resolved is for the referee to consult the applicant regarding the wording of the reference where dyslexia is concerned.

If a referee feels that it is essential to mention dyslexia, she should make this clear to the student and seek the student's permission. The student is entitled to refuse permission, and consequently the referee would be entitled to decline to supply a reference.

Referees are entitled to state that, in their opinion, the applicant is not suitable for the post in question; but it would be unethical for a referee to refer to the student's dyslexia in a negative light. As well as indicating briefly the student's strengths and limitations, the reference could also cover aspects of the student's dyslexia that may benefit from adjustments, assistance and/or training during employment.

The student's positive attributes should be mentioned in the reference. Dyslexic students who have progressed successfully through higher education will have developed a range of strategies for managing dyslexia. The reference should mention how the student works, and how these strategies may be used in employment. Above all, it should acknowledge that the student's achievement so far is evidence of his or her high motivation, persistence and determination against the odds.

CHECK POINTS FOR CHAPTER 21

With the increasing awareness of dyslexia, and acknowledgement of the strengths and talents dyslexic employees may bring with them, there are more dyslexic graduates in the workplace than ever before.

- Changes to the law mean that there is protection for dyslexic employees and job applicants against unfair discrimination.

- Employers have a duty to make reasonable adjustments to remove barriers in the way of dyslexic employees doing their jobs.

- Groups such as the Employers' Forum on Disability are looking for ways in which to include and enable disabled workers.

- The Access to Work scheme provides support in the workplace (employers and their dyslexic employees can benefit through this).

- Dyslexic students should look for careers which will neither over-challenge nor under-challenge them.

- There is plenty of advice available on choosing careers and on making job applications.

- The issue of disclosing dyslexia should be carefully considered: without disclosure there cannot be adjustment or support.

- Interviews give applicants the chance to show how they have developed positive and useful strategies to deal with dyslexia.

- Overall, organisation and time management are likely to be the greatest challenges for dyslexic employees in the workplace.

Tutors writing references for dyslexic students need to be honest and fair: they can usefully refer to the qualities and strategies that have helped the students to succeed in their degree studies.

Appendices

Believing that this book would be enhanced if it contained contributions from ex-students who were themselves dyslexic, we invited contributions. In the first edition these contributions were from Andrew Bullock, Colin Wilsher, Simon Batty and Stephen Martin. In the second edition we included a contribution from Fiona Zinovieff, while in the third edition we have also included contributions from Rose Wilsher, daughter of Colin, and Emily Newbury.

We have carried out the minimum amount of editing: we considered it better that these ex-students should speak for themselves in their own way. We are grateful to the British Dyslexia Association for giving us permission to reprint Fiona's article, *Working with Dyslexia*, which first appeared in the *BDA Handbook* for 2005. Thank you again to all our contributors.

APPENDIX I – WORK ORGANISATION, ESSAY WRITING AND EXAMINATION TECHNIQUES

A.B. Bullock, BA, MEd

Work organization

Planning time: At the outset, it should be remembered that several shorter stints of work are much more efficient than one longer session, which is often counterproductive. Thus it is better to work for shorter periods, but each day. Even pauses of five to ten minutes will restore attention. However, if this does not work, I have found through experience that there is little point in sitting over books in a dazed mood not getting on with reading them. So I will often change and do something completely different, or even take a 'power nap' of up to an hour but no longer. It is also efficient to take a day completely off current work. (I was always very active on Sundays but I set them aside for different activities. Now that is my working day!)

Many dyslexics glean much of what they know from listening to others. I became astute at asking questions of specific people who could answer my questions. At university I learnt so much more from lectures than reading books. Lectures, however, may well be a waste of time unless efficient notes are taken; and unless they are well taken, re-reading them can be well nigh impossible. I found that it was possible to learn simply by organising my ideas onto paper. Each student will function differently, but I certainly learnt more if I had made good notes, even if I didn't re-read them! Furthermore, having made a good set of notes, I can skim them and remind myself of the contents of the lectures in a brief space of time.

I found that the textbooks simply served to consolidate what I had learned from listening. Some books I have only read once; others I wish to re-read in order to learn and remember what I have learnt. I found that if I own them, which is expensive, then I can mark the books in such a way as to bring out the important points. Thus I make notes or underline in red, black, blue or green, scoring through words or lines with a yellow highlighting pen in order to make the words stand out. (I have found that Edding 1800 pens excellent for this because the ink does not bleed through even the thin paper of a Bible.) I find that I can simply scan the passage later and immediately be reminded of the key points that the author was getting at.

The other very useful tactic is the use of filing cards, especially when I don't own the original material. On these I can write the author, title, date and publisher for immediate reference. Card references may be made on books, articles, newspaper articles, experimental data or simply useful ideas for filing. Nowadays they can be computerised as well as being in a filing tray. It is a good idea if the card has on it the main gist of the book, results and then one's own ideas. Not only does the card concentrate one's own interpretation of the work, making one think of the main points that the author wished to put forward or portray, but it also helps me to remember the facts. It is vitally important that no more than the bare essentials are included. If more is required, one will need to go back to the original. Later on, I find that I can easily go back through all I have read and literally 'shuffle' the different points into a relevant sequence. Much of my 'brain work' is thereby accomplished on single filing cards. My card filing system, although limited by comparison with a modern computer, was a very fast access system. I could easily look up in one tray of cards all that I had read on my subject.

So having taken the information in and put it upon cards, I simply sorted it, reorganised it and added my own part. I then reproduced it, which was one way of 'essay writing'.

Essay writing

When I spoke to a group of dyslexic undergraduates, they insisted that their problem was not so much the organisation of their thoughts as the inability to convey the ideas in a way that reads well. Typical comments were: 'I know what I want to say but it never comes out on paper as I mean it to', 'You know you are as good as someone else, but you always do badly on paper' and 'It's getting it down that's the problem.'

My own hypothesis is that the writer may know what he wishes to say but that he may assume too much from his reader. He assumes that the reader knows the background or that he can guess it from a few words. One trouble with that is that those few words are not 'well picked words'. Thus what a brilliant author can convey in one neat sentence the dyslexic will need a complete paragraph. This can be exasperating. Even then, his reader may not follow what he wishes to say. The situation may not be helped by incorrect spelling or grammar or even not quite the correct word. However, in reality, it may be more likely that the point is inadequately presented; that is, that it is in one short sentence without any surrounding explanation. The dyslexic assumes that the reader will 'understand'.

Sadly, misunderstanding is often the case. Personal letters come back saying: 'I did not quite see what you were getting at' – when you thought that it was plain. Essays are returned with comments such as: 'Keep to the point.'

Thus, to avoid the reader having to follow the dyslexic's mental acrobatics, almost everything needs to be 'spelled out'. New points in the argument must be introduced, and one needs to couch the idea in suitable language. While writing, one must constantly keep the idea in mind that the reader does not know what one is talking about. Some idea which may never have occurred to other people may be pertinent to the argument. Putting it down in the middle of an essay will not convince anyone, even if they can understand it. The idea may even need a separate paragraph. This is a tedious way round the problem as writing is taxing enough without having to insert even more 'useless sentences'. However, it really is the only way to make others understand. (I have only found it possible through typing. I actually went to classes to touch type, which has been invaluable. I'm not sure if typing helps with spelling, but it certainly reduces the number of times I have to look while copying, like that awful experience of looking up at a black board for almost every letter of a difficult word, when anyone else takes in the whole word at one quick look. When I started to type, instead of having adverse comments on my essays, I began to get compliments!)

So the planning needs to be done in order that all the relevant points are included in the most appropriate order. It has been suggested that one might use a tape recorder in the process of essay writing. Having tried this method very briefly, I have doubts as to its usefulness. It is not easy to 'see' what has just been written. Furthermore, it is slow to transcribe. I have tried using voice recognition, but found it so much slower. The computer will type a word which sounds the same as a mistyped or misspelled one, but means something quite different. The result is that, on re-reading, my understanding is completely thrown by the changed word.

However, having once drafted out one's work, it may well help to see where it is lacking, by reading it onto tape and then listening to it!

In preparing an essay, it is helpful to take a rough sheet of paper and jot down in a list all the points that may be worth including. Ideas naturally come out in a haphazard order and thus need sorting. To do this I use either letters or numbers in order to group the ideas which should be included in the same section. Then the ordering of sections needs to take place so as to lead to a coherent essay. As I think about what is involved, so I think of more good ideas. With this system, these may easily be added right up to the place of the section finally being written. If I don't plan but simply write, new ideas become a clumsy insertion, which can be difficult to justify or rearrange neatly. To number pages as they are written is helpful.

Having once written it out, I go back through it, correcting as I feel fit. Although it is often nerve-wracking, I sometimes ask a friend to go through what I have written in order to correct the spellings and grammar or to make other suggestions. It will then need rewriting. This may happen two or three times in order that it may read properly. It is encouraging to know that even experienced authors may do this when writing books. This naturally is where typing is of extreme value, as it is so much quicker. One simply needs to look at what is being copied, not back and forth through the handwritten drafts. It is not only quicker but also substantially less tiring. Nowadays, word-processing packages greatly help this process.

Examination techniques

In the following section some of the special problems encountered in exams will be discussed: having to choose quickly which questions to answer, a lack of time to prepare answers, not being able to re-write what you have written and then the time pressure – all contribute to make exams difficult, especially when important outcomes are dependent upon the results. Thus exam technique is quite different from normal essay writing. In the group of dyslexics studied, worry was not necessarily a problem although, had it been, that would be very understandable. What is important is to get on with the task in hand, without letting one's mind wander due to the plethora of decisions to be made and so wasting time. I used to divide up the time available and mark my watch, so that I allowed the same amount of preparation time, writing time and re-reading time to each question – and stick to it, even if I hadn't finished that question.

Should the exam be an internal one, marked by tutors from the department, then it is important that one should get to know the tutors. Attendance at tutorials is important so that the tutors become aware that, although the answers may not be neatly expressed, the thinking behind them is probably very logical. Hence they will give you the benefit of the doubt, knowing how you would reply should they ask for further explanation.

Thus before starting, allow time to read the whole paper through completely. Exams often come in sections. The examinee is requested to answer so many questions from each section. It is important to follow this request, as otherwise if too many questions are answered from one of the sections, no marks will be gained from those not required. One must then either think which questions one can most easily answer – or which one knows least about. If two questions appear equally challenging, simply pick one, forget the other and get on with your choice. This procedure may be usefully practised prior to the exam by taking past papers and going out on a boat or punt or into the country to consider how you might best answer it!

Before answering each question try to plan out your answer. Use a scheme similar to the one for writing a formal essay but naturally abbreviate it by cutting the time on each part of the execution of the plan. Thus jot down ideas for an answer (remembering that trying to cover too much will result in a poorer answer), and order the ideas so as to make a logical sequence. If further points occur, it would probably be best to forget them unless one includes them in a skeleton continuation of a reply. Then write out your answer. It may be appropriate to allow time to draft out for the examiner how you would see the writing continuing had you had more time. It is important to allow sufficient time to read through your answer.

Some glaring errors may be spotted and corrected or, if time is too short, pointed out so that at least you are aware of them!

While in the middle of the exam, or any other work, concentrate upon the answer undertaken at that moment. Much valuable time can be expended by allowing one's mind to wander to a later question to be answered. Should, as so often happens, some good idea occur, then write it down in two or three words only on a separate note. It will then be a reminder of your thoughts when you come to that point. In the meantime you have not become distracted by this alien thought. I still do this even though I no longer take exams!

Finally, enjoy life at all times – even when waiting for your exam results!

Up to date – 20 years on

Following my MEd, I went into teaching. I found that working in the educational system meant that I was working with other teachers whose skills were frequently different from mine. Sadly, in order to get the most out of their department, they should have re-evaluated the skills of each member and reorganised job descriptions to fit the people, but I have found that one of my strengths – that of thinking outside the usual boxes – is often a problem. Sadly, people are sometimes threatened by having their preconceptions questioned.

My most interesting teaching work was teaching basic education in prison. There were clearly many prisoners who had had early learning experiences which contributed to their eventually being in prison. When testing them for dyslexia, I found that they had often masked their typical dyslexic difficulties, and so I would have liked to have tested their children, something which wasn't possible for me to do. While working in the prison, I was also teaching in primary schools, and I could see children drop out of there and reappear in the prison, where they then asked for help.

I tried several times to be accepted for an educational psychology course but was pipped at the post. When I once gave a lecture on the theory of intelligence tests to occupational psychologists, I found that, although I understood the theory, strictly speaking I was not qualified to administer the test, which was the reverse for them!

I have now retrained and become a parish vicar, which requires me to use my weaker verbal skills extensively. I could not work without being able to type onto a computer. I use mind-maps extensively for preaching or for funeral addresses (Visimap–Coco systems). It is so easy to rearrange what I want to say and it forces me not to write everything down verbatim. My other great fortune is to be married to someone who can support me, check my writings and work alongside in order to get them right, and, indeed, I now have four sons who can correct my work and support me as well.

APPENDIX II – DYSLEXIA IN MY LIFE

S.J. Martin, BSc, PhD, DSc

Discovery of dyslexia

After failing my O-level English language for the second time my mother forced me to go to private lessons in an attempt to improve my English. I needed English O level to enter university, and it was my private English teacher who, after reading an article on dyslexia in a popular woman's magazine, realised that I may be dyslexic. Despite this my school's headmistress refused to arrange to have me tested for dyslexia, saying that I was just lazy and not trying hard enough. However, via a series of friends we contacted the local Head of Education and he arranged a series of tests at school, which showed that I was dyslexic. I was nearly 18 years old. Only now did I realise why nobody could ever solved the crossword I used to do for the school magazine.

Sixth form

Even after I was confirmed dyslexic, little changed at school as some teachers believed that I now used dyslexia as an excuse. On the third attempt I passed my O-level English mainly through luck as

I had to write an essay on 'Your experiences with nature' and I had lots of them. My A-level Examination Board informed the school that no concessions would be given to dyslexics, except they would remark my paper if I was borderline between pass and fail. I was the only student to fail General Studies; this I attribute largely to not reading books or newspapers as I found reading difficult and always lost interest. In my other exams – maths, chemistry and biology – I managed to write very little and instead used lots of diagrams, equations and formulae to explain things; this is possible to a large degree in science subjects. Much to my headmistress's surprise I managed to get the required grades to enter university (Bangor) as well as having a very enjoyable sixth-form life.

University: the first two years

I welcomed the freedom that university offered, but as the workload increased I began to have difficulties in keeping pace with the other students. I spent lots of my spare time rewriting lecture notes, as these consisted of only a few key words which needed filling out. This was a time-consuming task which I did for my entire university life. I didn't mention my dyslexia and kept on trying harder but my marks were generally poor. So with nothing to lose I went along to a small dyslexics meeting at college. The meetings were informal affairs, mainly talking about problems and ways in which they could be solved. This resulted in my talking to my college tutor about my problems, and things started to improve. But the most valuable service was offered: a 24-hour free advice and help service which was always a great relief to me and other dyslexics. After starting my second term at college things greatly improved. Near the end of the second year I decided I needed a brain rest. I had also been asked to complete some work on forest birds. So I took the opportunity and asked my tutor if I could have a year's leave. As this is very unusual it caused a few problems but with advice from the Dyslexia Unit and full understanding of the situation by my tutor I was granted a year's leave.

The year off

Early winter was spent working on a remote Scottish island, spring working in a forest on birds and summer in China. I also did A-level geology at night-school. I kept in contact with college for advice on my work. Dyslexia lay very low that year as I had very little formal writing or reading to do. The year soon passed and I returned to college with a much more relaxed attitude and wider outlook on life in general.

The final year

Going back to college was easy as many of my old friends were still living in Bangor. Many of my teachers knew me on a personal basis and were very understanding and tried to help in various ways. The final year was more emphasis on development and expanding on ideas given in lectures. This suited me well and it was easy to keep up. I always listened to music while working as it helped me relax and work long periods (up to one hour) without a break. I settled down to my exams with a strong will to succeed. I now knew enough about exam technique from other dyslexics and teachers to devise my own method. This basically consisted of considering each teacher's exam separately and tailoring my exam essay to suit that person. I then wrote lots of practice essays and discussed them with the relevant teachers to refine the technique. This also allowed a personal contact between me and the department staff. Just before the exams the department decided to give me an extra hour for each three-hour exam if I wanted it. I was also able to do my exams in a small room which had a very relaxed atmosphere. I was rewarded with a good degree (upper second), and I had done it despite having been classed as almost illiterate for most of my school life. I had never read a book of fiction or fact and all my study was done directly from scientific papers and then I only read the summary. I consider my success at college to be due to four main factors: (1) my genuine interest in the subject, (2) my year's break, (3) the Dyslexia Unit, which helped at both personal and higher levels, and (4) the help from my department and especially my tutor.

After college

After college had ended I kept working and had my first research published, which was very satisfying even though it was only one page. After a trip to Nepal I was awarded a research scholarship to Japan and had to attend language school to learn Japanese for about four months. Learning Japanese was very difficult, as the major problem was not dyslexia but the lack of a formal English education. I still don't fully understand nouns, verbs, pronouns etc. I passed all my Japanese language exams except sentence pattern and construction. As my workload was light, so for the first time I started to read books – mainly translations of famous Japanese novels, as the words are simple and in big print and the chapters are short. In Japan I work mainly on my own through the medium of English, and when I write the dictionary and typewriter are my best friends. Even though I am dyslexic and always have to fight against the system, I have been rewarded for my determination. I take all the advice and help I can get and never let anyone look down on me.

Studying in Japan

After language college in Osaka, I was placed in a rural agricultural university deep in the mountains of central Japan to carry out studies into high-altitude beetles. I was the first Western student to attend the university, and my Japanese improved quickly.

I did an MSc (by research) course, which meant no lectures, tutorials etc. The research was mainly carried out independently high up in the Japanese Alps. During my spare time, I studied the biology of the local hornets with some mountain farmers. I achieved my first major scientific publication but not without a major struggle. I thought I could write it without outside help and it was returned three times from the journal to be rewritten. I almost didn't bother in the end, which may have been the beginning of the end of my scientific career. However, it was eventually accepted and reading the final printed version I realised how right the referees were after all. That was the first and last manuscript I sent off without getting it checked first.

The writing of my MSc thesis was a tricky job, but I managed to substitute a lot of charts, graphs and tables in place of written words. None of the examiners corrected the grammar in what little I did write in my thesis since they were far too polite and after all I was English and so must be right! I left Japan after three wonderful years to return to the UK and no job.

After Japan

I continued to write up my hornet and beetle research, which led naturally into submitting my hornet data as a PhD. However, the prospect of writing a several-inch-thick book was a nightmare; a three-hour essay was bad enough. I talked the idea over with the Zoology Department at Bangor and it was decided that I could do it part-time with a time limit of nine years. This was my cup of tea, since I could now work at my pace. I, of course, had to fund it but I registered and wondered what I had let myself in for.

Falkland Islands and a book

Around this time I was fortunately offered a job in the Falklands by a climber friend as a scientific officer on the fishing boats. This would earn me some money and provided me with plenty of spare time for my next project. I flew south with a case full of notes, maps and papers and my portable Japanese word processor. In between measuring and sexing squid and fish I wrote an English hiking guide to the Japanese Alps. This was hard work but great fun.

Unfortunately the various publishers liked the guide but said it would not have big enough sales to merit printing it. So it sits on a shelf at home waiting until I have some time to publish myself with the aid of computers.

Back to college

Now having the funds and renewed enthusiasm for my hornet work, I returned to Bangor University to tackle my PhD. After many discussions and careful reading of the college rules we realised it was possible for me to submit my thesis as a series of papers, published or not, as long as they were sandwiched between an introduction, methods and a discussion. This was of great help to me since now each piece of work was a small free-standing unit. I had become better at writing papers and had built up a network of colleagues who would check them for errors. These included continued support from my supervisors, Head of Department and Dyslexia Unit that had made it all possible. Fortunately the final exam is oral, my preferred medium.

Back to Japan

Within a week of obtaining my doctorate I was flying out to Japan funded by a Royal Society/Japan Society post-doc. research fellowship. This enabled me to continue my hornet research. This time I studied a rare species only found on the remote sub-tropical islands 1,000 km south of mainland Japan. Fortunately, my Japanese girlfriend, later to become my wife, accompanied me down to the island. This greatly reduced the language problem. There we spent over two years studying hornets, writing papers and diving on the coral reefs which ringed the island.

Back to college, again!

Before leaving Japan I was awarded another Royal Society grant, which allowed me to return to the UK and develop my ideas and write up my research. So it was another year in sunny Bangor working on my Japanese word processor (no spellchecker) churning out the papers and developing my hornet models. I still relied heavily on colleagues to check my work before submission to journals.

After the funding ran out I started to apply for more funding and jobs. We had our first child now, and so, being responsible parents, with no jobs in sight we took off for a six-month trip to the Far East. Based in Singapore we visited Malaysia and Borneo, where I collected hornet data, visited friends in Taiwan and relatives in Japan and returned to our island to go diving again. When the money ran out, we returned the UK and I applied for jobs and wrote up the new hornet data.

National Bee Unit

A month after returning to the UK I was offered a job doing research and development for the National Bee Unit. The work was based in Devon, well away from the main offices, and concerned the study of the parasitic honeybee mite, varroa. There was more paperwork in this job than any other I had done. But I also had a powerful computer with spellchecker and grammar-checker. I now never write anything without using the computer. It has speeded the whole process of writing enormously – I cannot imagine how I ever managed without it. I had an assistant who I delegated most of the letter writing, memos etc. to. However, I ran into major difficulties within the civil services when I was relocated to their main offices. My need to listen to music was seen as antisocial and the wearing of head-phones a health and safety issue. So for the first time since secondary school I had to take on a small group of ignorant bosses. I had to be retested for dyslexia and, since people's general awareness of dyslexia is much greater now, my bosses were told that I needed my music and my own room. This I was begrudgingly given, but unfortunately I never became an integrated member and my health deteriorated as my bosses made my life as difficult as possible.

Back to university, for the last time?

Although I was a successful scientist I was not a good civil servant and after seven years I moved back into university. My health quickly improved and I started to enjoy my research again. I got into a small highly motivated group of researches at Sheffield University, who were more than willing to correct my grammar and make constructive comments about my work. This is something that I had really struggled with in the civil services. I continued to conduct high-end research at the university and publish regularly.

During 2006 another milestone was achieved when I put together a collection of my 75 best publications. This formed my thesis, which contained over 550 pages of published research and for this I was award my senior doctorate (DSc). Looking back, I am so pleased that I persevered with those early papers and accepted the help of my friends and colleagues. Strangely the subject of my dyslexia rarely if ever comes up now, how times have changed for the better.

APPENDIX III – PROBLEMS WITH DYSLEXIA

S. Batty, BSc, MSc, PhD

School

When I entered my secondary school, I was automatically put in the bottom class. This was because my work wasn't of a very high standard: I could hardly read and could hardly write. I wasn't very good at maths; so consequently I was put in the bottom streams and not expected to do well. When I got to the fourth year, with it being a secondary school, most people went and did CSEs, and very few did O levels; the ones that weren't considered up to CSE standard were helped with remedial lessons, especially in English. I was immediately put into these remedial English lessons, and this is really where I learned to read, although it wasn't an awful lot of help apart from learning to read. I was put in for most of the CSEs, which I didn't work for, one reason being that I was told I was so stupid anyhow that I wouldn't get any qualifications. So, thinking that, I believed there was no point in doing any work anyway.

When I was 16, I got five CSEs. All of them were very low grades, fours and fives. I decided to carry on into the sixth form, at which point I was told I was so stupid I would never get any higher than CSEs and there was no point in staying on. But my mother forced the school to get in touch with the educational psychologist, who then tested me and found that I was dyslexic. Apart from then getting one or two extra English lessons with help from somebody who wasn't trained really in special English – and certainly not dyslexia – I got no other help from them at all. I proceeded to work through my sixth form doing O levels and one A level. I left the school with one O-level pass in biology.

On leaving school, I went to a College of Further Education. Here the staff were a lot more helpful. I was immediately put on a course of five O levels. Whether they expected me to pass or not they weren't sure at the time. They certainly didn't expect me to pass my maths or English. By the end of the year I had proved them wrong: I got my O-level maths, though my English was proving very difficult to get, and it meant hard work. I didn't get very much help in the O-level years, except that the college was very strict anyway, and you had to work. Then I set about doing three A levels and the general studies A level. This involved an awful lot of hard work (except for general studies where very little was required), but I did manage to get the A levels. I got help from lecturers giving me extra work, and marking that work for me, and I was given extra English lessons as well, both inside the college and outside the college. Inside the college the lessons really consisted of remedial English on one evening per week.

When I started my second year of A levels, I went to Lilian Henley, who was also in Northwich and who is a specialist dyslexia teacher. She helped very greatly indeed. And finally in the second year, that's the year I got my A levels, I got my O-level English; this was after seven attempts, every summer and every November since I left school! The work needed to get the A levels was specifically designed so that I could understand what I was doing; it wasn't designed just to learn the work, but to be learned in such a fashion that it had to be fully understood. This meant going over and over and over the work many, many times so that you got a full understanding of it.

The reason behind this was that if I was doing a section of work for the exams then I would be less liable to make a mistake because I understood what was happening, and, for it to work, all the parts you were doing would have to tie up, and, if it didn't in the end, you knew that you had made a mistake somewhere and you would go back and recheck it. I think that this did help quite considerably, but it did mean an awful lot of extra work for me to do. It meant many, many hours of revision; it meant no holidays for two years; it meant not going out for two years. But it was, in fact, the only way to get the work out. From here, and all the way through university, of course, the problem was that I knew the work orally well enough, but unfortunately I couldn't write it down, and this is a great handicap. I was supposed to get dispensation from the Examining Boards for my O levels and A levels, but I'm not very sure that this happened, as I believe they only give you dispensation if you fail your exams. As I probably passed them, just, I believe they weren't remarked; and I would have hoped to have got higher marks than I did.

University

The problems involved at university (Bangor) were similar to those found with the A levels, with a few exceptions. First of all, you couldn't work quite in the same style as you could for your A levels, or O levels. Instead of being able to go away and learn the work until you knew it backwards, the work had to be analysed, and I found this very slow going. Not only that; note-taking was erratic, or I could not get notes down, and I was finding I was having to go home and rewrite my entire set of notes in the evening. But, unfortunately, this just wasn't possible and, when I did my revision, time had to be taken up in rewriting the notes so that they were readable and legible. Overall, the problems were similar to those of the A levels in that I could do the oral work very easily indeed, yet the written work was very hard and I used to get very low grades for written work. This in the end led me to get a very low grade of degree indeed. If I hadn't been dyslexic, I would have wished to have got a much higher grade. At the same time I had involvements with the dyslexic department in Bangor, going to the odd meeting and doing tests for psychology students; and I had a number of chats, with Professor Miles especially, when I had great problems, which I certainly had near the end of the third year. This was because I was finding it impossible in many ways to get down the work that they wanted, yet I had an understanding of what they were doing. In the end I managed to get a third-class honours degree, which I'm still not very happy about.

Conclusions

Overall, I have found, over the last few years, that the way to get
my exam passes is to work extremely hard for them, to put in
many, many hours' overtime. One short cut that I have found is to
use symbols to represent phrases or long words. This cuts the time
used for note-taking and revising considerably, and by the end of
my degree I had got quite a set of symbols, which meant groups of
phrases strung together; this helped quite a lot. Another thing I did
which helped improve the readability of my work was to use word
processors to write up projects and coursework. The problem I found
here was that, unfortunately, there were very few word processors
that had scientific symbols on them, so it meant very involved work
just to get scientific symbols out. And, unfortunately, in the degree I
did, I wasn't given much dispensation because the people concerned
felt it very important that my writing skills were up to standard,
with chemistry being a profession.

Even in looking for a job the most important thing seems to be
writing skills. But of course nobody ever tells you that your dyslexia
is the reason why you won't even get an interview, but I suspect
that in a lot of the cases where I have been, or seemed to have been,
ideal for the job, this is why they do not want to give you the job
– because they suspect your reading and writing. Just as passing
exams involved a large amount of extra work so also looking for
jobs is going to be a problem. And it's debatable whether you admit
that you are dyslexic or not when you go for a job interview. It will
be interesting to see how many more interviews I will get if I didn't
admit I was dyslexic on my CV. However, overall, I have found
that if I want to get anywhere I have got to work very hard, but it's
also been very satisfying knowing that I can, and knowing that to a
certain extent my hard work has paid off.

Postscript

Since the first edition of this book, I have managed to follow not only
my chosen career but also had a varied and interesting life. In 1984
I was accepted at the Cranfield Institute of Technology to study for

an MSc in molecular electronics. As I only received a third for my degree, I had to undertake a one-year course on material science, which has subsequently been very useful on many occasions.

On successfully completing my MSc, I was accepted by Sheffield City Polytechnic to work for my PhD. This I completed in four years. The thesis took nine months of intense work to complete, but good planning and attention to detail and support from my parents and tutors made the completion of my PhD comparatively easy.

I then worked at Sheffield University for five years and managed to publish around 40 papers. My work was varied as my molecular electronics background meant I was both a chemist and physicist. I left academia in 1996 as I could not see a future with the university sector, despite being both a successful researcher and lecturer.

As I also have an interest in astronomy, I set up an astronomy centre in Norfolk called Fieldview. This has now been in business for ten years and is very successful. I also teach part time for the University of East Anglia and now also work part time for a company that solves and finds novel solutions to problems in the oil industry. My dyslexia makes me well suited to this as the job requires people who think differently.

Whilst being dyslexic has its obvious disadvantages where reading and writing are concerned, it also gives you some distinct advantages. Because I think differently I have been able to devise novel solutions to problems and because I know I am prone to make mistakes I have devised strategies to check my work. This makes me a careful and diligent researcher. I also have an unusual skill of being able to estimate. For example, the pricing of a task or the flow rate of a liquid can be estimated by just looking at the job. I don't know how this skill works, but time and time again it works.

My path to my goals was not straightforward, but I got there by any means I could. I took a contorted route that most may not think about but on the way I have become skilled in areas I would have never imagined, and these skills have all contributed to making me the kind of person I am. I have found very differing attitudes to dyslexia: yes, there are people who don't care, but in general I have found that once I have shown people I am not stupid they have been very helpful. Anyone with dyslexia who wants to pursue a science background should not be put off, but it does mean hard work and on the way you will probably pick up some strange skills. I have a chemistry degree but if pushed I could probably repair an oil rig or be a Unix network administrator. Rather than seeing dyslexia as a handicap, you should use the fact you think differently because you may be the person that can solve the impossible problem. Remember, some say that Einstein was dyslexic.

APPENDIX IV – A DYSLEXIC'S PROGRESS

Dr Fiona Zinovieff

Studying with dyslexia (1996)

I graduated from Bangor in 1994 with a first-class honours degree in psychology. I am writing this in the hope that others will read this and realise that dyslexic students are at least as good as other students and with a little help we might do even better!

Although my school career was filled with disparaging remarks such as 'Fiona must make more effort with the presentation of her work', 'Fiona's writing and spelling need attention', 'Her work lacks organisation' or 'She is careless', I was not diagnosed as dyslexic until I started university as a mature student. It took 14 years for me to decide to return to education, having decided that my problems at school were probably motivational. Once at college I began to notice that other people could read a page two or three times faster than me (a problem when sharing handouts or computer monitors). I also began to realise that my spelling was a problem. One lecturer told me that she just couldn't read work that was misspelled. A sympathetic tutor referred me to the Dyslexia Unit, where a formal assessment was arranged for me, and I was given information and help.

After I discovered that I was dyslexic, I felt the need to re-evaluate my situation. The good side was that I was to be given an extra grant to purchase a computer for word processing and spellchecking; the down side was that I realised that there were specific limitations on my abilities when I compared myself to others. I had already realised that I did not have the time to copy my lecture notes out in a more legible form, and I was struggling to keep up with the recommended reading, and this was only the first term of a three-year course. Obviously, I needed a survival plan to keep my head above water. The methods that I used to cope with the course are a rationalisation of my limitations and, more importantly, my capabilities.

The benefits that stem from being dyslexic

The most important thing to remember is that there are benefits that stem from being dyslexic. This might not seem immediately obvious so I shall explain. I read very slowly and frequently misread words, so I am constantly checking that what I am reading makes sense. Learning comes with understanding, so by having tried to understand what I am reading I have also been learning. I might read more slowly than non-dyslexic students, but I also read more efficiently. When I am thinking about an essay or a project, I find that my mind races around the problem as I try to relate ideas to what I already know about a subject. By imposing a structure on this and firmly abandoning ideas that are irrelevant to the question, I have often come up with a novel approach to an answer. I think that many dyslexics are good at lateral thinking, whereas the majority of people tend to think linearly. Without mechanically imposing a rigorous structure on a piece of work, this rush of associated ideas can result in confused and disorganised work, because writing is a strictly linear activity. With structure, these ideas can be harnessed to create original answers to old questions. This is an asset in university and can transform a competent answer into a first-class piece of work. In common with many other dyslexics, I find it easy to visualise ideas, and to remember diagrams and pictures. This is an advantage when making mind-maps for essay writing, or learning them for revision.

I have described the advantages first, as it is easy to despair on the bad days when the white spaces on the page dominate and the words won't come. It is important to remember that as a dyslexic my thoughts and ideas are as valid as the next person's, and the majority of my problems are focused on communicating through the written word. Although these problems cannot be solved, strategies for coping can be employed that minimise the workload and produce maximum benefit from the work that is done. I realise that the methods that I found useful might not help everyone, but I would recommend trying them out as they certainly worked for me.

Gathering information

I find it very difficult to scan a page for relevant information. I cannot judge how useful a text or journal paper might be until I have read a lot of it. How to select the most relevant material is a problem, but there are solutions. When faced with a list of books and papers recommended with a course, I found many of the lecturers would help me prioritise the texts. I asked which reading the lecturer would most recommend for each different aspect of their course; this helped me to reduce the list. When purchasing textbooks, I favoured those with good chapter summaries and introductions – I found these very helpful when trying to navigate through a sea of unfamiliar vocabulary and complex ideas. If I could anticipate what I was about to read, I found the process much easier. I found it easier to read and absorb information for writing essays than when I was just reading background material. This is because I was reading with a specific question in mind. This led me to conclude that past exam scripts might hold the key to improving my ability to focus on the background reading. Thus, as I read, I started to see how information could be used to answer certain aspects of different questions. This helped me to pick out the key themes of the courses and led me to appreciate how different ideas can be interlinked. I also found it beneficial to work in a small group with people reading alternative texts; we could then compare the information from different sources and select the most appropriate evidence for our arguments.

A good way of getting a broad and general understanding is to go to lectures – just think how many hours of reading has gone into preparing an hour's talk. Often lecturers provide an opportunity to ask questions, so try to think about the information that is being presented and then ask specific questions if you are having difficulties applying the new information to what you already know. But, however good a lecture might have been on the day, without notes much of it will probably fade or become confused. Initially, I found note-taking a nightmare, and I was trying to copy up my notes into a more presentable form. Within days I realised that this was far too time-consuming, and I should concentrate on making useful notes. After some trial and error, this is the system that evolved. During the lectures, I made an effort to try to print out names and terminology in capital letters, then if my notes were unintelligible I knew what or who I needed to look up in my textbooks. I find acronyms very hard to learn and easy to forget, and so I was wary of using a lot of abbreviations, although I shortened some words by omitting vowels. I used arrows to stand for phrases such as 'developing from this…' and I tried to lay out any comparisons schematically, but often this was impossible in the race to keep up with what is being said. I found it hard to listen and to attend to what I was writing; so I sometimes left gaps that I filled in from someone else's notes at the end of the lecture, or instructions to myself to read about a certain study.

At a later date, often at the end of a block of lectures on a certain subject, I would read through my notes, then insert headings and underline key words and names, then highlight definitive terms. When taking notes, I used broad-lined, wide-margined paper and I only used one side of each page. The margin is useful for adding comments or clarifications, and the wide lines make it easier to add underlining and still read what has been written. Often lecturers give strong hints about topics that are likely to come up in the exams – I noted these in the margin, and this often proved very useful! When I've put the notes into a ring file, there is a blank page beside each page of lecture notes. This has several advantages: brief notes about background reading can be juxtaposed to the related lecture material, the key points and names from each page of notes can be listed clearly and, if during revision these points have lost their meaning, there is a full explanation on the facing page.

When doing my background reading, I made extensive use of the photocopier, partly due to the time limits imposed by the library short-loan system but also because photocopying saved note-taking!

A useful feature of photocopiers is that print can be enlarged, also it is possible to copy onto coloured paper: both can help improve the readability of the text. When reading photocopies, I use a highlight pen to mark the key points so that I can remind myself of the contents without having to re-read it. I did make notes from journal articles that I found very difficult to understand as putting ideas into my own words sometimes helps me to understand.

Planning and writing

Brain-storming is a technique that I found particularly useful for imposing structure on a piece of writing. I started the exercise, after having done the reading, by writing the title of the work at the top of a large sheet of paper. I then dissected the title carefully, to check that I had included the right information and that I could use it to answer the question! Then starting in the middle of the page I wrote down the key points, each in its own bubble. Some points have closely associated ideas which form 'satellite bubbles'. I would then draw arrows between bubbles to link ideas, or use coloured lines to indicate contradictions in the evidence. Usually I found that the links between the ideas gave me a logical sequence to the paragraphs, and allowed me to group related ideas in a more coherent fashion, transforming the explosion of ideas into a logical linear format.

I then write using the word processor. I cannot overstate the value of this machine to me, despite being unable to type when I started the course and being completely computer illiterate. I still can't type properly, but then I get a huge satisfaction from producing legible, well-presented work without the agonies of copying, correcting, re-copying, re-correcting etc. Having entered a piece of writing, it is so easy to alter a sentence or move a paragraph. The spellchecker is invaluable, but not infallible. I have inadvertently added a few of my own spellings to the dictionary, or inserted the wrong word in the place of my misspelt words. I find it very hard to read from the screen and so always print up a rough draft. It is best to let some time elapse before reading it, as this reduces the chances of reading what you think you've written, as opposed to reading what you have really written. At this point I worked with a friend who would read what I had written and correct my spellings and also query any points that were not clearly expressed, and I would do the same for her (bar the spellings). This was a reciprocal arrangement and we both benefited from it. Not only did it improve our writing skills, but we also learned from reading another point of view. I would strongly recommend finding a work partner or a small group of like-minded individuals.

Revision strategies

The period before exams is a time of extreme anxiety and stress, which seems to make the dyslexia worse! Despite the advice, relaxation often seems impossible. Although it is necessary to impose some self-discipline and some sort of timetable, it is also important to recognise the times when some tasks seem impossible and to be flexible and try a different task. Before starting to revise, I read through all my notes for each course. I then decided which areas I really did not want to revise. By reading through the past exam questions and any specimen questions that were available, I made lists of the questions related to each specific topic. I then chose the areas that I intended to revise.

I only revised one topic more than the number of answers that I would have to answer; for example, if I had to write three answers, I would revise four topics. This might sound risky but the way that I revised allowed me to write answers for a variety of possible questions that may be set on any topic. When selecting the topics for revision, it is important to consider how likely questions are to come up and to be realistic in this guesswork. For example, if three lectures have been devoted to one topic and two other topics have been covered in another lecture, it would be foolish to revise one of the short topics and not the one covered in more detail. It is important to remember that often an exam question might reflect a theme that has run through a course rather than the content of two or three lectures. Having selected the topics, I then found a work partner for each topic.

I started revision by reading through my lecture notes and extracting all the key points, which I listed on the facing page. I took a very big piece of paper and wrote all the relevant exam questions at the top of the page. I put the most important issues relating to that topic into bubbles in the middle of the paper. I tried to restrict myself to only one idea, or definition, per bubble. I then tried to see a shape formed by the relationships between the central ideas, for example three core issues might make a triangle or two opposing theories might have evolved from one phenomenon, forming a seesaw shape with the observed phenomenon as the fulcrum. It is important that it is the relationships between the ideas that guide the shape, as it is the understanding of how the ideas relate to each other that give the flexibility to allow an answer to almost any question set. I then worked through my lecture notes and added in all of the key points and evidence presented. Each idea is put into a bubble close to the central issues to which it is related. It is often useful to discuss this with somebody else when trying to establish which are the most important issues, and whereabouts to place subsidiary issues. Often these bubbles are related to more than one idea, or have more than one interpretation. These are the links that will give an answer structure, leading neatly from one paragraph to the next.

Then I worked through the highlights of my background reading and added further bubbles to the plan, I tried to find alternative examples to the ones given in the lectures. As I often worked with somebody else, I would explain my examples to them and listen to them describe the points that they thought most worthy of inclusion. With hindsight I can now see that this was one of the most useful exercises of the process. Teaching somebody else is a very good way of learning; it not only helps you to understand the issues but also gives you a lot of practice in expressing them clearly. Your friend will let you know if you have failed to get the message across, giving you the chance to try a different way of explaining. Similarly when listening to your friend's examples, do so actively, and make sure that you understand why they are important and how they fit with the other issues.

At this point the page was usually a mess with loads of annotations and small paragraphs that were included in case of forgetting. The next stage was to re-write the mind-map to allow the examples and related ideas to be linked as easily as possible to the key issues. I would then rewrite the map using only one word for each bubble and excluding all of the paragraphs. Sometimes I drew the bubbles as a shape that might help to remind me of their content, for example the shape of a rabbit's head reminded me of a demonstration of the effect of language on perception. This might sound very laborious, but each time the plan is reorganised it reflects a deeper understanding of the issues, and understanding is necessary for learning. The links between the bubbles also serve as cues to the memory. I used colours to make different types of link, for example some links serve to illustrate a point whereas others are linked because they give contradictory evidence. I often made up mnemonics to help me to remember the subsidiary ideas surrounding the central issues. I would take the initials or, if possible, the first syllable and use them to make up a sentence. I found it helpful to go for a walk without any of my notes and to try to remember all the mnemonics; it isn't possible to cheat and have a quick look!

Having constructed a mind-map, I would then try to answer each question using the contents of the map. Different types of question demand different contents and it is important to decide which route through the map best answers each question. Not all of the information will be pertinent to all of the questions. Doing this with a workmate is again a useful exercise, as often there is more than one way to approach an issue. I made a mind-map for each topic that I revised. I must confess that I tried to select topics that had areas of overlap so that the same background reading could be used!

Exams

When sitting exams, I was allowed extra time on account of my slow reading and writing. I tried to make as good use of this as possible. At the start of the exam I carefully read every question twice before deciding which ones to answer. I then wrote out all of my mind-maps and mnemonics for all of the answers before I started writing. This takes time but it helped me to write organised answers, and it gives a bit of time to fill in any elusive memories. I then divided the remaining time equally between the questions, and started on my second best answer. I used a highlight pen to pick out the important parts of the question, taking care to check that I had found any 'either/or' instructions. I then worked out a route through the map that I had written down, and wrote an introduction to my answer, then systematically worked through the points until I was running out of time; I would then put a brief conclusion and leave that question. I then answered my strongest question, saving my least favourite until last. I have rarely finished any exam answer, and I have always come away knowing that I left out a lot of information, and to my surprise I have obtained several first-class papers.

I was very worried about my writing and spelling on my exam scripts. I felt very vulnerable without the protection of the word processor. However, I think that writing an introduction to an answer helps the examiner anticipate what is written. I was worried that my spelling would give the impression that I was confused about the terminology I employed, and so I tried to give a definition for each piece of jargon that I employed; then even if I had the word wrong the examiner would know that I had grasped the issues. At the end of the exam I put a note to the marker into each answer book explaining that I was dyslexic and that I wished the work was better presented and spelled too.

I don't know which of the above techniques was the most useful, but I have shared them with non-dyslexic students, who also benefited from them. I think that the most important thing is to direct yourself to the key issues. It is easy to be drawn into interesting side issues that are irrelevant to the course content. This is, of course, not a problem if you are doing a degree course to further an interest rather than to obtain a qualification. This all makes me sound like a naturally very methodical and organised person – one look at my desk would alter that opinion. I had to work very hard to impose this discipline on myself, but I was encouraged as the results were rewarding. At times you might find it all very hard going. Don't suffer in silence. Ask for help, then help somebody in return. Remember you too have a lot to offer.

Working with Dyslexia (2005)

Throughout my extended college career (BA and PhD) I evolved my own ways of working and to some extent I even developed the confidence to defend these methods. However, that was because I knew they worked in that environment, and so when I left academia for a post in a government organisation, where it felt that yet again good spelling equates with ability, I felt stripped naked of my ruses and strategies.

People and places

I have never been good at names, and here I was placed in a situation where I had to learn masses of people's names and also their job titles. There was no telephone sheet; so I couldn't crib off that because people's contact details were all on the intranet – I couldn't access their details, as I didn't know their names to start with. For years I have carried a small hardbound notebook with me as a sort of external memory; so now I made a point of writing down people's names and job titles and notes about where they worked or what they might expect from me or to do for me. Initially I was doing this privately, but eventually I found that most people are quite flattered by the interest and so it never seemed to be taken as a weakness! I also added other details that would help me remember them, although these might not always have seemed so flattering! Many of my revision strategies came back into practice – so I learned that Julie had the 'jewely' picture frame on her desk and Mr Hardy shared an unmistakable similarity with Oliver Hardy. I also drew a little chart of the immediate hierarchy in which I was working so that I knew who I should approach with problems or requests. I later found out that this is good management practice and is actually presented as an exercise in several courses!

I have learned to navigate myself around towns and even in the hills by relating places to landmarks. This does not work so well in large buildings – however, I do find that trying to keep my bearings with relation to the front of the building helps me set off in the right direction for the exit at home time! In the course of my work in different jobs I have had to visit many labyrinthine colleges and hospitals. If I have to meet someone, I always ask for explicit directions and write them down and stick them into my diary. If I can, I ask at the reception and, if possible, get them to telephone to get someone to meet me. If I find that I have to spend some time working in a new place, I try setting myself a variety of small missions and wandering around looking purposeful until I have mentally mapped the most important places. I find corridors confusing; so I do try to notice some distinguishing feature, especially where they join.

When making train journeys, I always print out the route details or get a copy at the ticket office. If I am driving somewhere unfamiliar, I do study the map first – and then I write out a list of the towns I am travelling through (and in brackets other towns on the same road). I try to guess what the road signs might say, for example 'M5 South' or the 'North-West'. Then I buckle my seatbelt and prepare to go round all the roundabouts three times reading the signs!

Time management

In my first job I was given a diary, which eventually became my greatest accomplice in the efficiency masquerade. It was one of those A5 diaries with a whole week across two pages. Through trial and error I learned to carry it with me at all times at work and to take it home with me in the evenings. In my work I often have to travel throughout the country meeting people, and so I learned to record not only the names and addresses of the people I was meeting but also their contact details for the day of the appointment. I also make a note of anything I should take with me – and if this is something I need to prepare I enter the task in my diary. For example, if I was going to be away for a few days, the entry for my last day in the office might say:

> Print report for G.A., get tape-recorder and tapes – check batteries, book accommodation, print map.

I try to leave enough time between appointments for getting lost and for refreshing myself on the reasons for the meeting – actually writing the times down really helps me plan my time. At first I tended to leave my diary at work but I find it really useful for checking in the morning if I need to be smart, or to leave earlier than usual. Also I find it reassuring to know that if I am going to be delayed I can let the right people know. Even more reassuring is that everybody uses diaries!

When I first landed in the workplace, I found the need to be accountable for my time very disconcerting. I have often found that apparently small tasks take an unexpectedly large amount of time – maybe this is because I tend to equate small with easy and so fail to notice how many steps they involve, or maybe it is because I tend to do them when I am at a low ebb and so performing at my worst. However, the old strategy of breaking tasks down into their component parts is wonderful, especially if you then put these smaller tasks onto a sheet headed 'To do list'. I regularly use to-do lists to encourage me because I can see progress and other people can see what I am doing. I can plan my time better because I can see how many small steps there are to a given task. It also helps me manage my more dyslexic moments without sinking into a slough of despair about it. For example I can choose easier tasks, such as making phone calls or photocopying when reading a large document might be too challenging.

Paperwork

On the spelling front, obviously first of all I got the spelling and grammar checker turned on – no spelling checker in the email meant that I composed most of my emails in the word processor and then cut and pasted. I asked my boss if she would check any final documents for me – I think that asking in the right way is important as, although she was aware of my problem, she was not sure what she should do about it – and so it is important to be explicit about the kind of help and feedback you want and to be brave if there are more corrections than you initially anticipated. It often proves to be a useful way of working as two heads are usually better than one, and quite often she had suggestions about the form or content as well as spelling mistakes.

Because I have had to learn to organise what I write, I use the outline view to build up a skeleton of the piece with various headings and sub-headings; this helps me stick to the point and present material in a more logical sequence. I have since found that this has an added advantage as it can be used as a discussion list when collaborating with other people. I also use it to make notes prior to meetings that can then be altered very easily to make a record of these meetings.

I have also learned when submitting expense forms that it is in my interests to take them in personally and have all those boxes checked – because otherwise it only comes back to me to fill in some omission or correction!

Finally

A new job or a new workplace presents new challenges for everyone, and this is especially true for dyslexic people. It seems to me that the stresses in starting a new job make for greater feelings of vulnerability, and these do not sit easily with the desire to give a good impression of competence for the role. I have made the decision to come clean about my dyslexia from the start. When I took up my most recent post, I was put in touch with an organisation called Access to Work, and, following an assessment, they provided me with software, a recorder, a scanner and, best of all, a large monitor so that I can enlarge all the electronic documents that I work with, which I found to be extremely helpful.

In my experience, although the problems of dyslexics are more severe and diverse than those of their non-dyslexic colleagues, very few if any are entirely unique and owning up to them often results in confessions of similar weaknesses in others. However, admitting to a problem is not a solution in itself – and many of us like to keep our darkest fears and secrets to ourselves – but identifying a specific problem is the first step to dealing with it.

APPENDIX V – TWO GENERATIONS

Colin Wilsher contributed to the first and second editions of *Dyslexia at College*, and we have included here the concluding paragraph from his 1996 piece – 'Characteristics of successful dyslexics' – alongside a contribution from his daughter Rose.

C.R. Wilsher, BA, PGCE, PhD

[The dyslexic child] must believe that literacy is only one part (unfortunately a very important part) of the world and that people are not judged by this alone. This does not mean that he should dismiss literacy as unimportant, but I feel it is far more important that he should preserve his self-image than that he should gain literacy skills. Admittedly, it is a value judgement of mine, but for my money I would rather have a happy, well-adjusted dyslexic who was successful at some things and had no literacy than a child who was unhappy, had low self-esteem and had not developed other skills, and was fully literate. Of course there is a compromise position which would hopefully capitalise on the best of both worlds.

Successful outcomes are usually seen when basic skills of literacy are brought up to at least a minimal level and where compensatory skills are maximised. In fact, many successful dyslexics never achieve a satisfactory level of literacy but their compensatory mechanisms have become so advanced that they gain notoriety in their chosen areas. The process should be viewed as a problem-solving one, in which the problem is the impact of the handicap. The resolution of these problems means that the individual is gaining important problem-solving skills that will stand him in good stead for any career in which problem-solving skills are pre-eminent over literacy skills. One might quip that non-dyslexics are at a distinct disadvantage because they enter the world of work without the benefit of advanced problem-solving skills.

Rose Wilsher BA (daughter of Colin Wilsher)

Having a father who is an expert in dyslexia means I was diagnosed soon after I started to learn to write. I think this has been very important to my academic success as, unlike many people I know with dyslexia, I didn't spend years thinking I was stupid because I couldn't spell or write neatly.

With the help (and funding) provided by the LEA and parents I achieved a 2:1 in psychology and am now studying for an MA in social work. Studying has usually been interesting though occasionally a struggle. I'm glad I stuck with it and am determined to succeed at my MA. Using the help offered by the dyslexia centres and the technological aids provided by my LEA and the care council has helped tremendously. I would strongly urge students with dyslexia to take up as much available help as they can, it can really make a difference.

Being a student with dyslexia is certainly easier than when my Dad was at university. Computers make spelling easier and stops handwriting being an issue. However, I have still faced occasional difficulties such as it taking a long time to receive my equipment and universities refusing to make allowances for grammar errors in essays.

Keep fighting for what you need and don't give up: it's worth it in the end!

APPENDIX VI – TURNING A MOUNTAIN INTO A MOLEHILL

Ms Emily Rose Newbury, BA

I tried but failed to do well at school and finished my studies to work. I felt relaxed in roles that did not require academic skill but nevertheless I was always a success in every post I held, which spanned from cleaning assistant to coffee shop supervisor. I then moved to north Wales and after unsuccessfully attempting to find employment I went to a college open day and signed up to an 'access to health' course. Within four weeks (after being assessed at my personal tutor's request) I was told I was dyslexic. By this time, I was 22 years old. Then, with the right help and knowing why written work took me hours I completed my access course at level three.

After the hardest year of my life (so far) at college, I applied to Bangor University and was accepted on the Criminology and Criminal Justice degree course. University has been the hardest but the best experience of my life (with the exception of motherhood). I studied a range of topics from psychology, social policy, law, methods of research to criminology. My final-year dissertation looked at the unwanted side effects of anti-social behaviour legislation on a rural housing estate and became a massive part of my life for a year in which I carried out my own research, helped to set up community initiatives in the area I was studying and finally wrote up the project.

Throughout this time and the rest of my degree, the Dyslexia Unit and its staff at the university gave me invaluable help. I sometimes felt like a fraud at university thinking that at any moment someone would say, I was in the wrong place because of the difficulties I had, but the staff at the Dyslexia Unit were always there with encouragement and practical guidance. I can now proudly say I finished university with a first-class honours degree.

While finishing my degree, I started applying for work early, which led to me starting work a week after finishing my last exam! I am now a Community Connections Worker helping people with a range of learning difficulties to become more involved in their communities and to have more active and fulfilling lives and relationships.

My university experience and the transition I took into work afterwards is still very vivid in my mind and I have been asked to write my thoughts on this subject from a dyslexic point of view. Dyslexia can have a great effect on an individual's ability to successfully study and negotiate the workplace; although, there are similarities between coping strategies used while studying and in the workplace: both environments create different pressures and challenges; so existing strategies have to be adapted. At university, it is often less easy to operate without discussing difficulties related to dyslexia than in the workplace but the stresses associated with coping with dyslexia are often felt more harshly in the workplace because deadlines are often irregular and given a short timescale. In both environments, knowing how to deal with stress and spotting personal indicators of stress is important to stop work becoming overwhelming and prevent the difficulties associated with dyslexia as being personally viewed as a disability.

I experienced the differences between university study and the workplace from the initial stages of entering the workforce. For example, even though it is recognised that the initial application stage can lower anyone's self-confidence this could have a more profound effect on a dyslexic individual. The rejection can be taken personally without being given clear guidelines on where and why the application has failed, despite knowing the probable reason is that they do not have the appropriate skills for the job. There is also a disadvantage from the point of view that it is considered common knowledge that the more jobs you apply for the better your chance of having a positive response. However, application forms generally include a lot of writing and time to complete; so being dyslexic means that a person is probably unlikely to be able to complete as many applications as another non-dyslexic individual.

Once I entered the workforce successfully, certain parallels still existed between work and study. I found it useful and important to try to focus on the parallels so that certain successful strategies I learnt to cope with study could be automatically applied to my new role. This increased my self-confidence in my abilities in the first stages of settling into my new workplace.

In my personal experience organisation is vital to being successful at university. Learning to timetable work effectively helps deadlines to be met on time and allows work to be proofread or redrafted if needed. Other preparatory measures can be taken, such as reading ahead of lectures and seminars and obtaining reading lists early (if available), meaning that time can be allotted to buying or transferring information into a user-friendly format. However, much to my disappointment even though organisation is important in the workplace, there is less opportunity to pre-plan the weeks. Therefore, there has to be a shift in focus on recording what has been done on a daily or weekly basis so that presentations or talks can be carried out at short notice.

I found that the university strived to help students, for example information could often be specially produced in different formats or one-to-one help could be given to students who needed it. However, this type of support is rare in the workplace due to the responsibility given to professional roles and the wide range of sources information is drawn from especially at seminars or conferences and the unlikelihood that the information could be available prior to the event. This can create a disadvantage because information has to be understood, often, in a short space of time with less opportunity to discuss material and its meaning.

Universities also try to create a level playing field, which does not exist in the workplace, for example specialist computer software is available at universities unlike in the workplace. Although students leaving university are encouraged to discuss dyslexia and associated needs with prospective employers at the earliest available opportunity, there is always the worry that an employer will opt for an individual who needs less support (luckily I was proved otherwise). Therefore, successful workplace strategies mean playing heavily on talents, such as lateral thinking, keen organisational skills, adaptability and utilising available IT packages to help with written work. University taught study skills, and advice gained from one-on-one tutorials was really important because it helped me realise my individual talents and provided a useful outline of my personal difficulties, which I then expressed positively in my new workplace to help my colleagues to understand dyslexia and to enable me to be an effective team player.

The hardest challenge for me at university was working in groups. In my experience, marks often relied heavily on group work, which was often organised and executed by a single individual in a group. Dyslexia for me means relying heavily on organisation and preplanning. This meant that I often carried most of the workload in group work because I worried about failing or having to write up work at the last minute. Group work then ended up being a disheartening exercise because of the added hard work I associated with organising a group plus producing written work compared to other group members who I felt had a greater ability to produce work on the spot and were less preoccupied with timetabling their schedules. In this sense, the workplace is positive because by contrast it often gives plenty of opportunity to work alone and receive recognition for this ability.

The workplace is generally a sharp learning curve whereas university gives an individual a lot of time to discover what works best for them. This can be both positive and negative. University allows an individual to know themselves well enough to go on to succeed in work, but there is the worry that due to certain difficulties a dyslexic individual may choose a job below their abilities because of concern about failing or letting down their employers. However, the workplace is often more responsive to success than university because of the way success is measured in a more practical way and because of the different ways in which targets can be met.

As a dyslexic individual, I find it important to be able to gage how well I am doing and to have an understanding of where I am going wrong. At university, this is easy because there is a clear marking system to judge your performance against and also feedback available from lecturers and help in understanding comments from personal tutors. However, in the workplace this is not available, and there is not necessarily the praise needed to feel confident within a role, and often more negative experiences are vocalised as examples of what not to do. In this situation, it is important to find ways to gain praise and an understanding of what is considered a good piece of work from colleagues and managers. This is when it becomes important to have the ability and confidence to ask if you have achieved something; this not only helps yourself but also can encourage a positive practice towards recognising good performance in the workplace.

To me being 'dyslexic' and in academia means that throughout university there is a need to learn how to think quickly and intuitively, to gain the best understanding out of all academic situations. In the workplace, this is invaluable because it draws together a mix of original thinking and unique concepts for planning work, which is accessible to both dyslexics and non-dyslexics. In professional roles an understanding of organisation, the ability to plan work realistically and being able to explain different methods of planning can be vital. I feel that these skills can be used in positions of responsibility to avoid panic over deadlines, reduce stress and to provide clear-cut reasons why you need to delegate work to other colleagues (if needed).

The strategies and skills I learnt through studying at university combined with having a positive view of dyslexia gained in a positive learning environment are beneficial in the workplace. Often being dyslexic means that a lot of forethought has to be put into how work is achieved, and so there is a clear awareness of the amount of effort needed to be put into doing something right. In the workplace, many people do not have this perception. Therefore, this can be used to gain confidence and to explain to others how work has been achieved and what has gone into it. This perception can also be used to gage the amount of work needed to do something quickly, which can help in designing projects or presentations because you can give a realistic view of timescales and what can actually be achieved. Based on my previous experiences I feel it is also important to say that this skill would probably not be gained by just being in the workforce; it is a positive skill born out of studying at a high level.

There are other skills picked up and learnt to cope with dyslexia and enhance academic ability, which can be adapted and used in the workplace; next, I will give three examples. First, brainstorming, mind-mapping and other planning methods learnt to create ideas to write essays are very useful in the workplace as they can help groups or individuals to plan reports, presentations and can be used to think of new concepts in an original way. Second, learning to have a working memory, the ability to hold information and reproduce it for exams is important to academic study and is an asset in meetings and presentations and can make an individual look and feel confident in their abilities. Lastly, note-taking is an art form, which can be honed throughout university and put to good use in any work role, whether it be taking messages or doing minutes for meetings.

The main challenge of being dyslexic and studying, which I faced, was coping with the pressures of essays and exams while trying to cope with dyslexic difficulties that were not necessarily understood by tutors, fellow students and myself. The workplace is similar; all the time there are challenges, which are often hard to solve. A simple recent example from my working life is people striking up conversation in my office while I am working, which I find incredibly distracting because it breaks my concentration and focus. Unfortunately, as I have discovered, there is often no way to get around this problem except for timetabling the times that people are quietest and speaking to managers about using flexitime so that there is time to work when it is guaranteed to be quiet in the office.

Certain challenges like the example I mentioned above mean trying to change the structure of the workplace to make it more accessible. An example of this is working from 9–5; although it is common practice in the workplace, at university the pace is more flexible and allows breaks when needed, especially for me because my degree relied heavily on the work I produced outside of lectures. Problems occur with the working day when the breaks are needed to increase concentration. Discussions with employers can allow a negotiation to break up a long lunch break into several breaks throughout the day, but this is an extra pressure to arrange once already started at work and can create difference between the individual and their colleagues. I think university should be used in a positive way to encourage students to think of practical needs their dyslexia will raise in the workplace. Personally, this example was one that was only realised once I was already there!

Hopefully, university teaches you valuable research skills. These can be used not only to add to any work role but also can be used to look for training to do with dyslexia in the workplace and to obtain information for employers and colleagues so that they have a clear understanding of what the needs of a dyslexic person are. The most important lesson I learnt through my degree was that a problem shared is a problem halved, in the workplace the same is true: unless dyslexia is discussed and understood, an individual's needs cannot be met and then they will find it hard to achieve any recognised success.

Finally, I would like to write that being dyslexic in the workplace has many positive sides. Nevertheless, I believe several stand out, for example having the ability to think 'outside the box', being able to recognise indications of stress in myself and others (after having to cope with the pressures of study at university) and being responsive to the needs of colleagues (after spending so much time coping and adapting to my own difficulties). This said, though, how positive an individual's experience is in either environment will depend on how they understand and learn to cope with their own difficulties. It is common sense really: the better you know yourself, the easier it is to explain your needs in a positive light to others and be confident that it does not effect your ability to strive and be successful in the workplace.

Notes

CHAPTER 1

1.1 The expression 'differently abled' was provided for us by Donald Schloss, of the Adult Dyslexia Organisation (ADO). It has always been ADO policy to encourage dyslexic people to 'think positive'.

1.2 The word 'allomath' was coined by Michael Newby. See Newby (2004) Chapter 13, p. 129. Newby writes (p. 123):

> Education has become a succession of standardised attainment tests and other markers which are used to produce league tables of performances in the basics. Pressure is exerted on schools to meet set academic targets, with financial and educational status depending on pupil performance. Stress has become a constant threat to both pupils and professionals.

1.3 This point is persuasively argued for in a book by Thomas West (1997). It has been proposed that the distinctive talents of some dyslexic people are the consequence of a distinctive brain organisation and that they can be particularly talented at tasks which implicate the right hemisphere of the brain as opposed to the left. This idea, however, remains a somewhat speculative one. Whatever the neurophysiological details, the important point is that those who are dyslexic should not underestimate their own abilities.

1.4 For assessing the very bright students we recommend in particular the Advanced Raven Matrices (Raven, 1965). The traditional concept of IQ, however, when applied to those who are dyslexic, is liable to present a misleading picture: the profile is likely to be uneven and an overall figure does not do justice to individual strengths.

1.5 There is good evidence that two eminent people in the field of literature, Hans Christian Anderson, the writer of children's stories, and the poet William Butler Yeats, were both dyslexic. For sources see Miles and Miles (1999, pp. 23–4).

1.6 Readers may be interested to look at the account of the Quaker prison reformer, Elizabeth Fry, as it appears in Miles (2006), Chapter 21. In one passage of her journal she writes:

> I know not what would have been the consiquence [sic] had I had any other than a most careful & wise mother & judicious

nurses, if I had been alarmed as too many are by falce [sic] threats of what might happen to me if I did wrong I know not what the consiquence [sic] might have been to me.

1.7   For evidence of the slow speed of dyslexic students when processing symbolic information see Miles (2006), pp. 92–4. In these experiments, the participants were presented with a sentence accompanied by a display. They were required to read the sentences and press one of two keys according to whether they did or did not match what was presented in the display. For example, in one case the display was a letter *b* separated by a short space from a letter *d* and the sentence was, 'The *b* is to the right of the *d*', for which the FALSE key had to be pressed. The average response time for the controls was between two and three seconds, whereas the average time for the dyslexic participants was higher on all the tasks, and particularly high – over five seconds – when the task involved judgements about *b* and *d* and about left and right.

For evidence of poor memorisation of sentences see Miles (2006) pp. 96–7. In this study, 48 college students took part, 24 of whom were dyslexic. Sentences were read out, which they were asked to repeat. If they repeated the sentence incorrectly, it was read out again, and a record was kept of how many repetitions were needed before they were word perfect. Overall, the dyslexic students required far more repetitions than the controls, and in some cases became tied up over an easy sentence but needed only one or two repetitions for a harder one. What was particularly interesting was that they had no trouble in recalling the gist of any of the sentences; their problem was that of achieving verbatim accuracy.

1.8   A businessman who was assessed as dyslexic at the age of 38 said that if he was handed a balance sheet and asked for his opinion he would either stall by saying that he would rather read it later or, in as casual a voice as he could produce, ask his questioner to tell him what was in it. He also mentioned his embarrassment when, as newly appointed president of a guild, he was asked, without notice, to read to the members the rules of the guild (see Miles, 1993, pp. 52 and 61).

1.9   Interestingly, some years ago a written report of this finding was given to a (non-dyslexic) typist in London for retyping. According to her version, the student had put 'corelated' for 'correlated' – a much less spectacular error. The typist's mistake is, of course, a striking example of the way in which most readers automatically correct misprints and misspellings. On one occasion this student had elected to dictate his examination answers to a typist so as to save him any worries over spelling. Many years later he told one of us (TRM) that he had wanted to use the word 'neuropsychological'. This completely defeated the typist who, in standard non-dyslexic fashion, asked him how to spell it! Not surprisingly, he replied, 'That's your job, not mine!'

1.10   Students who are still experiencing difficulty with the calculation aspects of mathematics may wish to consult Miles and Miles (2004).

1.11   For an account of the strengths and weaknesses of dyslexic musicians see Miles and Westcombe (2001).

1.12   For a telling account of how deep these scars may be see Edwards (1994). See also the personal accounts by dyslexic students in Preston *et al.* (1996).

1.13   *Butterworths Medical Dictionary* (published by The Butterworth Group, 1980) defines a syndrome as 'a distinct group of symptoms or signs which, associated together, form a characteristic clinical picture or entity'. Similarly, *Churchill's Medical Dictionary* (published by Konigsberg, 1989) refers to 'signs, symptoms, or other manifestations' and adds that the word is 'used especially when the cause of the condition is unknown'.

1.14   For a user-friendly account of recent brain research in relation to dyslexia the reader is referred to Beaton (2004).

1.15   For more technical details the reader may wish to consult Stein and Walsh (1997).

1.16   For evidence relating to phonological deficiencies in dyslexia the reader is referred to Snowling (2000).

1.17   In this connection see in particular Fawcett and Nicolson (1994), Chapter 6. The claim regarding the square-root rule is based on an extrapolation from a study of teenagers comprising six dyslexics and eight controls. The teenagers were tested on a computer game. The task was to navigate a Pacman icon around the fixed track of a computer maze, using specified key presses to move left and right, up and down. The critical question was how the skills developed with practice, and so extended training was given over a period of six months until each participant appeared to have stopped improving. A special study was made of the time needed for the children to eliminate errors. The mathematics which the authors use in support of their claim is complicated, and more details will be found in the chapter cited above.

   Although the numbers were small, the study was not just a one-off set of experiments; changes were studied over a period of six months. The authors claim, not unreasonably, that their study provided 'near optimal conditions for the development of automatisation' (p. 179). They make clear that the square-root rule is based on an extrapolation from the results they obtained, and are careful not to claim too much for it. Whatever else, however, it can still be regarded as a stark reminder of the extra effort that a college-level dyslexic student needs to give in order to achieve the same results as his non-dyslexic peers.

CHAPTER 2

2.1   In this connection, many investigators use the word 'co-morbidity', which by derivation implies that two *diseases* are jointly present. This terminology is potentially misleading: *morbus* is the Latin for 'disease' and, unless we want to think of dyslexic people as diseased, which clearly they are not, the expression 'co-morbidity' sets up the wrong associations: those who wish to say that dyslexic people are not disabled but 'differently abled' are logically committed to objecting to the term 'co-morbidity' in this context.

2.2   In particular David Pollak at De Montfort University in Leicester is leading the BRAIN.HE project, which aims to 'provide thorough and up-to-date information resourced from, and collated by, specialists in the field of education, psychology and, importantly, national and international support organisations for neurodiverse people run by neurodiverse people'. See www.brainhe.com/index.

2.3   The view that dyscalculia is a separate syndrome has been strongly defended by Butterworth (see Butterworth, 1999, for a theoretical justification and Butterworth, 2003, for his dyscalculia screening test). The issue of whether there are two separate syndromes is also discussed in Miles (2006), Chapter 22.

2.4   For these descriptions we have drawn principally on the American Psychiatric Association's *Diagnostic and Statistical Manual of Mental Disorders* (DSM IV; American Psychiatric Association, 1995).

College students and staff may be interested in Quinn (2001) on ADD and the college student; Colley and the Dyspraxia Foundation Adult Support Group (2000) on dyspraxia; Jamieson and Jamieson (2004) on students with Asperger's syndrome.

An excellent source of further information and links to relevant websites is the excellent BRAIN.HE site (**see note 2.2**). The Developmental Adult Neuro-Diversity Association (DANDA) is also pro-active in its mission 'To see that adults with developmental neuro-diversity reach their full potential and play a full role in society', and is another very useful source of information (www.danda.org.uk/).

2.5   For a full discussion of the issues of inclusivity in higher education see Pollak (2005).

CHAPTER 3

3.1   See Singleton (1999, pp. 81–2), who notes that as many as 43 per cent of university students who are known to be dyslexic have been identified as dyslexic *after* starting their course. These numbers would increase if fewer students were recognised as dyslexic during their years at school.

3.2   In this connection some educationalists have found it helpful to distinguish *norm-based* from *criterion-referenced* tests. Let us suppose that you are told you have scored at the fiftieth percentile: this figure would be norm-based if the intention was to compare your result with that of other people, or in other words with the 'norm'. If, however, the issue is *whether you have reached a certain level*, then the test is being used as a criterion-referenced test, and in your case this is perhaps a more helpful way of using the results. The point can be illustrated by means of an example from a quite different field – that of taking your driving test. Here your examiner will not be very much interested in your performance relative to that of others; what concerns her is whether your driving is up to a particular standard. The driving test can therefore be regarded as a criterion-referenced test.

3.3   In a paper entitled 'Do dyslexic children have IQs?', Miles (1996) calls attention to the many items in traditional intelligence tests which are affected by dyslexic limitations and which therefore cast doubt on the usefulness of a global, or overall, IQ figure. See also Miles (2006), Chapter 9, where the difficulties in assessing the intelligence of a dyslexic person are further discussed.

3.4   This view is associated in particular with the writings of B.F. Skinner and his followers. A good introduction to the many writings of Skinner is his book *Science and Human Behaviour* (1953). Skinner is at pains to point out the dangers of saying that a particular skill can *never* be learned if one has not explored to the full the possible ways of teaching it.

3.5   It has been found, for instance, that dyslexic college students performed considerably worse than their non-dyslexic peers on a test which required verbatim accuracy in the recall of sentences (**see note 1.7**); there are also tests where those who are dyslexic are quite capable of carrying out the necessary reasoning but which they fail because of slowness or inability to carry out calculation sums (see Miles, 2004).

3.6   See Gardner (1983), who argues that we should think in terms of 'multiple intelligences', including musical intelligence, emotional intelligence, inter- and intra-personal intelligences and so on.

3.7   *The Bangor Dyslexia Test*, Miles (1997), obtainable from Learning Development Aids, Wisbech, Cambridgeshire.

3.8   David Grant (2005, p. 19), in a very readable account of the underlying 'spiky' cognitive profile which many dyslexic and dyspraxic students have in common, illustrates how their specific limitations can lead to frustration. He uses a computer analogy:

> For many dyslexics and dyspraxics, it is as if they have a good-quality word processing package and graphics card, but limited memory and a slow processing chip. However, what it is not possible to do is to go to the nearest computing store to buy additional memory and a faster chip. It is a question of learning how to get around the limitations so that full potential is achieved.

3.9   From the beginning of the academic year 2006–7 it was expected that dyslexia assessment reports, and those for dyspraxia, would need to meet the requirements recommended by a working group set up by the Department for Education and Skills to clarify what would be acceptable evidence to qualify for the Disabled Students' Allowances (DSA). As well as specifying the range of tests which should be used for assessment, the working group's report makes recommendations on the format of assessment reports, the qualifications of assessors and what should be involved in assessors' training; the recommendations were introduced in a phased programme. Further information and the working party's report can be seen on the website of the Professional Association of Teachers of Students with Specific Learning Difficulties (Patoss): www.texticweb.com/patoss.

3.10   Some years ago, one of us (TRM) had occasion to test a girl whose mother was also dyslexic. A well-meaning psychologist had advised the mother to 'keep the landing light on at night' as a way of boosting her daughter's confidence. The mother made clear to us, however, that she regarded this advice as wholly irrelevant to her daughter's dyslexia!

3.11   For more detailed information about the DSA see *Applying to University for Dyslexic Students*, obtainable from the Dyslexia Unit, University of Wales, Bangor, Gwynedd LL57 2DG. Also see the booklet *Bridging the Gap*, produced by the Department for Education and Science; ask your Local Authority for a copy of this. (**Also see note 3.9.**)

3.12   At the time of writing, the system for applying for the DSA is beginning to change. Students in some Local Authorities (LAs) will be directed to the Student Loan Company, who are starting to take over the administration of the DSA. Our advice is to ask your LA what you should do, if you haven't already been told what the procedure is.

CHAPTER 4

4.1   The following is an example of a report which, however well meant, seems to us to show a lack of understanding and to be insufficiently constructive:

> I have just read …'s first essay written for my seminar in Tudor and Early Stuart Economic and Social History. I have given the essay a mark of DF and the 'D' element is mainly for trying very hard. I am bound to say that I am very worried by this case; so worried that I asked … whether she really considered that she ought to continue at university. My concern relates not to the historical material in the essay but to the almost total inability to express herself in intelligible terms. Sometimes this is clearly a matter of dyslexia but more often it is simply inability to put a straightforward proposition on paper. I simply cannot see that she has any chance of taking a degree unless there is a spectacular improvement. She has gone away to rewrite the worst and most obscure passages in the essay and she is seeing the woman who will help her with her dyslexia, in the near future, but I am bound to say that I take a very gloomy view of her prospects.

(This student eventually successfully completed her degree.)

4.2   Over the years, we have met large numbers of dyslexic students who have been successful at college despite having been written off as mediocre or stupid at an earlier age. For example, in the case of John (Miles, 1993, p. 21), a school report written when he was aged fifteen describes him as 'probably an average CSE prospect'; yet a few years later he was offered a place at university. Lilian Hartley, formerly secretary of the Cheshire and North Wales Dyslexia Association, gave us the following information about two boys assessed by TRM many years earlier: 'got a first at Loughborough and … a lower second at Portsmouth Polytechnic. Considering they were both classified by [name of county] at the age of nine as not being 11+ or Grammar School material their achievements are truly remarkable.'

In addition, we should like to quote some extracts from a confidential report made since that time on a dyslexic applicant to university:

> This boy's application is being made at the insistence of his parents and against the advice of the school. In spite of considerable help in school and a good deal of private tuition, he remains severely affected by the inability to express himself clearly, fluently and accurately in writing. How far the dyslexia on which both … and his parents lay such stress is a genuine medical condition is not for me to judge. The school has approached this with an open mind. The school was never confident about …'s potential to reach A level standard and it was only the strong parental support which he obviously enjoys which persuaded us to allow him to begin the course. His progress so far seems to bear out our misgivings … He works slowly and performs badly under test conditions. He finds concentration difficult, but attributes this to his dyslexia. Perhaps unfortunately he has been conditioned from an early age to pay great attention to this condition from which he believes he suffers … His parents have high expectations of … and are confident that in a higher education institution which will understand his condition and allow for his difficulties he could achieve degree status.

This student was admitted to university, despite weak A levels, on the basis of a high score on the Advanced Raven Matrices intelligence test. At the end of his course, he came very near to first-class honours, has now achieved a PhD and is a university professor.

4.3   Local (Further Education) colleges receive funding so that they can provide support (both equipment and individual study support) for their dyslexic students. These students are not normally eligible to apply as individuals for the Disabled Students' Allowance (DSA); the exception to this would be students taking HND (Higher National Diploma) or degree courses at the college.

4.4   For further information, ask for a copy of your local college prospectus.

4.5 DSA funding is available for eligible Open University students; in general, the Open University has been remarkable for its efforts to make its courses as inclusive as possible (visit www.open.ac.uk/inclusiveteaching). Particulars of courses are available from the Open University, PO Box 49, Milton Keynes MK7 6AD, or from the website: www.open.ac.uk.

4.6 For useful advice on this see *Applying to Higher Education for Dyslexic Students* (**see note 3.11**); in this booklet there is guidance on how to access the UCAS (University and College Admissions System) website.

4.7 There are many guides to degree courses, which are revised annually. Among these may be mentioned:

- *Into HE* (published by Skill). There is an online version of this (www.skill.org.uk) where you can also download or order other Skill publications. Chapter House, 18–20 Crucifix Lane, London SE1 3JW, Tel: 020 7450 0620.

- *The Push Guide to Which University* (updated every year, published by Nelson Thornes – and you can order it on the UCAS website). Visit the website (www.push.co.uk/pushguide/index.jsp) to find out about their online guide.

- *CRAC, Which Degree?* (a series dealing with various subjects). CRAC (Careers Research and Advisory Centre) has an excellent website (www.crac.org.uk).

- Trotman Publishing produces a good catalogue of books including the *Getting In* series (see also the UCAS website) and also publishes *The Student Book*, a guide to different universities with lots of informal info, *How To Complete Your UCAS Application* and *The Disabled Student's Guide to University*. Visit the website (www.trotman.co.uk) for details of Trotman books, and a lot of other useful information about applying to university. Order from: Trotman and Company, 2 The Green, Richmond, Surrey TW9 1PL.

4.8 For an account of a dyslexic student who has become a university lecturer in mathematics see Jansons (1988).

4.9 For a personal account of this distinctive skill see Aitken (1995).

4.10 There may, however, be risks for a dyslexic teacher in an environment where spelling errors meet with severe disapproval. For discussion on this visit the website of the Dyslexic Teachers' Association, set up by a dyslexic teacher for dyslexic teachers: http://thedta.tripod.com.

4.11 See McLoughlin *et al.* (1994). We regard this as an excellent book.

4.12 Information is available from:

- GAP, 44 Queen's Road, Reading, Berks. RG14BB; GAP Activity Project: www.gap.org.uk.

- Foreign & Commonwealth Office: www.fco.gov.uk.

- World Challenge Expeditions: www.world-challenge.co.uk.

- There is also a helpful book: *A Year Off...A Year On?* which details gap-year experiences, paid and voluntary study or travel opportunities. It is published by Lifetime Careers, regularly updated, and available through UCAS.

4.13 See Kershaw (1974), especially sections 178–81 and recommendation 23, p. 122.

4.14 We strongly urge selectors, when they interview dyslexic applicants, to make an extra effort to put them at their ease. A skilled interviewer can help the applicant to say what she wishes to say, while an unskilled one may cause her to retreat into her shell. Indeed, there is the risk that questions which are asked in all innocence (e.g. 'I see your referee says that you are dyslexic – what exactly does this mean?') may be perceived as threatening or as casting doubt on the genuineness of the dyslexia. There is a risk that sometimes such comments will reopen old wounds, since unsympathetic teachers may have expressed such doubts in the past.

CHAPTER 5

5.1 The figures for 1994/1995 and 2002/2003 are from the Higher Education Statistics Agency; visit www.hesa.ac.uk.

5.2 The contact details for Skill are given in **note 4.7 (and see note 5.4)**; ADO's website is www.adult-dyslexia.org; ADO has a helpline: 020 7924 9559.

5.3 This was the Special Educational Needs and Disability Act (SENDA) 2001.

5.4 To find out more about what the requirements of the Act may mean for dyslexic students, look on the Skill website (www.skill.org.uk). Skill, the National Bureau for Students with Disabilities, is an organisation active in promoting opportunities for young people and adults with disabilities, including dyslexia, in post-16 education or training. Skill publishes books and information leaflets on a range of topics relevant to students and teaching staff. Many of the information sheets are available for download from the Skill website.

5.5 For discussion on dyslexia as a disability see **Chapter 3** and **note 21.5**.

5.6 A fuller list of suggested recommendations can be seen on the ADSHE website (www.adshe.org.uk). See also in this connection Doyle and Robson's (2002) *Accessible Curricula: Good Practice for All*.

5.7 The whole issue of alternative assessment has been explored by the SPACE project (the Staff–student Partnership for Assessment, Change and Evaluation), which was funded by the Higher Education Funding Council for England. Writing about the initial findings of the project, Judith Waterfield *et al.* (2006) conclude:

We recognise that there may always remain a small group who will require something different as a response to an individual set of circumstances, a 'special arrangement' or a one off alternative. However, we believe that institutions need to adopt a more inclusive practice where traditional methods of assessment must be examined to better serve disabled students, other non-traditional students and students with a range of learning styles and experiences – in fact, all students.

5.8   See the SPACE website (www.space.ac.uk) for a fuller list of possible alternative assessments, many of which have been included in QAA (Quality Assurance Agency) Subject Benchmark Statements for higher education (www.qaa.ac.uk).

5.9   For some accounts of successful alternative assessment arrangements in practice in HE see McCarthy and Hurst (2001), Herrington and Simpson (2002) and Waterfield *et al.* (2006).

5.10   The Disability Rights Commission (DRC) has information on this; visit www.drc-gb.org.

CHAPTER 6

6.1   We are grateful to Michael Newby, himself a dyslexic and retired schoolteacher, for making this point clear to us.

6.2   From *Now We Are Six* (A.A. Milne, 1926, pp. 36–41).

6.3   A diary especially designed for students, with a lot of useful information, links and tips, is The Palgrave Student Planner, compiled by Stella Cottrell, and it is well worth considering for next year. Look on the Palgrave website for details (www.palgrave.com/skills4study).

6.4   There will be advice available at college on managing your finances, perhaps as part of the college Student Services (there is a Student Money Adviser at Bangor, for example); the Students' Union may also be able to help you. There is also plenty of practical information and tips available online, for example: www.studentcalculator. org.uk, www.missyourmum.com, www.interstudent.co.uk, www. nusonline.co.uk, www.allaboutstudents.co.uk. The website www. dyslexia-college.com has useful advice on general organisation and on strategies for study as well as links to other relevant sites.

6.5   For examples of errors in spoken English on the part of dyslexic teenagers, see the account of Eileen Stirling's work in Miles (2006, pp. 88–89).

6.6   For example, see Collins Letter Writing (2005) and also Burton and Humphries (1992).

CHAPTER 7

7.1   Goodwin and Thomson (2004).There is a very useful CD-ROM to go with this book.

7.2   Some dramatic reports of these scars have been published in Janice Edwards's book *The Scars of Dyslexia* (1994). See also Riddick (1996) for an insight into the issues related to living with dyslexia.

7.3   Some readers may also like to refer to Miles (2004), *Dyslexia and Stress*. This book includes a chapter by Dorothy Gilroy ('Stress factors in the college student'). There is also a chapter by Gerald Hales in which he describes the stress conundrum ('anxiety creates mistakes; mistakes make me more anxious'). Nearly half of the chapters in the book are written by dyslexic contributors, who describe the various sources of stress they have experienced. Michael Newby's chapter ('Dyslexia without stress') contains some forward-looking suggestions as to ways in which stress can be avoided or minimised.

7.4   For further suggestions in this area see Gilroy (2004) and Scott (2004).

7.5   There is also relaxation music available online for downloading, or as CDs and cassettes. For example visit: www.calming.org/music.

7.6   To start with, you could visit the website: www.studenthealth.co.uk, which covers general health, first aid, diet and exercise, treatments and drugs, as well as travel health; the site also recommends books with useful information in this area.

7.7   The following report once came into our possession:

> I would pass … [non-dyslexic student] for 1 question reasonably attempted and she knew when she had gone wrong by saying so. As for … [dyslexic student] – forget it, is he simple or something?

This 'simple' student went on to obtain a lower-second-class degree.

CHAPTER 8

8.1   See **Chapter 5** for reference to the increased numbers of dyslexic students taking degree courses.

8.2   The implications of the DDA are discussed in **Chapter 5** (with regard to educational institutions) and in **Chapter 21** (as they affect employment).

8.3   The following is a striking indication of the sensitivity felt by some dyslexic students: two of them had met at one of these meetings and afterwards recognised each other at a sports club. Both were worried in case it became necessary to reveal to their friends how they came to know each other.

From time to time, though very infrequently, we have met dyslexic students who themselves found it difficult to be sensitive to the needs of fellow dyslexics. On one occasion some half-dozen dyslexic students were attending a study group when a seventh student, known to very few of them, but himself dyslexic, entered the room and said, 'Ah! Here are all the thickies.' No harm was intended by this quip, but the speaker had clearly not appreciated that any reference, even a joking one, to being 'thick' was likely to reopen old wounds.

8.4   See, in this connection, Morgan (1994).

8.5   Stephen Martin, who contributed **Appendix II** to the present book, has given us permission to reproduce a typed letter which he wrote to DEG shortly after his graduation. We have left it unedited.

Dear Mrs Gilroy,

I hope this letter finds you and your family in good health. This letter has got a duel purpose;

– firstly find enclosed some copies of the project which you so kindly corrected along with a corrected copy and a typed copy for copmarasion. I hope you will find them of use, sorry about the delay in sending them but resonly I've been very busy.

– the reason for been busy is that on the 9th of April I am leaveing for Japan to start a 2 year scholarship which I have been awarded. It is with the Japanese Government (Monbusho). Basicaly they are giving me money about 168,000 yen per month to do anythink I want to, so I've decided to do high altitude entomology thats looking at bugs on top of mountains in Japan, not bad eh.

They is only one snag Thats a promblem, for the first six months I learn Japanese at a language school. So a bought a learn Japanese book but as let I've not got past lesson one. The main promblem is the english its all nouns and verbs etc etc and I can't T rember what is the diffrence. Still it should be interesting. I'm going with two other people both Oxford graduates and both with firsts so it looks like I'm going to be with some pretty brainy people but no-dout I'll soon bring them down to my level.

Since arriving back from Nepal & Northen India where I had a brilliant time, hope you got the card, I've been all over the country Aberdeen–Southamton and every where in between. I've just finished typing and compiling three reports; Chinese Entomological' High Stand Natural History, and Fluted Peak thats the mountain we whent to climb in Nepal. Its been a long struggle but now its all finished it feels good. I also had to turn down an interview with the B.B.C at Bristol but I've got to go back in two years time' also I've been offered a part-time job at a new field center near use's so there' s been plenty going on. Well its about time I was going' I hope to see you on my return with lots of new tales to tell. Keep the good work up and give my best whishes to the dsyelixia group. Thery is still hope for use let. Dsyelixics rule O.K.

PS. the only problem with typing is the mistakes are much more easy to spot as you can't t cover them up with bad handwriting.

See **Appendix II** to find out what has happened to Stephen since he went to Japan.

8.6 See Robinson (2003) for a discussion of the challenges and benefits associated with setting up a student group.

8.7 For further discussion of the counselling needed by dyslexics see Miles (2006), Chapter 17. See also Scott (2004).

8.8 ADSHE (the Association of Dyslexia Specialists in Higher Education) has drawn up guidelines for good practice in arranging services for dyslexic students at college level. The guidelines cover many aspects of support and issues arising, and have been formulated after national consultation visit: www.adshe.org.uk.

CHAPTER 9

9.1 Hales (1994, p. 183).

9.2 For further discussion see Palinscar and Klenk (1992).

9.3 Some educators have spoken in this connection of 'neurolinguistic programming': see, for instance, O'Connor and Seymour (2000) and Scott (2004).

9.4 There has been a great deal written in this area. This includes accounts of the stresses experienced by some dyslexic students (Miles, 2004). See also Scott (2004) and Carroll and Îles (2006).

9.5 For example see Herrington (2001).

9.6 See Stacey (1994b).

9.7 In this connection see also Sumner (2006). Neither the suggestion that dyslexics are 'right-brained' nor the suggestion that individuals have a preferred and fixed learning style are supported by firm evidence. At Bangor we have used various learning style questionnaires with students, in both individual and group sessions. The questionnaires are useful primarily for generating discussion and awareness, rather than for encouraging individuals to classify themselves as particular types of learner. Mortimore (2003, p. 271) speaks of helping students to expand their repertoire of learning skills, and we have found that students are always interested in considering the different learning processes available to them, and discussing how they would be appropriate for different tasks. They also enjoy identifying the strategies that they already use and realising that these are valid ways of learning: often they will comment that they had thought 'it was just me' – as if their strategy, however successful, was not quite worthy of academia. See also Cottrell (2001) particularly pp. 165–6.

9.8 See Stacey (1994a).

CHAPTER 10

10.1 See Grant (2005, p. 93) who has an interesting chapter on sleep – and speculates that 'when someone has an active life but a working memory deficit … there is a backlog of unfinished work by the end of the day.'

CHAPTER 11

11.1 See Cottrell (2003), Chapter 6.

11.2 Burton (1976), section 4.1.

11.3 See Buzan and Buzan (2006) and Cottrell (2003).

11.4 See the guidance on recording lectures from Skill (www.skill.org.uk/news/policy/word/guidance.doc).

11.5 See Meredeen (1988).

11.6 *Listening Books:* available from the National Listening Library, 12 Lant St, London SE1. See www.listening-books.org.uk. Also see Calibre Cassette Library: www.calibre.org.uk.

11.7 Lewis Carroll, *Alice's Adventures in Wonderland*, Chapter 12.

11.8 See in particular Buzan (2006a).

11.9 Buzan (2006a, pp. 91–8).

11.10 This is often termed 'Meares Irlen Syndrome'. You may sometimes meet the description 'scotopic sensitivity syndrome' which was used by Irlen (1983). There is controversy, however, as to whether this term is theoretically justified (**see note 11.12 below**).

11.11 Such a pack can be obtained from I.O.O. Marketing Ltd, 56-2 Newington Causeway, London SE1 6DS (www.ioo.org.uk). The introduction to this pack, *Intuitive Overlays for Use by Teachers and Optometrists*, written by Dr Arnold Wilkins of the MRC Applied Psychology Unit, Cambridge, is very helpful. See also Wilkins (2003). Those interested in this area may also like to explore Asfedic tuning (see www.tintavision.com).

11.12 Exactly *why* coloured filters and coloured lenses should sometimes be beneficial is not clear. Since some dyslexics, but by no means all, experience these kinds of visual discomfort, it is doubtful whether they should be classified as part of the dyslexia syndrome. Research and discussion continues, for example see Evans and Drasdo (1991) and Evans (1993, 2005).

11.13 Reading Rulers can be purchased from Crossbow Education; visit their website at: www.crossboweducation.com/Eye_Level_Reading_Ruler.

CHAPTER 12

12.1 For a useful list of such words see Cottrell (2003, p. 155).

12.2 Main (1980).

12.3 We recommend *Roget's Thesaurus of English Words and Phrases* (2004). Also, as well as the thesaurus in Microsoft Word, which we know students use as much as a spelling tool as a thesaurus, there are now several online thesauri, for example http://thesaurus.reference.com/.

Students are often interested in synonyms, etymologies, shades of meaning and the like – perhaps because these aspects of language are intellectually challenging. In the same way, students can become very interested in advanced mathematical concepts, even though they find the mechanics of calculation difficult and tedious. It is important for the tutor to try to give students the confidence to exploit these new interests in their written work. In addition, group discussion of synonyms and shades of meaning may help to make them aware of distinctions which they would not otherwise have noticed.

12.4 This is best done on a one-to-one basis, as the tutor's initial criticisms may unavoidably have to be somewhat negative. It is important for the tutor to call attention – as tactfully as possible – to imprecise or immature language and discuss ways in which it can be improved.

12.5 Many examples of good paragraphing will be found in Imhoof and Hudson (1975). This is now hard to find, although copies are still available. Useful guidance on paragraphing can also be found in Palmer (2002) and Northedge (2005).

12.6 In this connection we recommend in particular Berry (2004), Fabb and Durant (2005), Bell (2005) and Day and Gastel (2006).

12.7 See also Berry (2004) and the chapter entitled 'Preparing a bibliography'; Fabb and Durant (2005), 'Putting together a bibliography'; Bell (2005), 'Keeping records and making notes'; and Day and Gastel (2006), 'How to cite the references'.

CHAPTER 13

13.1 There are some entertaining exercises in Palmer (2002) and Peck and Coyle (2005).

13.2 These examples are drawn from Kirkman (1992, p. 177). In the appendix he presents six different versions of three scientific topics which are then analysed for clarity and simplicity.

13.3 These are set out clearly in Dykes (1997).

13.4 Spelling dictionaries are useful here as they indicate the spellings of verbs when they are extended from the root.

13.5 If there are any dyslexic readers who have failed to detect the differences between the last three sentences, they should look carefully at the placing of commas. Shortly before the publication of the first edition of this book we came on the following passage in *The Times* (4 January 1986): 'The ashes of J.B. Priestley ... are to be buried in the Yorkshire Dales parish of Hubberholme, where he had many friends on April 19.' As written, this implies that he had no friends on other days; a comma after 'friends' is essential!

13.6 These will be found in Kirkman (1992).

13.7 For example, Day (1989, pp. 160–1) writes: 'Do not be afraid to name the agent of the action in a sentence, even when it is "I" or "we".'

CHAPTER 14

14.1 Our experience is confirmed by others: see Farmer *et al.* (2002, p. 208): speaking of the students she works with, a dyslexia tutor says: 'Mostly they don't complain about spelling but they're generally quite pleased when you do it ... especially the first years think that their spellcheckers are going to fix it, it's only after you've tried a spellchecker they know it doesn't.'

14.2 Mnemonics are, of course, possible, for example the letters of the name JASON are also the first letters of the months from July to November.

14.3 For a very useful chart of Greek (and Latin) word parts, particularly useful for students of the sciences, see Miles (2005). This is a very readable account of the influences on and changes in the history of English spelling.

14.4 Regarding the relationship of pronunciation to spelling see **note 6.5**.

14.5 Books on spelling written specifically with the needs of dyslexic learners in mind include: Brand (1985), Miles (1998), Thomson and Watkins (1998), Cooke (2002) and Hornsby and Shear (2006).

14.6 For example, Collins COBUILD Advanced Learners English Dictionary (2006) (with CD-ROM).

14.7 For example, *Henderson's Dictionary of Biological Terms* (London: Prentice Hall, 2000) and the *Oxford Dictionary of Nursing* (Oxford: Oxford University Press, 2003) (a pocket version is also available).

14.8 One that is especially recommended for dyslexic learners is: *Pergamon Dictionary of Perfect Spelling* (now revised and updated, published by Barrington Stoke, 2005).

14.9 In particular, there is a range of Franklin spellmasters and wordmasters. Details are available from Franklin Educational Distributor's Association, Bingham-Gurney, Old Commerce House, Pentrecagal, Newcastle Emlyn, Carmarthenshire, Wales SA38 9HX. Visit: www.ukspellcheckers.com.

CHAPTER 15

15.1   For documentation see, in particular, Miles (1993).

15.2   Readers interested in the mathematical problems which may accompany dyslexia could consult Miles and Miles (2004), where the contributors discuss these problems from many different angles and in many cases make practical suggestions for overcoming them.

15.3   The Dyscalculia and Dyslexia Interest Group (DDIG, based at Loughborough University, www.ddig.lboro.ac.uk) has produced guidelines for students on choosing a 2-line scientific calculator: http://ddig.lboro.ac.uk/documents/calculator_guidelines.doc. Research on a multimedia calculator for dyslexic people was carried out by Sue Flynn at Coventry University. The intention was that the operations (addition etc.) should be demonstrated visually for the user to see what was happening, thus reducing the risk of pressing the wrong button. Visit: www.agocg.ac.uk/reports/graphics/26/node17. htm.

15.4   Some useful help with the basics of mathematics will be found in Henderson (1998) and Henderson and Miles (2001).

15.5   See **note 15.3** for the website of the Dyscalculia and Dyslexia Interest Group, which includes a guide to maths books that are appropriate for students as well as links to further websites where you can find free resources in the form of basic courses, some with step-by-step worksheets on various aspects of mathematics and statistics. There are a number of basic statistics guidebooks available, for example Rowntree (2000), but before you buy any book do look at it to ensure that the layout and the text are user-friendly.

CHAPTER 16

16.1   There are various sources of useful and informed advice:

- AbilityNet is an excellent source of information: www.abilitynet. org.uk/content/abilitynet/advice, AbilityNet PO Box 94 Warwick CV34 5WS, Tel: 0800 269 545, Email enquiries@abilitynet.org. uk. AbilityNet also produces a large number of dyslexia-friendy helpsheets on various aspects of word processing useful for dyslexic students.

- Emp Tech (Empowering Access through Technology) has a very user-friendly website with comprehensive coverage of equipment and software, as well as links to further information: www. emptech.info/index.

- The British Dyslexia Association (BDA) also provides computer information sheets: www.bdadyslexia.org.uk/sitemap, The British Dyslexia Association, 98 London Road, Reading RG1 5AU, Helpline: 0118 966 8271.

- Dyslexic.com, as well as promoting eqipment and software, provides advice and a support forum: www.dyslexic.com.

- British Educational and Communications Technology Agency (BECTA), Milburn Hill Road, Science Park, Coventry CV4 7JJ, Tel: 01203 416994. BECTA promotes the use of IT in education and learning.

16.2   These are available from www.accessableworld.com.

16.3   For information on spellcheckers see **note 14.9**.

16.4   Examples are the *Que Quick Reference* series, *Rough Guides*, *Idiots' Guides* and so on.

16.5   For more on the use of computers in this way see Laycock (1994).

16.6   For a discussion on this point see Morgan (1994).

16.7   West (1997).

CHAPTER 17

17.1   See, for example, the advice on assessment arrangements in the *Code of Practice for Disabled Students* at the University of Wales, Bangor: www. bangor.ac.uk/ar/main/quality/firstpage.

17.2   Skill has a useful information booklet on examination arrangements for disabled students. Visit www.skill.org.uk.

CHAPTER 18

18.1   For a brief outline of this research see Miles (2006, p. 88).

18.2   These figures were quoted in an article in the *Times Higher Education Supplement* (4 June 2004).

18.3   Psychologists have traditionally distinguished 'long-term memory' from 'short-term memory'. However, there is no simple theory as to how our memories work.

18.4   The results of TRM's research (**see note 1.7**) illustrate this.

18.5   In an early experiment on mental imagery, Galton (1883) asked a number of eminent contemporaries to 'think of some definite object – suppose it is your breakfast table as you sat down to it this morning – and consider carefully the picture that rises before your mind's eye' (p. 255). There were 100 replies, some of the subjects reporting that they had very vivid mental imagery; others, virtually none. This appears to be an area where there are wide individual differences, not necessarily associated with dyslexia.

18.6   See Baddeley (1999, p. 286).

18.7　See Buzan (2006b, p. 53). Using a room that you know well to 'peg' the things that you want to remember is the 'Roman Room' technique. Also see O'Brien (2000, p. 96), who suggests visualising a familiar journey, during which you 'peg' things to landmarks en route.

CHAPTER 19

19.1　In this connection see Shone's (1984) *Creative Visualisation* and Levin's (2004) *Sail through Exams*.

CHAPTER 20

20.1　The word 'adjustment' is now used in preference to 'concession', although some institutions prefer 'accommodation'.

20.2　See Singleton (1999, p. 138). One of the present authors (DEG) was a member of this working party, which has been a milestone on the road to the development of greater understanding of the issues which arise for college students with dyslexia.

20.3　While it is true that any examination candidate may have an off day, there is reason to think that, because of their disabilities in the area of language, dyslexic students are particularly vulnerable. For an account of how things can go wrong on a bad day see in particular Hampshire (1981). Susan Hampshire is, of course, a particularly striking example of a dyslexic person who has achieved success.

20.4　National policy, however, at least in Great Britain, still seems to reflect some uncertainty on this matter, since many grant-giving bodies do not make awards to students who have not obtained first- or upper-second-class honours. This is, in effect, to use the student's degree class not as a certificate of achievement but as a means of predicting her future performance.

CHAPTER 21

21.1　The Association of Dyslexia Specialists in Higher Education (ADSHE) has produced on its website some useful and informed guidance for students and their mentors on placements in nursing, teaching and social-work settings: www.adshe.org.uk.

21.2　See, for example, Reid and Kirk (2000), Morgan and Klein (2000), Bartlett and Moody (2000), Fitzgibbon and O'Connor (2002) and McLoughlin *et al.* (2002).

21.3　For example, the TUC (Trades Union Congress) has published a book 'for union reps, employees and their bosses' (Hagan, 2005).

21.4　Recent data published by the Association of Graduate Careers Advisory Service (AGCAS) allow comparison between the first destinations of dyslexic graduates with those of other graduates. In

2003, 50.3 per cent of graduates with dyslexia entered full-time paid work, compared with 54.6 per cent of non-disabled graduates, with higher percentages of graduates with dyslexia entering management and administration occupations, and occupations associated with professional and technical work, than non-disabled graduates. See Croucher *et al.* (2005).

21.5 The British Dyslexia Association (BDA) has an advice sheet on dyslexia in the workplace (www.bdadyslexia.org.uk) which explains how dyslexic people may be disabled:

> The DDA [Disability Discrimination Act] defines a disabled person as someone with 'a physical or mental impairment which has a substantial and long-term adverse effect on his ability to carry out normal day-to-day activities'. Dyslexia does not always affect a person's ability to carry out normal day to day activities. Dyslexic people can often reduce the effect of their disability if they are able to do things their way. However, if they cannot do this for any reason the effects can be disabling. When the Bill was being debated in parliament, the government made it clear that they thought severe dyslexia was covered under this law.

21.6 This is a Jobcentre Plus scheme (www.jobcentreplus.gov.uk). There are Disability Employment Advisers at these job centres who can give advice to job applicants and employees who are disabled.

21.7 Visit the website: www.employers-forum.co.uk.

21.8 A leader in this field is Key 4 Learning (www.key4learning.com), which has also produced a Hidden Disabilities Toolkit for the workplace. For tutors who are interested in specialising in workplace assessments and advice on adjustments, there are now 'Dyslexia in the Workplace' courses available, for example those offered by the LLU+, London South Bank University.

21.9 The value of having a workplace assessment is stressed by Close (2006), who emphasises that 'one size does not fit all' and that recommendations for aids and support need to be appropriate to the employee and compatible with the tasks/duties of a particular post.

21.10 Your CV is an account of what you have done so far, in terms of qualifications obtained, employment history, and other aspects of your life that have given you experience and skills which are relevant to employment; 'CV' is short for the Latin *curriculum vitae* (life story). There is a great deal of information and guidance available on making applications and on writing CVs: visit, for example, the graduate careers website: www.prospects.ac.uk.

If you find the advice confusing, speak to your Careers Adviser or your dyslexia support tutors, who should also be able to help you.

21.11 Skill, the National Bureau for Students with Disabilities, has plenty of useful information on issues concerning employment and training. Visit the Skill website (www.skill.org.uk) for their information sheets or contact Skill, Chapter House, 18–20 Crucifix Lane, London SE1 3JW, email: info@skill.org.uk. Tel: 0800 328 5050 (the Skill information helpline).

21.12 For a discussion of the strengths and abilities which are often associated with dyslexia see Reid and Kirk (2001, pp. 74–5): this points out that not all dyslexic people will have *all* the strengths that are often associated with dyslexia.

21.13 Prospects (www.prospects.ac.uk) has some very good advice on going for interviews.

Recommended books
on study skills

Although the reference section which follows contains details of all the books mentioned in the chapter notes, we thought it would be helpful if in addition we provided a separate list of recommended books on study skills. This will enable readers to pick out immediately the books which are most relevant to their needs. The list includes some books not referred to in the main text.

Allison, B. and Race, P. (2004) *The Student's Guide to Preparing Dissertations and Theses*. 2nd edn. Abingdon: RoutledgeFalmer.

Bell, J. (2005) *Doing Your Research Project*. 4th edn. Milton Keynes: Open University Press.

Berry, R. (2004) *The Research Project: How to Write it*. London: Routledge.

Burton, S.H. and Humphries, J.A. (1992) *Mastering English Language*. Basingstoke: Palgrave Macmillan.

Buzan, T. (2006a) *Speed Reading*. London: BBC.

Buzan, T. (2006b) *Use Your Head*. London: BBC.

Buzan, T. (2006c) *Use Your Memory*. London: BBC.

Buzan, T. and Buzan, B. (2006) *The Mind Map Book*. London: BBC.

Casey, F. (1993) *How to Study: A Practical Guide*. Basingstoke: Macmillan.

Collins Letter Writing (1995) *Collins Letter Writing*. London: Collins.

Cottrell, S. (2003) *The Study Skills Handbook*. 2nd edn. Basingstoke: Palgrave Macmillan.

Cottrell, S. (2006) *The Palgrave Student Planner*. Basingstoke: Palgrave Macmillan.

Day, R.A. (1989) *How to Write and Publish a Scientific Paper*. Cambridge: Cambridge University Press. Now updated: see below.

Day, R.A. and Gastel, B. (2006) *How to Write and Publish a Scientific Paper*. 6th edn. Cambridge: Cambridge University Press.

Dixon, T. (2004) *How to Get a First*. Abingdon: Routledge.

Dykes, B. (1992) *Grammar Made Easy*. Sydney, NSW: Hale & Iremonger.

Fabb, N. and Durant, A. (2005) *How to Write Essays, Dissertations and Theses in Literary Studies*. Harlow: Longman.

Imhoof, M. and Hudson, H. (1975) *From Paragraph to Essay*. London: Longman.

Goodwin, V. and Thomson, B. (2004) *Making Dyslexia Work for You*. London: David Fulton Publishers Ltd.

Kirkman, J. (1992) *Good Style: Writing for Science and Technology*. London: Spon.

Levin, P. (2004) *Sail Through Exams*. Basingstoke: Open University Press.

Meredeen, S. (1988) *Study for Survival and Success: Guide Notes for College Students*. London: Chapman.

Miles, E. (2005) *English Words and Their Spelling*. London: Whurr.

Northedge, A. (2005) *The Good Study Guide*. Milton Keynes: Open University Press.

O'Brien, D. (2000) *Learn to Remember*. London: Duncan Baird Publishers.

Ostler, C. and Ward, F. (2000) *Advanced Study Skills*. Wakefield: SEN Marketing.

Palmer, R. (2002) *Write in Style: A Guide to Good English*. 2nd edn. London: Routledge.

Pechenik, J. and Lamb, B. (1994) *How to Write About Biology*. London: Harper Collins.

Peck, J. and Coyle, M. (2005) *The Student's Guide to Writing*. 2nd edn. Basingstoke: Palgrave Macmillan.

Peelo, M. (1994) *Helping Students with Study Problems*. Buckingham: SRHE & Open University.

Rowntree, D. (2000) *Statistics Without Tears: An Introduction for Non-Mathematicians*. London: Penguin.

Seely, J. (2002) *Writing Reports*. Oxford: Oxford University Press.

Whitehead, E. and Mason, T. (2003) *Study Skills for Nurses*. London: Sage Publications.

Useful websites

We thought that it would be helpful to collect together the Web addresses that we have mentioned in the course of the book. They are listed here in the order in which they were first noted.

www.brainhe.com/index

www.danda.org.uk

www.texticweb.com/patoss

www.open.ac.uk/inclusiveteaching

www.open.ac.uk

www.skill.org.uk

www.push.co.uk/pushguide/index.jsp

www.crac.org.uk

www.trotman.co.uk

thedta.tripod.com.

www.gap.org.uk

www.fco.gov.uk

www.world-challenge.co.uk

www.hesa.ac.uk/pubinfo/student/disab0203.htm

www.adult-dyslexia.org

www.space.ac.uk

www.qaa.ac.uk

www.drc-gb.org

www.palgrave.com/skills4study

www.studentcalculator.org.uk

www.missyourmum.com

www.interstudent.co.uk

www.nusonline.co.uk

www.allaboutstudents.co.uk

www.dyslexia-college.com
www.calming.org/music
www.studenthealth.co.uk
www.adshe.org.uk
www.listening-books.org.uk
www.calibre.org.uk
www.ioo.org.uk
www.tintavision.com
www.crossboweducation.com/Eye_Level_Reading_Ruler
www.skill.org.uk/news/policy/word/guidance.doc
thesaurus.reference.com/
www.ukspellcheckers.com
www.ddig.lboro.ac.uk
ddig.lboro.ac.uk/documents/calculator_guidelines.doc
www.agocg.ac.uk/reports/graphics/26/node17.htm
www.abilitynet.org.uk/content/abilitynet/advice
www.emptech.info/index
www.bdadyslexia.org.uk/sitemap
www.dyslexic.com
www.accessableworld.com
www.bangor.ac.uk/ar/main/quality/firstpage
www.adshe.org.uk
www.bdadyslexia.org.uk
www.jobcentreplus.gov.uk
www.employers-forum.co.uk
www.key4learning.com
www.prospects.ac.uk

References

Adams, M. and Brown, S. (2006) *Towards Inclusive Learning in Higher Education*. Oxford: Routledge.

Aitken, G. (1995) From an orthopaedic surgeon. *Dyslexia: An International Journal of Research and Practice*, 1 (1): 55.

American Psychiatric Association (1995) *Diagnostic and Statistical Manual of Mental Disorders*. 4th edn. International Version. Washington, DC: American Psychiatric Association.

Baddeley, A.D. (1999) *Essentials of Human Memory*. Hove: Psychology Press.

Bartlett, D. and Moody, S. (2000) *Dyslexia in the Workplace*. London: Whurr.

Beaton, A.A. (2004) *Dyslexia, Reading and the Brain: A Sourcebook of Psychological and Biological Research*. Hove: Taylor & Francis.

Bell, J. (2005) *Doing Your Research Project*. 4th edn. Milton Keynes: Open University Press.

Berry, R. (2004) *The Research Project: How to Write It*. London: Routledge.

Brand, V (1985) *Remedial Spelling*. Baldock: Egon.

Burton, S.H. (1976) *Using English*. London: Longman.

Burton, S.H. and Humphries, J.A. (1992) *Mastering English Language*. Basingstoke: Palgrave Macmillan.

Butterworth, B. (1999) *The Mathematical Brain*. London: Macmillan.

Butterworth, B. (2003) *Dyscalculia Screener*. Windsor: NFER-Nelson.

Buzan, T. (2006a) *The Speed Reading Book*. London: BBC.

Buzan, T. (2006b) *Use Your Head*. London: BBC.

Buzan, T. and Buzan, B. (2006) *The Mind Map Book*. London: BBC.

Carroll, J.M. and Iles, J.E. (2006) An assessment of anxiety levels in dyslexic students in higher education. *British Journal of Educational Psychology*, 76: 651–62.

Close, S. (2006) Dyslexia and Technological Aids in the Workplace. *Patoss Bulletin*, 19 (1): 65–8.

Colley, M. and the Dyspraxia Foundation Adult Support Group (2000) *Living with Dyspraxia*. Hitchin: The Dyspraxia Foundation Adult Support Group.

Collins Letter Writing (1995) *Collins Letter Writing*. London: Collins.

Cooke, A. (2002) *Tackling Dyslexia the Bangor Way*. 2nd edn. London: Whurr.

Cottrell, S. (2001) *Teaching Study Skills and Supporting Learning*. Basingstoke: Palgrave Macmillan.

Cottrell, S. (2003) *The Study Skills Handbook*. 2nd edn. Basingstoke: Palgrave Macmillan.

Cottrell, S. (2006) *The Palgrave Student Planner*. Basingstoke: Palgrave Macmillan.

Croucher, K., Evans, M. and Leacy, A. (2005) *What Happens Next? A Report on the First Destinations of 2003 Graduates with Disabilities*. Sheffield: AGCAS. Downloadable from www.agcas.org.uk/committees/disabilities.

Day, R.A. (1989) *How to Write and Publish a Scientific Paper*. Cambridge: Cambridge University Press. Now updated: see below.

Day, R.A. and Gastel, B. (2006) *How to Write and Publish a Scientific Paper*. 6th edn. Cambridge: Cambridge University Press.

Doyle, C. and Robson, K. (2002) *Accessible Curricula: Good Practice For All*. Cardiff: University of Wales Institute, Cardiff (UWIC).

Dykes, B. (1997) *Grammar Made Easy*. Sydney, NSW: Hale & Iremonger.

Dyslexia Unit, University of Wales, Bangor (2006) *Applying to University for Dyslexic Students*.

Edwards, J. (1994) *The Scars of Dyslexia*. London: Cassell.

Evans, B.J.W. (1993) Dyslexia: the Dunlop test and tinted lenses. *Optometry Today*, 33 (13): 26–30.

Evans, B.J.W. (2005) Case studies: The need for optometric investigation in suspected Meares–Irlen syndrome or visual stress. *Opthalmic and Physiological Optics*, 25 (4): 363–70.

Evans, B.J.W. and Drasdo, N. (1991) Tinted lenses and related therapies for learning disabilities – a review. *Ophthalmic and Physiological Optics*, 11 (3): 206–17.

Fabb, N. and Durant, A. (2005) *How to Write Essays, Dissertations and Theses in Literary Studies*. Harlow: Longman.

Farmer, M., Riddick, B. and Sterling, C. (2002) *Dyslexia and Inclusion: Assessment and Support in Higher Education*. London: Whurr.

Fawcett, A.J. and Nicolson, R.I. (1994) Speed of processing, motor skill, automaticity and dyslexia. In A.J. Fawcett and R.I. Nicolson (eds.), *Dyslexia in Children: Multidisciplinary Perspectives*. Hemel Hempstead: Harvester Wheatsheaf.

Fitzgibbon, G and O'Connor, B. (2002) *Adult Dyslexia: A Guide for the Workplace*. Chichester: John Wiley & Sons.

Galton, F. (1883) *Inquiries into Human Faculty and its Dvelopment*. London: Dent.

Gardner, H. (1983) *Frames of Mind*. London: Heinemann.

Gerber, P.J., Ginsberg, R. and Reiff, H. (1992) Identifying alterable patterns in employment success for highly successful adults with learning disabilities. *Journal of Learning Disabilities*, 25 (8): 475–87.

Gilroy, D.E. (2004) Stress factors in the college student. In T.R. Miles (ed.), *Dyslexia and Stress*. London: Whurr.

Goodwin, V. and Thomson, B. (2004) *Making Dyslexia Work for You*. London: David Fulton Publishers Ltd.

Grant, D.W. (2005) *That's the Way I Think*. London: David Fulton Publishers Ltd.

Hagan, B. (2005) *Dyslexia in the Workplace: A Guide for Unions*. London: TUC.

Hales, G. (1994) The human aspects of dyslexia. In G. Hales (ed.), *Dyslexia Matters*. London: Whurr.

Hales, G. (1995) Stress factors in the workplace. In T.R. Miles (ed.), *Dyslexia and Stress*. London: Whurr.

Hampshire, S. (1981) *Susan's Story*. London: Sidgwick & Jackson.

Henderson, A. (1998) *Maths for the Dyslexic: A Practical Guide*. London: David Fulton Publishers Ltd.

Henderson, A. and Miles, E. (2001) *Basic Topics in Mathematics for Dyslexics*. London: Whurr.

Herrington, M. (2001) Adult dyslexia: partners in learning. In M. Hunter-Carsch and M. Herrington (eds) *Dyslexia and Effective Learning*. London: Whurr.

Herrington, M. (ed) and Simpson, D. (2002) *Making Reasonable Adjustments with Disabled Students in Higher Education*. Nottingham: University of Nottingham (available on the University of Nottingham website).

Hornsby, B. and Shear, F. (2006) *Alpha to Omega*. 6th edn. London: Heinemann.

Imhoof, M. and Hudson, H. (1975) *From Paragraph to Essay*. London: Longman.

Irlen, H. (1983) *Successful Treatment of Learning Difficulties*. Paper presented at the annual convention of the American Psychological Association, Anaheim, California.

Jamieson, J. and Jamieson, C. (2004) *Managing Asperger Syndrome at College and University*. London: David Fulton Publishers Ltd.

Jansons, K.M. (1988) A personal view of dyslexia and of thought without language. In L. Weiskrantz (ed.), *Thought Without Language*. Oxford: Oxford University Press.

Kershaw, J. (1974) *People With Dyslexia*. London: British Council for the Rehabilitation of the Disabled.

Kirkman, J. (1992) *Good Style: Writing for Science and Technology*. London: Spon.

Laycock, D. (1994) The technology needs of the dyslexic adult. *Ability*, 11: 7–9.

Levin, P. (2004) *Sail Through Exams*. Maidenhead: Open University Press.

McCarthy, D. and Hurst, A. (2001) *A Briefing on Assessing Disabled Students*. York: Learning and Teaching Support Network (LTSN) (now available through the website of the Higher Education Academy: www.heacademy. ac.uk).

McLoughlin, D., Fitzgibbon, G. and Young, V. (1994) *Adult Dyslexia: Assessment, Counselling, and Training*. London: Whurr.

McLoughlin, D., Leather, C. and Stringer, P. (2002) *The Adult Dyslexic: Interventions and Outcomes*. London: Whurr.

Main, A. (1980) *Encouraging Effective Learning*. Edinburgh: Scottish Academic Press.

Meredeen, S. (1988) *Study for Survival and Success: Guide Notes for College Students*. London: Chapman.

Miles, E. (1998) *The Bangor Dyslexia Teaching System*. 3rd edn. London: Whurr.

Miles, E. (2005) *English Words and Their Spelling*. London: Whurr.

Miles, T.R. (1993) *Dyslexia: The Pattern of Difficulties*. London: Whurr.

Miles, T.R. (1996) Do dyslexic children have IQs? *Dyslexia: An International Journal of Research and Practice*, 2 (3): 175–8.

Miles, T. (1997) *Bangor Dyslexia Test*. 2nd edn. Wisbech, Cambridgeshire: LDA.

Miles, T.R. (2004) (ed.) *Dyslexia and Stress*. London: Whurr.

Miles, T.R. (2006) *Fifty Years in Dyslexia Research*. Chichester: John Wiley & Sons Ltd.

Miles, T.R. and Miles, E. (1999) *Dyslexia: A Hundred Years On*. Ballmoot, Bucks: Open University Press.

Miles, T.R. and Miles, E. (2004) (eds) *Dyslexia and Mathematics*. London: RoutledgeFalmer.

Miles, T.R. and Westcombe, J. (2001) *Music and Dyslexia: Opening New Doors*. London: Whurr.

Milne, A.A. (1926) *Now We Are Six*. London: Methuen.

Morgan, E. (1994) Can dreams come true? *Dyslexia Contact*, 13 (1): 8.

Morgan, E. and Klein, C. (2000) *The Dyslexic Adult in a Non-dyslexic World*. London: Whurr.

Mortimore, T. (2003) *Dyslexia and Learning Style* London: Whurr.

Newby, M.N. (2004) Dyslexia without stress. In T.R. Miles (ed.), *Dyslexia and Stress*. London: Whurr.

Northedge, A. (2005) *The Good Study Guide*. Milton Keynes: The Open University.

O'Brien, D. (2000) *Learn to Remember*. London: Duncan Baird Publishers.

O'Connor, J. and Seymour, J. (2000) *Introducing Neuro-linguistic Programming*. London: HarperCollins.

Palinscar, A. and Klenk, L. (1992) Fostering literacy learning in supportive contexts. *Journal of Learning Disabilities*, 25 (4): 211–25.

Palmer, R. (2002) *Write in Style: A Guide to Good English*. 2nd edn. London: Routledge.

Peck, J. and Coyle, M. (2005) *The Student's Guide to Writing*. 2nd edn. Basingstoke: Palgrave Macmillan.

Pollak, D. (ed) (2003) *Supporting the Dyslexic Student in HE and FE: Strategies for Success. Proceedings of a One-day Conference*. Leicester: De Montfort University.

Pollak, D. (2005) *Dyslexia, the Self and Higher Education*. Stoke-on-Trent: Trentham Books.

Preston, M., Hayes, J. and Randall, M. (1996) *Four Times Harder*. Birmingham: The Questions Publishing Company.

Quinn, P.O. (2001) (ed.) *ADD and the College Student*. Washington, DC: Magination Press.

Raven, J.C. (1965) *Advanced Progressive Matrices*. London: H.K. Lewis.

Reid, G. and Kirk, J. (2001) *Dyslexia in Adults, Education and Employment*. Chichester: John Wiley & Sons.

Riddick, B. (1996) *Living with Dyslexia*. London: Routledge.

Robinson, P. (2003) Confessions of a group support tutor. In D. Pollak (ed.), *Supporting the Dyslexic Student in HE and FE: Strategies for Success. Proceedings of a One-day Conference*. Leicester: De Montfort University.

Roget, P.M. (2004) *Roget's Thesaurus of English Words and Phrases* (prepared by George Davidson). London: Penguin.

Rowntree, D. (2000) *Statistics Without Tears: An Introduction for Non-Mathematicians*. London: Penguin.

Scott, R. (2004) *Dyslexia and Counselling*. London: Whurr.

Shone, R. (1984) *Creative Visualisation*. London: Aquarian.

Singleton, C. (1999) *Dyslexia in Higher Education: Policy, Provision and Practice. Report of the National Working Party on Dyslexia in Higher Education*. Hull: University of Hull.

Skinner, B.F. (1953) *Science and Human Behaviour*. New York: The Free Press; London: Collier Macmillan.

Snowling, M.J. (2000) *Dyslexia*. 2nd edn. Oxford: Blackwell.

Stacey, G. (1994a) Dyslexia from the inside: Or some ways to make the most of your dyslexic mind. *Dyslexia Contact*, 13 (1): 12–13.

Stacey, G. (1994b) My brain is wired differently. *Dyslexia Contact*, 13 (2): 18–19.

Stein, J.F. and Walsh, V. (1997) To see but not to read: The magnocellular theory of dyslexia. *Trends in Neuroscience*, 20 (4): 147–52.

Sumner, P. (2006) The labyrinth of learning styles. *Patoss Bulletin*, 19 (1): 52–7.

Thomson, M.E. and Watkins, E.J. (1998) *Dyslexia: A Teaching Handbook*. 2nd edn. London: Whurr.

Waterfield, J., West, B. and Parker, M. (2006) Supporting inclusive practice: developing an assessment toolkit. In M. Adams and S. Brown (eds), *Towards Inclusive Learning in Higher Education*. Oxford: Routledge.

West, T.G. (1997) *In the Mind's Eye: Visual Thinkers, Gifted People with Learning Difficulties, Computer Images, and the Ironies of Creativity*. Buffalo, NY: Prometheus Books.

Wilkins, A. (2003) *Reading through Colour*. Chichester: John Wiley & Sons Ltd.

Index